THE UNIVERSITY OF
WINCHESTER

HUNTING
IN BRITAIN
FROM THE ICE AGE
TO THE PRESENT

BARRY LEWIS

To my wife Kat and daughter Zoë Elsa Lewis (Peanut)

First published 2009

The History Press
The Mill, Brimscombe Port
Stroud, Gloucestershire, GL5 2QG
www.thehistorypress.co.uk

British Library Cataloguing in Publication Data.
A catalogue record for this book is available from the British Library.

ISBN 978 0 7524 4802 2

Printed in Great Britain

Contents

Preface

In early 2006 I was looking for a book that did not exist. What I was looking for was a book about hunting from an archaeological, historical and cultural perspective that covered all the periods that humans have been in the British Isles – even encompassing the recent (relatively speaking) change in attitude towards sport hunting. Even better if such a book should cover changes in legislation regarding hunting with dogs and how we got there. I wanted to know what had led us to this critical junction when the Hunting Act 2004 (see Appendix II) saw this activity banned. I wanted to better understand our relationship with hunting, the oldest human endeavour and one that was absolutely critical to our survival and that had played a key role in human evolution and the evolution of human invention. Hunting must have been one of the first areas where humans wanted to strive for something; to hunt bigger, faster animals or perhaps even smaller, more difficult, specialised but tasty prey and all this against a backdrop of, at times a rapidly changing climate. I felt that there ought to be such a book and it was a surprise that there wasn't. So I decided there and then that I should do the decent thing and write it.

It was not an area where I have a particular specialised knowledge; my career and interests were leading me towards specialising in the Upper Palaeolithic and in the field of rock-art and landscape archaeology, but since no one else, it seemed, had a specialist knowledge of hunting from all periods either, I concluded the subject was fair game.

It became apparent during the writing of this book that this was not going to be an easy task. Some eras, particularly those covered during the Pleistocene (from *c.*2 million years to 10,000 years ago) and early Holocene (from 10,000 years ago), were better studied in this regard but others, such as later prehistory, essentially from the Neolithic through until the arrival of the Romans, were far less well researched on the subject of hunting. It was apparent that the reasons for this were largely ideological and political in nature, as much as for any other reason – it was a subject area that academia seemed uncomfortable with. Much better to concentrate upon the pattern of field systems and settlement, the pottery, the lithics, the movement of goods and people, and the trading and ritual lives of people in the past, than to engage in a subject area that was morally grey and that was potentially academically, publicly and politically distasteful. This sort of thinking seems to permeate the research throughout all of the later periods too, including the Roman period.

However, from the Roman era there was a written historical dimension that featured hunting that had to be considered and was less easy to ignore. It was also difficult to ignore the landscape evidence of medieval forests and parks and therefore academic archaeological forays, albeit limited in nature, were made into the subject. More often than not, most of these researches looked at the economic aspects of medieval forests and less so at the purpose and role of hunting in society at the time. There are a few pioneers though, as we shall see, who grappled with the more distasteful elements of the subject, such as the ritual of unmaking, and produced high quality academic work free of the guilt and almost apologetic stance that was sometimes taken and that pervaded some of the earlier studies.

Consequently, this book was in some ways difficult to write because the prior research was simply just not done or was very limited in scope. For example, much of the historical and archaeological literature touches upon the importance of hunting dogs in the Iron Age and Roman periods, yet there is little detailed information about this topic. And yet, in some ways it was an easy book to write for it is so vast a subject that I could only lightly touch upon hunting through all of these very disparate and complex periods. What I hope this book will achieve is debate; it is much needed. This subject area is remarkably fertile ground and yet is barely touched upon in the mainstream of archaeological research and thought and, as I think I have shown here, albeit briefly, hunting was a core element of human life, culture and society in Britain; and it still is in so many ways. Equally importantly, it was critical in our view of landscape and the way we understand land tenure that to continue to ignore the role of hunting through all of these ages would be to continue to severely impoverish the disciplines of archaeology and history.

Naturally enough, when writing a book there are so many people to acknowledge. In this instance there are some very exceptional people to thank, people who gave freely of their time, their thoughts and material, such as photographs, illustrations and references. Chief amongst these people and in no particular order are George Nash (friend and colleague) for photos and offprints, and Dr Naomi Sykes who provided me with useful offprints of her work. Naomi's work has enriched parts of this book considerably. Iain Soden at Northamptonshire Archaeology, a friend and former colleague, has advised me along the way about the process of writing and publishing, and provided useful information on medieval hunting that arose from his earlier work. Thanks to Ian Wall and the staff at the Creswell Crags Visitors Centre, especially Marie Smith, who allowed me to photograph the rock-art in Church Hole Cave and material in their collection just at a time when they were about to embark upon their move into the new museum and visitor centre. Lloyd Laing, Nottingham University, kindly supplied images of Pictish symbol stones. Claire Pickersgill at the University of Nottingham Museum allowed me access to photograph items in the collection there.

My colleagues and friends at Trent & Peak Archaeology also deserve a special mention: Lee for allowing me to photograph his Aurochs discovery, his critical eye, his support and suggestions; Howard for his unstinting support and useful suggestions; David Knight for his suggestions; Jenny Brown for her advice on lithic technology and references. Most especially, though, I must thank them for their forbearance, especially during the final weeks of writing – their indefatigable support allowed me the time to finish this book.

The Spectator magazine must also get a big thank you for allowing me to reproduce one of their covers (19 April 2008), and the artist who took the photograph for it, Amanda Lockhart, both for permission to reproduce the same and also for allowing me to access other amazing photographs of hunting that she took.

I must also give thanks to Paul Bahn for a useful email that confirmed that I might roughly be on the right track where horses were concerned. Paul Taçon of Griffith University, Queensland, also provided me with useful information about horses in post-contact Australian rock-art. Paul Pettitt, Sheffield University, supplied me with a couple of useful pointers and references for me to chase.

There are an awful lot of other people who helped and offered advice and photographs and so on and if I have not mentioned you by name it does not mean I am any less grateful. Finally, I must thank my wife Kat for her support. She had to put up with me writing this throughout her pregnancy and first few months of Zoë's life. It would have been a much more difficult task without that support. It only remains for me to say that I take full responsibility for any inaccuracies or mistakes I have made.

I

Introduction

Hunting, as we understand it even today, encompasses a world of tradition and deep human knowledge of animals, their behaviours and their habitats, which informed key hunting and subsistence strategies that played an important part in human development and evolution – a fact that seems too often overlooked in archaeology. Also overlooked is the relationship between people and seasonality, what grows best and when it grows best; because to understand seasonality was to understand when and where your prey might be in a given time of the year. Watching and studying the seasons did not start when people planted the first crops; it was already an important part of life when modern humans hunted the tundra for reindeer and the post-glacial boreal forests for giant deer (Irish elk). This book hopes to take the first step towards redressing this imbalance, for the first time providing a synthesis of hunting through all the ages of human existence in Britain. The aim of this? To firstly provide a joined up account of the 'history' of hunting by humans for the British Isles, to join up all the disparate periods and to examine the effects hunting had on the landscape. Landscape archaeologists today remain focused primarily upon agriculture as the activity that shaped our landscapes since the Neolithic, explaining features and settlement patterns and change as an artefact of this. But what of the effects of hunting on the landscape? Here I argue that some of our concepts of land-use, landownership and stock ownership, even our laws that relate to trespass, owe their origins to hunting, which I hope will provide a clue as to why the act of hunting and the issues surrounding it are still so emotive today.

Throughout much of human history hunting was not a sport but a necessity. The very existence of all humans and their earlier hominid ancestors, in one form or another, was dependent upon hunting, gathering and fishing. These three critical elements to human survival were essential for many more millennia by far than our current, more comfortable mode of settled agricultural subsistence. Without proper strategies, knowledge of prey animals and their behaviours, an understanding of the environment and landscapes that animals and humans shared, and the development of the correct tools and weapons, we humans would not have been able to survive for as long as we have. Hunting was not just for food but also for clothing and became one of the primary reasons that our ancestors, *Homo antecessor* and *H. heidelbergensis*, managed to colonise Britain during interglacials around half a million years ago. Hunting was a cultural imperative at the core of our existence and soon became synergistic with religious experience, art, human relationships and relationships with the landscape. Hunting was inescapable and deeply redolent of, and tied to, human experiences of the natural world. Here I will argue that in the Neolithic the formal rules of hunting and human relationships with landscape and agriculture was the basis of atavistic interactions with ancestry, defined by knowledge of the natural world and has shaped our concept of land tenure since.

In some parts of the world hunting is still as important to a number of rural communities in developing nations, at different stages along the road to social and technological development, as it once was in prehistoric Britain. It was, after all, especially when considered against the length of human occupation of the British Isles, only comparatively recently when the first farmers appeared in the Neolithic some 5,000 years ago, spelling the beginning of the end for our hunter-gather-fisher lifestyle as the prime means of our subsistence existence. During the Neolithic this change in the way we made and consumed food came at a price, for free time and leisure time were eroded and people became reliant upon staple foods for the first time. It is a misconception that farming brought with it more leisure time – it was always the hunters who had the benefit of more free time. It was this reliance on farming that made humans vulnerable to disaster, and the single major factor that impacted upon societies at this time was sedentism. For settling in one place and investing labour and time in growing crops and raising livestock meant that when things went wrong, such as plant and livestock diseases or the failure of crops due to weather, all that investment of time in food sources was threatened. Sedentism also means that local game resources may be affected by over-hunting in such lean times because the group is less able to travel further to hunt. When humans did travel to hunt then this might bring them into conflict with other groups of people at these critical times. Also during the Neolithic, the relatively narrow range of crop types available to people meant that there was likely to be increased cases of malnutrition within settled groups. Indeed, it is probably more amazing, in spite of all these problems, that human society stuck it out with farming at all!

Someone once said that society is never more than three meals away from anarchy, and there has never been a more correct truism than when applied to modern Western society. Imagine a scenario where a series of diseases or weather-related disasters wiped out all of our grown crops and domesticated livestock (in a world where climate change driven by global warming wreaks increasing numbers of weather-related disasters, this seems all too possible); in other words, if our food supplies dried up, how many of us do we think would have enough knowledge to seek out wild edible plants, berries and fungi, or to track game and hunt it in sufficient quantity to feed our families? Only a very small handful is the answer. Cities would be the first places to feel the effects of this. In such a scenario it would probably be the end of civilisation as we know it and certainly the end of cities as people tried to migrate to the country. Many tens of millions, even hundreds of millions of people would die as a result of conflict, starvation and disease. Granted, this is an improbable occurrence, but it does illustrate a point: in modern Western Europe only a very small number of people have the knowledge and skill to hunt to survive.

Yet hunting for necessity, by varying degrees, was in one form or another a relatively common practice, until fairly recent decades, in the countryside. A fair proportion of this hunting, especially by the masses of country people, was poaching – not necessarily out of a love of the sport of poaching, although there is a strong element of that, but because much of the land was, and indeed still is, owned by relatively few people: the large landowners. It is large landowners that invariably control the hunting rights upon the land that they own, even if, as in many cases, the land is farmed by tenants. The nature of this type of land tenure arose in the last few centuries, not by accident but by design. This situation arose through passing a series of laws that enabled the already rich and powerful aristocrats and men of wealth to accumulate and control more and more land. The enclosures, for example, allowed the wealthy to appropriate common land that by right and tradition was used for its wood resources, farmed for arable and grazed by those who lived on or near the common. This process began in the twelfth century when many parks and forests were created, but in the periods 1450–1640 and 1750–1860 the enclosures were at their height. The wealthy aristocratic landowners usually owned common land but the rights that the commoners had upon these particular parcels were ancient and had become enshrined in laws and were almost inalienable. But by the time of the Enclosure of Commons Act 1876 (a piece of environmental protecting legislation that was designed to halt the enclosure of common land), the wealthy landowners had by dint of their wealth become Members of Parliament, lawyers, law lords or were long established by familial descent in the House of Lords. To rescind the commoners' rights to these lands for grazing sheep, an especially profitable enterprise, or to intensively farm them to feed the burgeoning populations of the towns and cities, now requiring the extra calories to fuel the Industrial Revolution, was too tempting to resist. This process did not happen suddenly and start overnight in the eighteenth and nineteenth centuries, nor indeed in the twelfth century; in one form or another, I believe, it had already started in prehistory as people began to put down roots in a single location and to farm the land. Inevitably there have always been powerful people who were able to control and dominate others, and in so doing they learned that there were advantages to owning and controlling a finite resource like land. This then puts pressure upon the land and in turn pressure mounts upon perceived resources like game, which eventually become appropriated or 'owned' and then contested. I hope to show in this book how this process 'evolved' – for lack of a better word.

In some places in the UK there is a long history of hunting, the New Forest for example, a place where hunting in one form or another has continued unbroken since at least King Cnut's proclamation of Forest Law in the early eleventh century. At Creswell Crags there is a tradition of hunting that is even longer, although not continuous nor by design. Hunters, ancient and modern, have used the gorge since the Ice Age; Mother Grundy's Parlour at Creswell Crags has evidence of Neanderthals using and probably hunting in the locality up to 50,000 years ago – modern humans were certainly camping and hunting there 30,000 years ago. In the eighteenth century a duck pond was created by the Duke of Rutland to shoot birds there. Today the gorge is part of the Welbeck estate, and shooting game birds in the gorge has resumed as a regular feature of the shooting season. Similarly, in Cheddar Gorge, Somerset, the ninth-century king, Edmund, hunted there as humans had done for many millennia before him.

Today hunting faces new challenges in Britain as, seemingly, town and country are locked in a war of attrition, of differing attitudes and ideologies, of cultures diametrically opposed to one another, each politically active in seeing one way of life victorious over the other. I am, of course, talking about the 'Pro' and 'Anti' sides of a protracted debate, recently turned into a form of guerrilla warfare played out in the British countryside and the House of Commons over the issue of the right to hunt animals, primarily foxes and deer with horses and dogs. The pro-hunters seek the continuation of their centuries-old, traditional way of life, the right to hunt on horseback, using dogs. The anti-hunt campaigners, fighting a campaign that started in the first half of the nineteenth century for animal welfare, fought for a ban that they won in 2004 and came into law in February 2005 (Appendix II contains the full wording of the bill). The hunts still continue, albeit in a diluted fashion as drag hunts or using the dogs to flush but not kill. Country people continue to fight the threat of further controls that they believe will fall upon shooting and eventually fishing. The anti-hunters, wanting to end the killing of all animals by all methods of hunting, controversially persevere in monitoring hunts and lobbying Parliament and the public to see an eventual ban on all 'blood sports'.

Somewhere in the middle of this sits politics, and deeply juxtaposed views of class, ideology and society. Sometimes the issue surrounding animal cruelty can seem somewhat obscured by the fog of war. The increasing urbanisation of the UK population in the last century and decades of improved education has led to an intellectualising of the issues surrounding hunting and animal cruelty. Also the nature of the anti-hunt argument is particularly persuasive because of the obvious and easily made point that to *not* kill animals is a better, more progressive idea. This stance can be made to seem somewhat ironic if it is linked to a lack of comprehension or a myopic understanding of where food, particularly meat, actually comes from and how it arrives on ones plate. Some of these issues explain the reasoning for the trend of being 'anti'. The middle classes in towns and cities are the new social and intellectual elite that have emerged over the course of the last century. Many of this group view hunting as an unnecessary and barbaric sport that holds us back developmentally as human beings. Also central to their view of hunting as an upper-class sport is the perceived control and domination of large parcels of the countryside under the ownership of a few wealthy landlords, which stands at odds with certain egalitarian ideologies traditionally associated with the recent middle classes; that the countryside should be for all to enjoy and not be under the control of the few who can legally exclude them from it. I say egalitarian, but many of the politically anti supporters who view the right to have full access to the countryside as inalienable, are sometimes people who, ironically, measure their wealth by the value of the properties they own riding on the back of the recent house price boom. On the other hand, the pro-hunters, who perceive themselves as sons of the soil, close to landscape, nature and a primeval world closely allied to the seasons, want to maintain their way of life, to continue to hunt. Some elements of the countryside population who are supportive of hunting do align themselves to an older social elitist worldview, and it is this in particular which can alienate them to the urban populations: 'the townies'. The maintenance of country estates with a view to hunting over them and of farms too, and the right to hunt with dogs and shoot game with the wider public excluded from accessing the privately owned countryside, is also perceived as fundamental and inalienable. But who is right? Which side should win the argument? No one can know this yet.

There are too many factors that can come into play to save the day for the pro-hunters, such as the growing trend for knowing where our food comes from; the growth of organic farming and locally farmed or home-grown and produced foods could prove to be a useful tool in the pro-hunting argument. Ironically, the same middle classes, from whom some elements of the anti-hunt ideology and anti-hunting movement grew out of, support much of this type of farming and produce buying. This group may yet come to view hunting as a way of procuring good quality, healthy wild foods as a 'green' and sustainable source of animal protein. Such a notion might, in the development of understanding food and hunting, see a change of view on the whole issue of blood sports as a means of vermin control. For example, there is a rise in the number of people keeping their own chickens in towns and cities, but there is also a rise in the number of urban foxes – this is clearly incompatible to chicken rearing. As a result of this, people who keep chickens, and their neighbours and friends, all now have an understanding of the damage that foxes can do to not just the odd chicken once in a while but to the whole coop. Therefore, we may yet come full circle.

2

The Earliest Humans and
What They Hunted

The Ice Age context of human evolution and migration to Britain

In order to understand the long lineage of hunting from its earliest origins in the Palaeolithic in Britain, it is necessary to start at the very beginning of the human occupation of the British Isles, and to understand the longer palaeoenvironmental and human evolutionary background to this occupation. To do this means looking broadly at the Pleistocene, the geological epoch that was associated with what we know as the Ice Age, starting 1.8 million years ago and ending 10,000 years ago at the start of the Holocene, or 'wholly new' age. The Ice Age was not really a single event but a series of cold-stage events interspersed with warmer ones, or 'Interglacials' – arguably we are living through one of these events now, for there have been periods between cold stages or glacials that were longer and warmer than we are currently experiencing today. To complicate matters somewhat, there is a further series of subdivisions within the Pleistocene that were much shorter periods of warming called interstadials and cooling (stadials) that are sandwiched in the larger sequence of glacials and interglacials. Colour plate 2 clarifies this sequence somewhat.

Within this 'dance of the Ice Ages' there is a discernable pattern of advancing and receding ice sheets. Their leading edges pushed or pulled a broad margin of environmental and climatic conditions that, dependent upon topography, elevation and other factors, provided suitable habitats for various types of animals. With this came an ebb and flow of rising and falling sea levels, that during the glacials was sufficiently low as to allow animals to come and go from the Continent across what is now the North Sea and was then Doggerland (hence the Dogger Banks or North Sea Plains), a broad plain dissected by river channels.

For much of the Pleistocene, Britain can be thought of as a peninsula occasionally inundated by the sea, allowing these migrations to take place during some of the cold

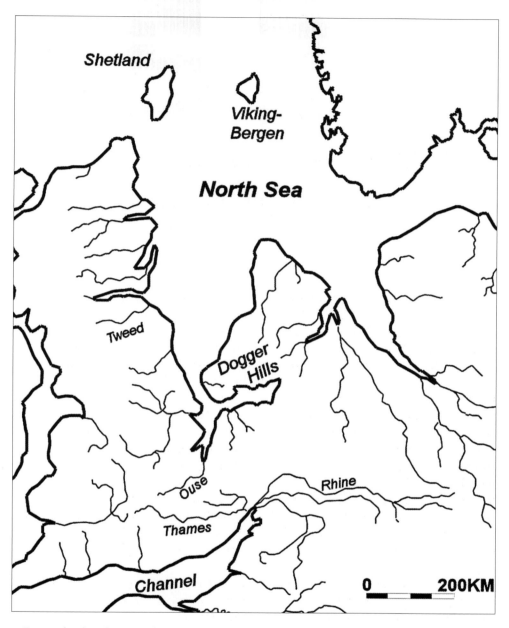

1 Doggerland at the end of the last Ice Age (Early Holocene), when Britain was connected to the Continent by a broad plain dissected by river channels

2 Lower to Middle Palaeolithic, Mode II hand axes (one on right is a replica). (Objects photographed courtesy of Creswell Crags Heritage Trust)

3 Mode II flake tools. (Objects photographed courtesy of Creswell Crags Heritage Trust)

phases. Eventually, and inevitably, these animals were followed by hominids. The evidence that they left behind was sparse, often only amounting to a few stone tools that were churned up by the erosional actions during later warm phases and the extra meltwater they created. This removed the tools from their primary depositional context. Of course, and thankfully, there were some sites that were fortuitously largely missed by this process, such as Boxgrove, Surrey, and Pakefield, Suffolk, where the evidence for early human activity is still intact and reasonably *in situ.*

In this chapter I will examine the human occupation of Britain during most of the Pleistocene and the environmental context in which early hominids lived, and say something about the way they subsisted during this time. A sketchy look at the key migrations out of Africa will be necessary to understand the evolution not only of humans but of hunting and subsistence, and how these strategies changed over time. An important body of evidence from Europe will also be considered because of its direct relevance to Britain, either to fill in the gaps or to flesh out the sparse evidence that we have here. The next chapter will look at the Upper Palaeolithic evidence in more detail because its relative richness permits a more in-depth approach.

Pakefield, Suffolk, has the earliest evidence of human occupation in the British Isles, dating to 700,000 years ago. Indeed, Pakefield represents the earliest evidence of human activity in north-west Europe (in other words, anywhere north of the Alps at this time). These hominids lived in a Mediterranean climate, similar to that of their contemporaries that were known about in southern Europe. This indicates, with the evidence provided by later sites (although, still all within the Anglian Glaciation or earlier) like Boxgrove, Waverly Wood and Westbury-Sub-Mendip, that humans colonised areas of northern Europe during times when the climatic conditions were favourable to their lifestyles, i.e. during warm Mediterranean-like periods.

At Pakefield, these hominids were exploiting flint pebbles from an adjacent river channel and their tools were found in sharp condition, indicating that there had been little lateral movement or disturbance of the burial context of these objects. Around the site, on the banks of the river channel, which supported hippopotamus, was marshy ground with pools and reed vegetation and alder trees. Oak woodland could be found on the nearby higher ground. There was also open grassland supporting *Mammuthus trongontherii* (steppe mammoths), *Stephanorhinus hundsheimensis* (an extinct rhinoceros), *Megaloceros savini* (a giant deer larger than caribou), *M. dawkinsi* (a species similar to *savini*), and *Bison schoetensacki* (bison). Predators, including *Homotherium sp.* (Schimitar toothed cats), *Panthera leo* (lions), *Canis lupus* (wolves), and scavengers, such as *Crocuta crocuta* (spotted hyena), were also found here. This was a rich environment for early humans with a good range of plant and animal resources and a local source of easily procured flint from the river gravels.

Thirty-two worked flints were found at Pakefield; these included a flaked core, a crudely retouch flake and waste flakes. The assemblage lacked formal tools but this is consistent with the so-called 'Mode I' technology, which comprises pebble tools,

4 Map of Lower Palaeolithic sites mentioned in text

flakes and choppers worked using hard hammers and stones. The authors of the Pakefield site report (Parfitt *et al* 2005), point out that this is a provisional interpretation as the flint material represents a small sample size. However, the use of those stone artefacts point to butchery of carcasses but it is unclear whether or not this indicates hunting. It could be that they were scavenging the carcasses that died of natural causes or that were hunted by predators. In Germany, a fortuitous survival of sharpened wooden lances up to 2.8m long, dating to around 400,000 years ago, suggests that early humans were capable of hunting. A similar spear tip dating to around 410,000 years BP (Before Present) was also discovered at Clacton-on-Sea nearly a century ago. At Boxgrove such a thrusting weapon dated at around 500,000 years may have pierced a horse scapula. The rarity of this type of survival of wood implements of this age, and their even more remarkable discovery, indicates that it is just possible that the Pakefield humans were hunters – we just do not have the direct proof yet. The relevance of these strands of evidence will be discussed later.

Around 200,000 years later, the site of Boxgrove provides more evidence, including a human tibia and two teeth and a far more extensive range of tools that allows us a better insight into the lives of early humans in the distant prehistory. Comparisons of the teeth and the tibia with other known specimens means that it is possible, even from such fragmentary remains, to fairly accurately reconstruct what the skeleton would have looked like. For instance, the thickness and length of the tibia points to an individual that was 1.8m tall, probably male and quite muscular. Other information provided by the robust nature of the tibia suggests that these archaic humans were used to being busy and were probably constantly on the move. The Boxgrove specimens can be placed within the species range of *Homo heidlbergensis* (first discovered in, and hence named after, Heidelberg, Germany), probably showing similar characteristics of both *Homo erectus/ergaster* and archaic *Homo sapiens*; perhaps even, in terms of physical appearance, size and cranial capacity, occupying a mid-point between them. The cranial capacity of the Boxgrove specimens was perhaps very similar to that of *erectus* and archaic *Homo sapiens* (around 1220 CC). Their general appearance would be fairly tall, robust and physically very powerful and large-bodied, sharing many of the physical characteristics of more advanced humans. The difference, compared to modern humans, would be most startling above the shoulders as they possessed large prognathic faces, sloping foreheads and massive projecting brow-ridges.

The occurrence of these hominids within Europe at this time raises issues about their place in the fossil record, in terms of the evolution of later hominids, including ourselves, but more particularly *Homo neanderthalsis*. It is beyond the scope of this book to examine all the arguments in detail but a brief overview of hominid evolution, development and migration within Europe and, in part, out of Africa, is permitted as these matters are quite closely tied with the evolution and development of hunting.

Since the discoveries of the earliest hominids (descended from the human *homom* family) and hominins (descended from ape lineage), there have been various 'models' to explain how each species developed, evolved and then became numerically marginalised by natural mechanisms such as volcanoes, earthquakes, tsunamis and disease; subsequently being succeeded by a more evolved species who pushed them even further aside and so on. Many models have themselves become marginalised and disassociated in favour of new ones that better explain how some hominids, such as *Homo erectus*, fared better. I shall try to avoid the use of 'models' here and give only the best information that seems to fit the facts, thus borrowing from the models currently used by scientists to explain how it was that Britain came to be colonised by a succession of hominids over the last 700,000 years. The books mentioned in the Select Reading List will point the interested reader in the right direction if these models are of interest.

Equally, what constitutes a human 'cultural package' that is the behavioural traits and indicators of a culturally advanced human, such as art, burial of the dead and acts of commemoration surrounding death, are often discussed and are equally, if not more controversial than theories about evolution and diasporas. The current arguments as to the number and type of cultural signals for art and burial that Neanderthals displayed (or did not display) in the Paleontological/archaeological record are especially subject to a great deal of heated discussion; particularly in recent years. Here these ideas will be briefly examined because these traits could reinforce the argument that hominids in Britain around 400,000 years ago may well have been practising hunting as well as scavenging.

All fossils that date earlier than 1.8 million years ago come from Africa. There is no doubting that Africa is the likely home of the earliest human ancestors and, if further proof were needed, our closest living relative, the bonobo chimpanzee, is still to be found there. This means that the human colonisation of the rest of the world must have radiated outwards from Africa as populations expanded their ranges and their ecological niches. Eventually, over 1 million years later, they made their way to northern Europe and Britain. The precise timing of these migrations is controversial, but evidence suggests that the very earliest migration may have happened 1.8 million or more years ago and was likely to have been either *Homo ergaster*, an ancestor of *Homo erectus*, or *Homo habilis* – the so-called 'handy man'.

There is another earlier fossil, a jaw fragment dating to 2.3 million years ago that seems to belong to the genus *Homo* but, as yet, cannot be fully classified as a distinct species and therefore it is uncertain where this may fit in. Within the fossil record, just after 1.9 million years ago, it seems that there was a species that fairly closely resembled modern humans –*Homo erectus*. Turkana Boy, a 1.6 million-year-old fossil of an adolescent male, remains the most complete fossil of *Homo ergaster/erectus* discovered and was found in 1984 on the west shore of Lake Turkana in Kenya by Kamoya Kimeu. The fossil was excavated by Richard Leakey, Alan Walker and Kamoya Kimeu. The discovery at that time put the fossil of *Homo erectus* at an intermediary position in the human family, between the first upright hominids and man. Turkana Boy represents an earlier *erectus*, in other words, a *H. erectus/ergaster* hybrid, and it was this species that left Africa first about 200,000 years before.

There are some very close anatomical resemblances to modern humans but crucially, had Turkana Boy lived to maturity, he would have made 1.8m tall (see Fig. 5 for cranial comparisons). He also possessed a large brain that was roughly double the size of his predecessors, and his remains bore a very close resemblance to the first hominid fossils found in the Middle East, Asia and Europe. The stone tool technology that these humans took outside of Africa with them was the Mode I technology, consisting of simple pebble tools found at sites like Dmanisi in Georgia and dated to nearly 1.8 million years old. A newly published site at Sima del Elefante, Sierra de Atapuerca in northern Spain, reports the earliest dated hominin in Europe, dating to 1.2 to 1.1 million years old. There is a suggestion that in this region *erectus* later evolved to become a new species, *Homo antecessor*, whose remains were also found in this area. Interestingly, Dmanisi is viewed as the 'gateway' site for human dispersals into Asia and Europe. However, there are potentially older sites in Indonesia and

South Asia that use the same tool types, and at Dmanisi a fossil there was discovered to have closer resemblance to a predecessor of *erectus*, the smaller *Homo rudolfensis*. A theory put forward to explain this is that this was the result of an earlier dispersal that ended in extinction, so Dmanisi could have been the gateway for more than one diaspora. This raises questions about the environmental and social background of these hominids and the triggering reasons for their migrations out of Africa, which recent research is beginning to answer but is beyond the scope of this work to answer in detail (but see Select Reading List).

Firstly, *Homo* had to develop a large enough brain and a body able to cope with the stresses and demands of prolonged walking, including the physical ability to transfer heat. Then *Homo* had to be adaptable in the methods of seeking food and processing and cooking it, and thus the ability to make and use fire was a key adaptation, allowing hominids to better utilise roots and tubers, which in some instances can give a 40+ per cent calorific advantage over uncooked foods. Fire also gave heat, light and protection to *Homo* as they expanded their range. Cooperation, communication and social cohesion were undoubtedly of extreme importance amongst early hominid groups and ensured survival and food procurement. It was probably foraging that was the crucial advantage in terms of food procurement that allowed the expansion of the human range and not hunting at this time. More human-like social structures were necessary too, especially where they related to food-gathering strategies. The 'Grandmothering theory', which highlights the importance of older females as primary carers and food providers, utilising and imparting knowledge of things like improvements in processing and cooking foods, was an evolutionary adaptation that

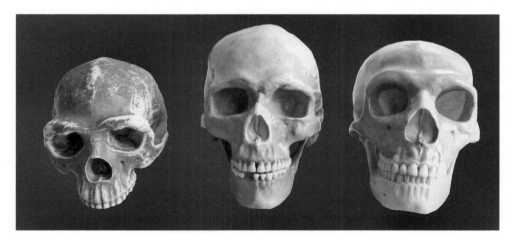

5 Skull cast of *Homo erectus* (left), *Homo sapiens sapiens* (middle) and *H. Neanderthalsis* (right). Note the difference in cranial sizes. Neanderthals had a larger brain than modern humans (*Homo s. sapiens*). There was a noticeable difference in terms of facial features if *H. erectus* were compared to modern humans, but the difference between the Neanderthals and moderns was less marked. (Casts photographed courtesy of Creswell Crags Heritage Trust)

may have led to delayed maturity and longer fertility in females. The imparting of knowledge was a key social strategy and allowed humans to 'learn' behaviours and patterns relating to animals, plants and seasons that exceeded a single human life length. Grandmothering, and the social improvements it brought to early humans, may have generally prolonged human life expectancy.

It is believed that hominid groups numbered around 50 individuals and that there was, even in this early stage in human social development, a sexual division of labour. It is most likely that male hominids hunted whilst women were the carers of children. Hunting was a risky and physically arduous activity, having the potential to injure or kill women (the primary care-givers to the children) and children. The lives of these groups were spent in a constant seasonal migration, visiting places in certain seasons for certain commodities. In times of more extreme hardship groups would probably break up and form into smaller ones, and knowledge was disseminated over time, from one group to another in this way. More will be said of this later.

The climatic and environmental background to these dispersals needs to be considered as it explains how and why humans ended up in northern Europe during the Pleistocene. With Ice Ages (glacials) giving cooler and dryer conditions in parts of Africa, the Sahara Desert expanded and during warmer, wetter interglacial conditions it contracted. This has led to the Sahara being described as a 'pump', forcing migrations during the drier phases and pulling some humans back during wetter, warmer times. *Homo erectus* was considered to be a tropical mammal, preferring to remain in the zone 20° to 30° above and below the equator; whilst north of 40° latitude *Homo* was faced with belts of temperate forest and dry, cold deserts which, given the limited technology available, would have made them difficult places to survive in. Even just below 40° latitude, diurnal variations in temperature, length of day in winter and seasonal temperature variation and rainfall would make the growth cycles of plants and animals difficult to get to grips with, thus having consequences for the acquisition of food resources. There were topographical barriers too, with the mountain ranges of Taurus and Zagros massifs blocking migrations via the Near East and Anatolia route; the only landlocked route. Sea routes, such as the narrow Gibraltar Strait, even at glacial maxima was still a considerable sea gap and probably too difficult to negotiate – as was the even greater distance between Sicily and North Africa. The best route it seems was via the narrow Bab-el-Mandeb Strait, which recent undersea mapping has shown that at glacial maxima this crossing between Ethiopia and the Arabian Peninsula was only a few kilometres wide.

The landscape of Africa that *Homo* was used to occupying and exploiting was open woodland and grassland or savannah, a mosaic environment that was fairly geographically widespread, at times spanning a belt from West Africa to northern China. There were few, if any, of the desert barriers one would today find blocking these migration routes. These dispersal corridors were important, as was a degree of longer-term climatic stability to allow *Homo* to slowly cover distances over a period of several generations. This inching across the globe viewed in terms of a human lifespan is incredibly slow, but in terms of generations and given the timescales we are discussing here it is nothing. It has been calculated that allowing for an expansion rate of 10km a generation, *Homo* populations could have reached Indonesia from East Africa in only 25,000 years. Consequently these climatic, environmental and chronological factors have given rise to variation amongst *H. erectus* groups, leading to a South-east Asian *erectus* and a Chinese *erectus* each showing slight differences, which are sometimes exclaimed as an argument for a new species of *Homo* to be declared. In Europe, as noted earlier, *erectus* may have evolved into *H. antecessor.*

Putting these early hominids into Europe proper requires that a Mediterranean climate had to become established for a prolonged period, over a considerable area that included southern Europe, the Near East and extending as far north as the Caucasus. *Homo* could cope and adapt to these conditions and over time learnt critical seasonal routines and was able to penetrate into northern Europe, but only when conditions allowed – just as we saw in the evidence at Pakefield. Occasional *ex situ* stray finds of Lower Palaeolithic age artefacts from other parts of Britain had, until the unequivocal *in situ* evidence from Pakefield, provided the only evidence that indicated archaic humans were in Britain at this crucial time. At 700,000 BP we are probably looking at *Homo antecessor* as the people who had penetrated this far into northern Europe. Discoveries of fragmentary fossil bones displaying a unique blend of early *ergaster* and later *sapiens* from Gran Dolina, again in the Sierra de Atupuerca region of northern Spain, have been dated to 800,000 years, and a 700,000-year-old skull has been found in Ceprano, Italy, and these were given the species designation *Homo antecessor*, which means 'explorer' or 'Pioneer Man'. There is some 5–600,000 years separating fully fledged *antecessor* from *erectus* in this region, according to the results of recent research from Spain.

Later migrations came too and these people carried a newer toolkit with them, one that was characterised by ovate hand axes or 'Acheulian' hand axes, named after the site where they were first discovered and classified in Acheul, France. *Homo heidelbergensis* (archaic *sapiens*) migrated from Africa at some time prior to 500,000 years ago; evidence that this species was in Europe comes from a number of sites dotted around the Continent, including Mauer, Germany, and at Boxgrove, England. *Heidelbergensis* represents a split from *erectus*, an evolution that might have eventually led to *Homo neanderthalsis* in Europe as a regional variant. Flakes were an important by-product from hand axe manufacture and were used as cutting and skinning tools. This evolution took place as early as 500,000 years ago, at about the time *Homo heidelbergensis* left Africa, but certainly by 200,000 years Neanderthals had colonised much of central Europe and northern central Europe, as far north as Scandinavia and Britain and even as far south as Israel.

The Neanderthals were better adapted to the cooler northern latitude climate. Neanderthals left a rich archaeological record behind and one that pointed to highly evolved social networks. These were a culturally rich range of artefacts and archaeological signals – much richer than was seen before. Aside from burying their dead with ochre there was further evidence of their artistic abilities. Neanderthal artefacts included art such as a triangular block of limestone bearing cupules covering a burial of a child at La Ferrassie, France, and dating to 50,000 BP and the *Masque de la Roche Cottard*. The masque is flint block that already had a natural human-like appearance, which was then further modified by inserting bone splinters in the 'eye' sockets. The object was found on a former bank of the River Loire within a context containing evidence of a camp, discarded faunal remains and tool working. There have been long and protracted debates that argued *Homo sapiens sapiens* (our species) developed in tandem with the Neanderthals in separate parts of the Old World but with a limited exchange of genes. This argument is believed, by some, to have been settled through genetic studies and a re-evaluation of the fossil evidence. Current thinking states that modern humans are likely to have evolved in Africa, migrated and eventually replaced the Neanderthals around 30,000 years ago – the 'total replacement theory'. How this replacement happened is still poorly understood or explained: was it violence and thus genocide that made the Neanderthals extinct? Was it not possible for Neanderthals and moderns to reproduce? Did they become marginalised by the more intelligent 'moderns' and eventually become extinct? Interesting evidence, obtained from the growth layers (cementum layers) of the teeth of animals hunted and killed by Neanderthals and moderns at this time, suggest that modern humans were more migratory, seasonally following game and hunting prime specimens, whilst the Neanderthals were more sedentary and tended to stay put. The evidence showed clear dark and light banding of the cementum in the modern camps, indicating they hunted at certain places in winter and others in summer, whilst the mixed bandings in Neanderthal camps showed permanent occupation of camps. It may have been this and the competing interests of the moderns making incursions to hunt in their territories that helped the demise of the Neanderthals. Conventional wisdom points to the latter. However, there still exists a school of thought that I broadly agree with, which suggests that *Homo sapiens*, after leaving Africa, are unlikely to have marginalised their well-established counterparts, with whom they have so many cultural and social affiliations and similarities, but may have integrated by mating. It has been pointed out that there is a lack of genetic evidence to support this but, sharing as we do upwards of 98 per cent of our DNA with chimpanzees, it would be difficult to argue that current methods are refined enough to spot a variance in DNA with our even closer hominid relatives, especially given the lapse of time that these genetic divergences occurred. One thing that genetic studies have shown us (in conjunction with the fossil evidence) is that there would be little visible difference between Neanderthals and ourselves. Skin pigments, as compared to white Europeans, would be very similar and ginger hair is the most likely colouring for Neanderthals. These traits can be found in modern humans today, as can projecting brow ridges and receding chins in some population groups and individuals. Famously, a recent televised experiment showed that an individual (in this instance the writer and broadcaster Alan Titchmarsh) made up as a Neanderthal, dressed in twenty-first-century clothing and walking down a modern city street, barely drew a second glance – he just looked a bit unfortunate.

One of the big questions that, so far, remains unanswered is whether *Homo antecessor* or the later *Homo heidelbergensis* wore clothes; perhaps made from the skins of the

6 Grave slab from La Ferrassie, France. This triangular block of limestone bearing cupules covered a burial of a child, demonstrating that Neanderthals too had a rich culture. (Barry Lewis – object photographed courtesy of Musée National de Prehistorie, Les Eyzies, France)

7 The *Masque de la Roche Cottard*, a modified flint block with bone splinters inserted to create the eyes. This was found in a secure riverside Mousterian context and is further evidence of the creative abilities of Neanderthals. (Barry Lewis – object photographed courtesy of Musée National de Prehistorie, Les Eyzies, France)

animals they killed. Archaeological and paleontological thought on this matter seems to fall on the side of 'probably yes'. This is one of the reasons why these hominids got this far north at some of the cooler times and accounts for the adaptability of *Homo* to live, hunt and expand their ranges over great distances. This and their ability to construct even simple shelters of branches or skins meant that they could cope with bad weather. Also, flint scrapers found in many tool sites suggest that working hides could be one of their uses. In some instances, use-wear patterns on scrapers consistent with scraping hides have been detected.

This brings us to modern humans: the most recent hominid to migrate out of Africa during the Pleistocene. The beginnings of our evolution started in Africa, certainly 160,000 years and possibly as far back as 200,000 years ago. Studies involving mitochondrial DNA (mtDNA), genetic material passed only through the maternal line, tell us that we can retrace our lineage to a single woman: the 'mitochondrial Eve' who lived in east Africa around 200,000 to 150,000 years ago. Fossil evidence is close behind in supporting this with the discovery of a subspecies of *Homo sapiens* in Herto, Ethiopia, that dates back 160,000 years, and a controversial re-dating of remains found at Omo Kibish, Ethiopia, to about 195,000 years. The diaspora of *Homo sapiens* out of Africa happened, relatively speaking, quite recently and with great rapidity, with remains at Skhul and Qafezeh in Israel dating to between 120,000 and 90,000 years and are the earliest modern human remains found outside of Africa. Then as far away as Australia there are remains that date to around 50,000 years old (possibly up to 60,000 years old, though these dates have yet to withstand further scrutiny) and along the way, following the sea coasts of South Asia, East Asia and South-east Asia, there are a string of dated sites that fall within the range of 65,000 to 50,000 years. This shows that modern humans had colonised Asia, South-east Asia and Australasia within a maximum of 15,000 years and probably within 10,000 years. In Europe modern humans penetrated about 40,000 years ago and their tool culture is the Aurignacian. Currently the earliest site known is Bacho Kiro, Bulgaria, with a date of 43,000 BP.

For a proportion of the early Upper Palaeolithic modern humans lived alongside the Neanderthals. In parts of Europe there is argument about the level of tool complexities that existed within the hominid populations at that time. The Mousterian in France was more complex than that of Britain, of that there is no doubt, but 90,000 years ago, in Seclin in Pas de Calais, France, there were blade tools from prismatic cores that are the same as those found in the Upper Palaeolithic some 50,000 years later. The tool industries of the Aurignacian are found where Neanderthals are found too, suggesting some form of cultural exchange or parallel development in technologies (see Chapter 3). Certainly in parts of northern Spain and north-western France there is evidence of Neanderthals and moderns living side-by-side for three to five millennia and sharing broadly the same tool technologies. In Britain, the earliest modern humans it seems arrived around 35,000 years ago. A partial human maxilla was discovered in Kent's Cavern and a number of leaf point find spots, including Creswell Crags and Beedings, Sussex, may point to *sapiens* being in Britain at this time. However, the maxilla is not 100 per cent certainly a *sapiens* jaw and the leaf points could be of Neanderthal origin. At a single site in Britain – Bamford Road, Ipswich – there is a suggestion of an overlap, where small ovate Levallois hand axes of the Acheulian Tradition were found within the same stratigraphic unit as a few leaf points and blades that typify the early Upper Palaeolithic. It has been argued, based upon the finer nuances of the Aurignacian flint tool assemblages, that a two-phase dispersal can be discerned: one a 'pioneer' dispersal; the other a more developed one, rather than a single wave of advance that had previously been postulated. Other researchers suggest that these early human incursions are more like pulses that were separated by periods when no humans were present. This is all further complicated by the morphological features of the Swanscombe skull (the so-called Swanscombe Man, who is probably a woman form Barnfield Pit, Kent) which, dating to the period 350,000 to 400,000 years ago, should be more 'Neanderthal-like' but is actually slightly more 'modern' in appearance. This makes the point that there are still many outstanding questions surrounding the issue of human evolution and the placement of Neanderthals and early modern humans within the perceived human lineage.

In the next chapter this early modern human colonisation of Britain will be discussed in more detail because of the special relevance of the advances displayed in the lithic and bone implement assemblages, and the impact this had on hunting in Britain.

Early humans: from scavenging and foraging to hunting

Hard, direct evidence of hunting during the Middle and Lower Palaeolithic in Britain is difficult to come by, and the clues we have come from a few cave sites and even fewer open sites. This is because subsequent glaciations, such as the Devensian, the last one that occurred in Britain, which had its maxima around 12 KYA, has scoured away many of the sediments of interest to us. Even where ice did not cover the landscape, the huge volumes of melt-water transported sediments and debris modifying much of the periglacial landscape, moving the evidence from its depositional context. Many of the clues of human activity we do have from this period were found in gravel quarries, where tools were trapped within the gravel terraces of rivers when they were formed during the interstadials and interglacials. Stadials and glacials then came along, sometimes creating vast thick ice sheets. Subsequent reworking, both by glacial melt-water during interstadials and interglacials, and the early phases of later interglacials and the developed rivers during interglacials, can move stone implements far from their depositional context. It is only by understanding river terrace formation and the subsequent erosional and depositional processes that interpretations about their age and context can be attempted – a difficult process. For example, at Fulbeck Quarry in Lincolnshire a rare Ipswichian faunal site (*c*.125,000 years old) was discovered during quarrying work that led to the recovery of remains including *Hippopotamus amphibious*, now only found in Africa.

Cave sites are perhaps our best resource for finding tools and ecofacts enabling us to paint a picture of life in the Pleistocene. In these environments, which suffered less of the erosional damage of subsequent glaciations and the general longer-term weathering processes, evidence is sometimes abundant and *in situ*; whilst even well-preserved open sites tend to show a degree of post-Pleistocene weathering or have been subject to geological disturbance such as freeze-thaw processes, land slips, erosion of sediments, colluviation, water erosion and alluviation. Not to mention human processes that can disturb the rare and delicate burial contexts of Palaeolithic material such as quarrying, building, agriculture and landscaping activities to name but a few. Where caves have suffered disturbance to their important deposits this is invariably the result of humans interfering or excavating within them. In the last two centuries particularly, people have recognised that caves held the remains of early humans and now extinct animals and they have 'quarried' those important sediments for that evidence. Cave excavation techniques in the nineteenth century included removing hard stalagmitic flowstone floors in caves to get at the softer fossil and artefact-bearing sediments below by using liberal doses of TNT to blast it out. This highly destructive technique was used in the caves at Creswell Crags gorge.

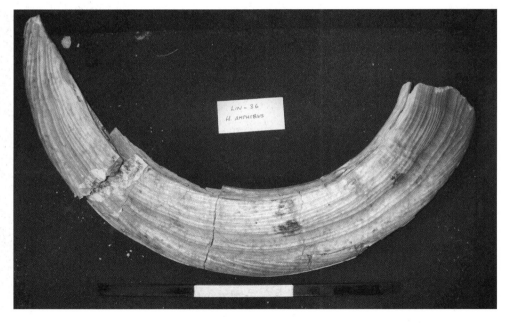

8 Tusk of a hippopotamus (*Hippopotamus amphibious*), one of a number of animals found in Ipswichian levels at Fulbeck Quarry, Lincolnshire, dating to around 125,000 BP. This indicates how warm the climate was during the interglacial period of this cold phase, as this animal is now only found in Africa. No evidence for humans has been found for Britain during the Ipswichian. (Barry Lewis – photographed from collection of Creswell Crags Visitors Centre, courtesy of Creswell Crags Heritage Trust)

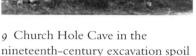

9 Church Hole Cave in the nineteenth-century excavation spoil heap (left). Excavations were sometimes conducted using dynamite to break the flowstone floor. Armstrong and Garfitt excavating outside Mother Grundy's Parlour (right), using a more careful methodology. (Pictures courtesy of Creswell Crags Heritage Trust)

10 Excavation by Sheffield University outside Church Hole Cave, 2007 season

In the late nineteenth century photographs show huge piles of discarded earth piled up outside Church Hole Cave.

Nevertheless, a considerable amount has been learned from excavations in British caves, both from more recent excavations such as those at Pontnewydd Cave in Dyfed and at Pin Hole Cave Creswell Crags, and a re-examination of earlier excavated material which is part of the rationale of an ongoing project at Church Hole Cave conducted by Sheffield University led by Dr Paul Pettitt. This data has been supplemented by studies of a few remarkably productive open sites like Boxgrove, where flint tools and butchered bones were found in a fresh condition. Boxgrove is a rare example of an open site that has seen little disturbance of its important deposits by the previously described destructive processes. These and a very few other sites have provided evidence of the subsistence strategies employed by these early humans. Evidence from Continental sites provides additional information that fleshes out the British picture.

Wooden spears or javelins were discovered dating to *c.*400,000 BP in 1995 at a Pleistocene site in Schöningen, Germany – a very rare survival, they are made of spruce (*Pincea sp.*) wood. Grooves were cut into the spearhead end that might well have been made to insert sharp flint pieces. They resembled modern javelins, with long tapering ends and their lengths varied from 1.70m to 3.2m, and if the setting of flints into the shafts could be proven then they could be the earliest known composite weapons. Until recently, composite weapons were thought to be the invention of modern humans dating to the late Palaeolithic, but discoveries in the Near East have changed this. A discovery of a broken Levellois point embedded in the neck of an ass in Syria dates to the Middle Palaeolithic. The Schöningen spears were found in conjunction with many flint implements and the remains of a number of butchered animals. Before this, a single thrusting spear was found in the 1940s in Lehringen, Lower Saxony, Germany, embedded in the ribs of a straight-tusked elephant, dating to 125,000 BP.

It seems likely, given what we now know of the cultural sophistication of the *Homo antecessor/heidelbergensis* that were in Britain at this time (*c.*700 and 500,000 years ago), that they were using similar weapons to hunt larger game. A single spear tip made of yew was discovered in waterlogged deposits at Clacton-on-Sea in 1911 and was recently dated to 410,000 BP. Certainly their 'Mode I' stone tools were capable of manufacturing and sharpening wood and providing flint pieces to set into the javelins, and they were capable of capturing, at least some of the time, larger game as evidenced from their butchery sites. The evidence for this is most compelling from Boxgrove and Hoxne, Suffolk; here the butchery marks made by human hands with stone tools were incised onto the bone before the remains were scavenged by carnivores such as hyenas. Also at Boxgrove a punctured shoulder blade of a horse was discovered, and subsequent experiments have shown that this damage is consistent with an injury inflicted by a wooden javelin. Here, at these sites at least, *Homo* was not the scavenger.

Recent research into chimp behaviour on the edges of the Savannas of Senegal shows that even primates can manufacture rudimentary thrusting weapons. Here chimps have been seen, and recorded on many occasions, to use sticks sharpened with their teeth to stab bush babies through tree holes where they lie hidden within the tree. This seems to be a recent adaptation, done mainly by the females and copied by the young, to supplement the protein in their diets. Interestingly, the environmental conditions and adaptive behaviours noted here are reflective of the situation early hominins found themselves in during the Miocene, about five million years ago: pushed to the edges of the forest, on the fringes of the Savannah, having to adapt to the hotter, dryer climate by extending their home range whilst exploiting and adapting to new opportunities. Here the chimps learned to do it within a few generations, so *Homo*, even as far back as the early Pleistocene (1.8–1.5 million years ago), must have been at least as capable, adaptive and inventive. Certainly the chimp behaviour in the Senegal took people by surprise for the speed at which they were able to adapt to their situation at the edge of the forest – something previously thought to have been unlikely.

What of hunting strategies in the Lower Palaeolithic? The answer is ambiguous at present, but one thing that is clear is that in order to initiate a successful hunt, particularly using group participation, some form of communication is critical. Neanderthals we know were probably able to talk, at least to some extent, as they possessed a hyoid bone – a critical anatomical part found within the throat that is required in speech. In Neanderthals the morphology of the hyoid was fully modern in appearance, meaning that it differed sufficiently from those of Apes to provide compelling evidence that they could speak. However, it has been noted that the shape of the base of the Neanderthal skull may have meant that the voice box was higher up in the throat, as it is in developing infants of modern humans, which means they may have had a limited range of vocalisations – similar to those of a child in fact. Recently, genetic studies have shown that Neanderthals, as suspected, possessed the 'Fox P2 gene', which in our genus is thought to be responsible for advanced speech. *Homo heidelbergensis* or *Homo antecessor* probably did not possess the power of advanced speech but instead may have relied upon hand signals, a sign language if you like, to communicate during a hunt. The benefit of this is that it is a silent and effective way of communicating while hunting, and it is probably during hunting that it developed as a primary means of communicating complex information between hominids at other times.

In recent decades, studies of deaf children who attended schools where sign language was not permitted and who had no prior experience or exposure to sign language soon developed their own means of communicating by signs with each other – a phenomenon well known since Deaf Schools were first formed in the nineteenth century. It seems reasonable to expect that early humans, such as *Homo antecessor*, who were capable of making wooden spears 400,000 years ago, were quite capable of gesturing and making shapes with their hands to communicate complex information – particularly where important group activities such as hunting were concerned.

It has already been stated here that group sizes for *H. antecessor*/*H. heidelbergensis* were around 50, and that in times of lean they would split into smaller groups and transmit knowledge that way – to exploit new resources and landscapes. The model of subsistence that was practised was a mobile subsistence strategy; the core tenet being maximum reward for minimum effort. But this no doubt held a different meaning to these earlier humans than to more modern human hunter-gatherers; moving through the landscape from one camp to the next, exploiting resources around it to a point where it no longer becomes efficient to carry food back to the camp so they would move on again. This strategy hinged around what they could carry day-to-day and for early *Homo*, who probably lacked the ability to make an efficient bag to carry foodstuffs gathered on the plain or in the forest, or for mothers to carry their babies, this was a quick almost daily change of camps.

The pathology of the Boxgrove tibia, as mentioned earlier, points to constant movement, particularly walking. This strategy is not unlike modern primate behaviour, which is an almost daily round of moving from one camp to the next within a geographically specific home range. Home ranges for *Homo* would be much more extensive than for chimpanzees, whose lush forest ranges can be just five miles square, and able to support a family group fairly easily. Such movements, though seeming opportunistic, are far from it – apes recognise landmarks and their pattern of movement is guided by familiar paths and places – something that early *Homo* would certainly have done. As time passed, and from the evidence of tooth-wear patterns and lithologies of the stone tools they carried, it becomes clearer that early *Homo* employed a simple gathering strategy. The tooth-wear evidence showed that they had learned to exploit roots, root vegetables and occasionally meat, and the lithology of their stone tools showed that they had transported suitable stones some distance from their sources. It is possible that these groups had a 'home base', from where some of the males, leaving the women caring for the children and gathering close by, would go off on extended expeditions to hunt or gather more specialised items.

Fire is the key to making meat digestible for humans; we are simply unable to digest large quantities of raw meat and, until fire was a regular feature of human subsistence lifestyle, early *Homo* would not have needed to hunt much. Aside from sporadic and unreliable evidence dating, in one instance, to 1.6 million years old from Koobi Fora, Kenya, the regular or generalised use of fire appears around 500,000 years ago. That would certainly cover much of the period we are interested in for Britain, with the Boxgrove material supplying good evidence of hunting and butchery and therefore the likely use of fire to process the meat. It is not clear if we could push back the use of fire to encompass the Pakefield hominids, some 200,000 years earlier.

Into the Middle Palaeolithic the evidence for hunting is clearer and more unequivocal. At first there is evidence of scavenging of horse carcasses by *Homo s. neanderthalensis* in the earlier portion of the Middle Palaeolithic (*c.*125,000–95,000 BP) in Italy. The bones and skulls were cracked open by stone tools and this was one of the ways that allowed Neanderthals to expand their range of foods from edible plants and small mammals. By the latter part of the Middle Palaeolithic, around 55,000 BP, bones were appearing in rock shelters and caves representing animals of prime reproductive age, indicating a shift from scavenging to hunting of large game. The prey included bison, aurochs, reindeer, ibex, mammoth and antelope. Crucially, there is no obvious archaeological signal of a technological revolution taking place at this time accounting for this shift; although, as we have already seen, the use of spears either for thrusting or even throwing was probably common by this time. Newer strategies were employed that led to making food sources more reliable. This led to increased population that in turn provided more manpower for communal hunting. One of the emergent strategies in the communal hunt was to control the direction of herds into kill zones and this was instrumental in accounting for high numbers of kills. The early Middle Palaeolithic kill site of La Cotte de Saint Brelade in Jersey was a mammoth kill site where the animals were driven over a 30m-high headland and butchered at its base. This is dramatic and early evidence of human cooperation, and the archaeology here shows that this happened on two separate occasions – demonstrating that this was no fluke. Five woolly rhinos were amongst the butchered carcasses.

What of the landscape? I have touched upon the fact that even primates could recognise landmarks and that they used familiar paths and places to navigate within their environment. The evidence suggests that early *Homo* did too. A concept of landscape and of territoriality seems to be a likely facet of their make-up and, again, something we know that primates are possessed of (territoriality at least). It is not impossible to suppose that as a local group became established in an area or a 'territory', defined by familiar landmarks and encompassing a range of resources that they knew were to be found there, they became protective of it to an extent. Having familiar landmarks, pathways and route ways through the landscape would also be important. It is reasonable, therefore, to assume that early *Homo* had a concept of a form of ownership or guardianship of the resources within the area defined by known places and landmarks. This goes beyond the familiar reasoning for primate territoriality, which is traditionally viewed as hinging upon the protection of breeding females from perceived rival males from other groups. Although it could be argued such guarding of females is the starting rationale for protecting a territory, a development of herd-based aggression that is so familiar to us modern humans, even today. But in early *Homo* it was subsistence necessity that drove this form of territoriality. I do not want to get into too much detail about this issue but interested readers are recommended to look at Bo Gräslund's book *Early Humans and their World* for further detail. This territoriality is in essence a way of laying claim to land, of ownership, or, as Bo Gräslund put it:

> Low technology human societies also lay claim to land in some way, in the form of shared, exclusive or direct rights of exploitation or ownership, which superficially reflect inherited behaviour. The rather approximate concept of territoriality that we meet in mobile hunter-gatherers is not unlike that of chimpanzees and other primates. I view the strict territorial concepts of many later sedentary societies as hefty cultural enhancements of a more original and flexible notion of land use.

The concept of territory is of interest here as it defines a place or space where a group can find all, or nearly all, of the resources it needs to subsist and survive. The group will define that space with reference to landmarks and pathways through the landscape. Such places might be defined on a cultural level as symbolic reminders that have a type of permanence, perhaps even down the generations. Australian Aborigines attach stories or creation myths to special places that require defining in some way and these places might have their own song, which itself will be passed on, and down through kin and totemic lines. Whilst this perhaps overcomplicates how earlier *Homo* might have viewed such places in the landscape, it does raise the possibility that they are likely to have viewed some places and some defining territorial landscape markers as symbolically significant. Certainly, the significance of places and the symbolic associations that were attached to them grew deeper over time so that by the time we reach Cro-Magnons in Europe, some 45,000 years ago, such concepts were already highly evolved. More significantly, I believe such concepts were intrinsically bound up with hunting. This is a point that will be discussed and expanded upon in further detail throughout this book, as I believe this is a central tenet in how humans defined landownership and land appropriation. Ultimately, these concepts make up part of the human condition and probably made sedentism and agriculture possible.

3

Times of Transition: Hunting in a Rapidly Changing Landscape

In the early Upper Palaeolithic, termed the Aurignacian period (or Gravettian period, as it is called outside of France), anatomically modern humans, the so-called Cro-Magnons (named after the Abri Cro Magnon rock shelter where their remains were first found, see Fig. 11) made their first incursions into Europe and Britain. As discussed earlier, the pace of their migratory progress was nothing short of blistering compared to their predecessors, probably helped by their larger brains (although they are slightly smaller than Neanderthal brains), their better vocal and language abilities and adaptability to extreme climates, which enabled them to colonise the colder northern latitudes. Generally they were probably better suited to the concept of seasonal migration and to-ing and fro-ing with the seasons than earlier *Homos*. Also touched upon in the last chapter was that in Europe, and probably in Britain, the Cro-Magnons were living alongside their Neanderthal counterparts. What is relatively unknown was whether they lived side-by-side in peace or in conflict. Some palaeontologists have suggested that the 'moderns' pushed them aside and may have even caused the extinction of the Neanderthals, perhaps by warfare. However, there is evidence to suggest that in some places, such as in Israel (the cave sites of Mount Carmel for example), they lived closely for many thousands of years. Skeletons from the caves of Tabun and Kebora contained the remains of Neanderthals, possibly even variants within this species, whilst only a few hundred metres away at the cave site of Skhul and from Qafzeh (20km from Tabun), skeletons here were a lot less Neanderthal-like, their skull morphologies possessing more modern features.

The Franco-Cantabrian region straddling either side of the Pyrenees was another place where modern humans and Neanderthals lived close to each other. Eventually the Neanderthals retreated to the slopes of the Pyrenees, perhaps hanging on in the Iberian Peninsula until around 28 KYA. Significantly, the Franco-Cantabrian region possesses a rich body of rock-art that began shortly after the disappearance of the Neanderthals. The question here is does this amount to evidence of gene flow

11 Cro-Magnon shelter, Les Eyzies, France

between species or something else? There has been some debate as to which species – Neanderthals or Sapiens – had the richer artistic and cultural assemblages at this time, and whether this translates into the emergence of this rich legacy of parietal and mobile art in this region. Even here in Britain there is tentative evidence in the form of the seemingly Châtelperronian assemblage at Bamford Road, Ipswich, which may show that the two species rubbed along together for a time at least. It seems likely that if the two species were living in close proximity then there must, as a minimum, have been a sharing of ideas. There are some tell-tale signs in the differing tool assemblages in use that suggest Neanderthals were probably copying, to some extent, the Cro-Magnons or even vice versa. There are suggestions that Neanderthals were on the way to behavioural modernity, in areas such as the manufacture of bone tools, and that this is evident within the Châtelperronian assemblages even before modern humans arrived in Europe, according to Nick Barton (*Ice Age Britain*, 2005: 114). It is even possible that the Neanderthals developed the earlier facies of the 'Aurignacian' toolkit and that the Cro-Magnons copied it and ran with it; developing it along the way. One explanation, based upon some of the current evidence, is that Neanderthals may well have been assimilated into the Cro-Magnon gene pool; that there was some gene flow as well as information flow between species. Further work on Neanderthal genes may yet shed more light on this – certainly there is a suggestion that the gene

12 Map of the seven British Aurignacian finds locations dating to *c*.32,000 to 28,000 BP

37

for speech may actually have been transmitted to us from Neanderthals, the 'Fox P2 gene' mentioned earlier. Another strand of evidence, as we have seen, is that the Neanderthals were hafting and using Levallois points as projectile weapons in the Levant.

In Britain, as in the rest of northern Europe, there was no early Aurignacian tool industry evident – only a later Aurignacian. There are seven sites with a western (Atlantic seaboard) distribution including Fynnon Beuno, North Wales, the Severn Estuary, Paviland, Hoyle's Mouth and Nottle Tor in South Wales, and at Uphill Quarry, Somerset, where a bone point was discovered. All these sites seem to fit within a narrow band of occupation dating to between 32,000 and 28,000 years ago. Climatic deterioration at the onset of a stadial, drove human occupation away from Britain for several thousand years.

The Aurignacian tool industry is believed to have had its origins in the Balkans region, or at least the industry was there by the time anatomically modern humans arrived about 45,000 years ago. But more than just being a tool assemblage, the Aurignacian was a pattern or system of identifiable and tangible behavioural signals deduced in the archaeological record that was consistent, broadly, over a span of 18,000 years (45,000 to 27,000 years ago). The tool industry was typified by a turning away from the earlier Mousterian flake-based tools to a blade-based one, with retouching – trimming the flint edge to create tools such as knives – becoming the dominant tool form. This is not to say that there were no blades in the Middle Palaeolithic, only that at around 45,000 to 43,000 years ago blade production sharply increased and flakes declined. This is critical to the story of hunting, because this change represents a revolution in weapon-making, with the new blade technology showing a critical shift to hafted (composite) weapons. The use of the easier to make blade tools represented a significant saving in time when it came to weapon-making because hafting the flint into cut notches using resin glue made a reusable weapon. The cutting edge of the spear tip could be significantly increased in this way. Again, it is important to point out that in the earlier period, the Middle Palaeolithic, there is some evidence that Neanderthals used this method too (the Schöningen spears dating to 400,000 years), but it was in the Aurignacian that the method really started to come into its own.

Scrapers were also a common tool type, but unlike the earlier Mousterian-type scrapers the Aurignacian ones were again based on blades and were smaller, sometimes fitting comfortably under the thumb, and were not unlike 'thumbnail scrapers' found in later prehistory. These sorts of scrapers were easier to use and capable of finer work. Tools such as burins for boring holes into hide, bone, ivory, antler or wood were also appearing in the archaeological record. In general the blade led to an increase of tool forms upon which it could be based and this led to a proliferation of a broader range of specialised tools in use at this time. Naturally enough, all these distinctive subcategories of tools point to an increased sophistication in producing worked ivory, antler and bone tools, and ornaments or adornments. In Geissenklösterle, Germany, for example, Aurignacian levels revealed an abundance of debris associated with working bone and ivory. The debris showed how these materials were cut, sawn, ground and polished and the waste was associated mainly with flint burins. Microwear analysis of the burins showed that they were indeed used for this type of production.

Perhaps more importantly from a hunting point of view was the creation of bone and ivory points with modified bases (termed split-based ivory and bone points), assumed to have been made thus for hafting. They were made from long thin splinters separated from a straight beam of antler or mammoth tusk by using a sharp piece of flint to cut a pair of parallel grooves deeply into the material and then prising out the splinter. This is called the 'groove and splinter technique'. It is quite clear by the way they were made that they were designed to fit onto the end of a wooden or antler shaft to make a composite throwing spear or a short dart. Barbed points were a highly specialised type of weapon; in effect a hunting harpoon, useful for fishing and spearing medium to large-sized game.

In addition to developing hafted composite spears, and probably emerging in tandem with them, an entirely new and critical hunting device appeared that meant that humans could throw their spears further, more accurately and with far greater force than ever before – the atlatl or spear thrower. The actual evidence for a spear thrower does not appear in the archaeological record until the Solutrean (about 21,000 to 19,000 years ago), but the appearance of these highly evolved implements at least indicates that they were likely to have been in use in the Aurignacian too. A spear thrower is a device made of wood, bone or antler with a short hook-like attachment at one end. This is used by resting the hollowed tip of a spear-end against the hook and laying it along the shaft; secured by thumb and forefinger the spear can then be cast with greater force, distance and accuracy. In Combe Saunière, France, a small hook of antler was found which, in this instance, was bound and set in resin to a shaft. Other examples were found in late Upper Palaeolithic contexts, some of which were quite ornate. Australian Aborigines used the spear thrower with deadly effect and the first European colonists' descriptions of their use attest to their effectiveness in hunting. Interestingly, Aborigines used the spear thrower for other purposes, such as for digging up edible roots and even for butchery.

To dwell upon the Aborigines again for a moment, another tool that they used was also found in the European Solutrean (21,000–19,000 BP) – the boomerang. At the site Oblazowa Cave, Poland, an ivory implement, if interpreted correctly, is a boomerang and was capable of returning to its thrower and probably had a range of 200m – and was accurate in a skilled throwers hand.

It is clear then that at this critical period in modern human history, in the few millennia after they arrived in Europe, hunting was becoming an increasingly sophisticated endeavour, with the proliferation of more advanced composite weapons and new ways of extending their range (spear throwers), and some new weapons appearing (the boomerang). What is important to note is how these changes went hand-in-hand with the advancements in flint technology – better flint tools helped manufacture better weapons. So if the Aurignacian and Solutrean periods represent something of a watershed for modern humans in terms of technology, then what of the hunting strategies they employed? How did these strategies differ from those employed by their Middle Palaeolithic cousins?

Advances in weapons we have just seen meant increased power and range and improved accuracy, especially to spear throwing. This gave greater flexibility in modifying old and developing new hunting tactics. Herds of animals could then be manipulated to have individual animals separated out and killed, or groups of animals could even be intercepted and killed in large numbers. The development of seasonal specialisation was one key feature of hunting in this period (see Chapter 4 on human–animal relationships for more on this).

In previous periods Neanderthals, it is believed, stayed put in their territories and hunted the same area consistently for long periods of time. This narrowed the range of their diets somewhat and probably meant that certain animals were locally over-hunted. Modern humans by comparison were more mobile and hunted far larger territories. The evidence for this comes from the seasonal tooth cement layers on the prey animals that were hunted (see previous chapter for a fuller explanation). It may be for this reason that modern humans and possibly Neanderthal/human hybrids ultimately survived their Neanderthal counterparts.

Sometime during the Upper Palaeolithic the bow and arrow was probably developed, although the evidence for this is largely circumstantial, as no direct evidence for them has been found. Flint assemblages from this period point to the possibility, but as there seems to be no definitive 'arrowhead' that belongs to this time it is hard to prove. Arrows, if they did exist, were likely to be composite weapons with flint blades and fragments set into resin. The first solid evidence for the use of the bow and arrow comes from the early Mesolithic and its appearance at this time suggests that such a weapon would have evolved and developed in the preceding period. There are a number of aurochs known in Britain which show evidence of having been hunted in the Mesolithic using bow and arrow. One from Bleasby Quarry in the Trent Valley, Nottinghamshire (shown in Colour plate 4), was found in conjunction with three microliths from an arrowhead, which were in close proximity to the vertebrae of the animal. This aurochs was one of at least two animals found in the silts of a palaeo-channel, indicating that these aurochs had died trying to escape their hunters or had died in a flood sometime after the event.

Animals hunted in the Ice Age

From the Aurignacian through to the Magdalenian periods there was a wide variety of species hunted by Cro-Magnons. We have examined some of the species that were hunted by earlier humans in the Lower to Middle Palaeolithic periods and how they varied, due to environmental factors, through time. Game species also varied over time due to the environmental conditions imposed upon the landscapes by the Ice Age from the early Upper Palaeolithic and into the late Upper Palaeolithic. For much of the late Ice Age animals were free to roam back and forth across what is now

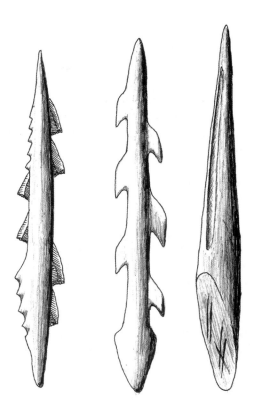

13 Magdalenian bone spear points. (Source: http://commons.wikimedia. org/wiki/File:Proyectiles_oseos_ Magdaleniense.jpg; artist: José-Manuel Benito Álvarez)

the North Sea and these migrations and the spatial pattern of habitats used by horses, reindeer, bison, elks, giant deer, mountain hares and aurochs would have been studied with interest by the humans who relied upon them for food. Since the start of the Devensian Glaciation (*c.*122,000–18,000 years ago) Britain was not always inhabited by humans due to the extremes of cold during the stadials and the interglacials. It is notable also that animals such as the musk ox (*Ovibos moschatus*), and possibly polar bear (*Ursus maritimus*), and woolly rhinoceros could be found right up to the Late Glacial Maximum (LGM) of *c.*18–20,000 years ago. However, there is a striking contrast just after the LGM when these specimens become rare – indicative of just how cold this stadial was.

Perhaps the best known of the Late Glacial animals is the impressive and now extinct Mammoth (*Mammuthus primigenius*), and its remains have been found at a number of British sites, including Creswell Crags and Paviland Cave, Gower, Wales. Preserved remains of mammoths from Siberia, Russia and Alaska, combined with parietal art from the Continent, such as the drawings at Chauvet Cave and engravings and drawings at Rouffignac, France, means that we know how these creatures looked. Interestingly, when the media discusses Ice Age rock-art it endeavours to show mammoths as a primary image of that period; yet it is far from the most numerous of the animals shown in rock-art. Related to modern elephants, but in many ways startlingly different, mammoths possessed a long outer coat of coarse fur and a short dense undercoat. They also had a good covering of fat (up to 8cm thick), all of which provided much-needed protection from the harsh cold environment. Their tusks were huge and twisted, sometimes touching at the tips, and were used for digging into the snow to get to the vegetation below it. The tusks were also valued by humans for making ornaments, examples of which have been found at Paviland Cave on the coast of the Gower peninsular, such as the fine bracelet and thin rods discovered with the Gravettian remains of the so-called 'Red Lady' of Paviland.

Mammoth tusks, bones and teeth are, from time to time, discovered in the gravel quarries of the Trent Valley. The mammoth became extinct here by around 11–12,000 BP, due to a rapidly warming climate leading to a change in the vegetation it required. Mammoths became extinct perhaps considerably later in Siberia, where colder conditions prevailed for longer and human hunters were more dispersed. Hunting it was thought was unlikely to have contributed to its demise, but a new study on the Megafauna of Tasmania indicates that the link between climate change and extinction may be less clear than previously thought, with many creatures becoming extinct two millennia after humans arrived there during a time of stable and favourable climatic conditions. This, allied with the data from mainland Australia at 46,000 years BP, when 90 per cent of the Megafauna became extinct, coincides with the arrival of people there, indicating that human intervention plays a greater role in animal extinctions than had previously been thought. The human appearance in the environment, perhaps in conjunction with climate change, was a double-whammy on the Megafauna of Australia and Tasmania. There are indications, yet to be fully researched, that this may have been the case elsewhere, including Europe.

Bison (*Bison priscus*) were certainly present in the British Isles in the earlier part of the Devensian (last) Glaciation, but there is debate about whether they were there in the latter part of the Devensian, at about the time the rock-art, which is in the Magdalenian style, was created in Church Hole Cave, Creswell Crags (dated to *c.*12,000 BC). Here a bison is supposedly depicted on Panel III, with its horns pointing into the darker recesses of the cave. The figure, now described as a bovid, could be of an aurochs (*Bos primigenius*), as the latest dated specimens of bison come from Beckford, Worcestershire and Kent's Cavern, Devon and date to 27,700 BP. However, the figure does more closely resemble a bison than an aurochs but this again presents a problem – aurochs are woodland species and at this time are unlikely to be this far north (later, in the Mesolithic, aurochs were fairly common in this area). The other possibility, of course, is that if the people who visited Church Hole were part of a group of people that had travelled from further afield. Could the most parsimonious explanation be that they were depicting something they had seen and hunted elsewhere? At 27,700 BP the bison was certainly familiar to early Upper Palaeolithic hunters in Britain, but not so in the late Upper Palaeolithic. Perhaps the artist belonged to a nomadic group that travelled from, or had contact with, people in the Paris Basin or Ardennes region.

14 The Bison. Church Hole Cave, Creswell Crags. The head can be seen at the right, which is part bas-relief with the clear engraved line showing the back of the animal and a vertical line at the front showing the foreleg. (Barry Lewis – courtesy of Creswell Crags Heritage Trust)

Another interesting anomaly thrown up from the rock-art at Church Hole is the depiction of the red deer (*Cervus elaphus*), another woodland species found further to the south where a few specimens were discovered. In the south they were the inhabitants of the birch woodlands. In the Creswell Crags area at this time steppe-tundra conditions prevailed, and again indicates that people had brought the images of red deer with them. A single faint horse engraving is also on the roof of Church Hole; its small but faint and very typically late Upper Palaeolithic head perhaps utilises the natural form of the rock surface.

What these depictions highlight is that the hunters who occupied and created the rock-art at Creswell Crags were capable of, and probably were, travelling great distances in seasonal migrations that took them south and east. As will be shown later in this chapter, it is entirely possible that they travelled some 600km as far as the Paris Basin, perhaps even further, and brought with them images of bison, a creature that was probably unknown at this time in Britain. From the south they brought images of red deer. What this indicates is that Creswell Crags was an important aggregation locale.

Most commonly hunted during the Late Glacial it seems was reindeer (*Rangifer tarandus*), its presence an indicator of how cold it was during the Late Glacial era.

In Creswell Crags the most commonly hunted animal, perhaps for its fur for making clothes, was the mountain hare (*Lepus timidus*). Both the reindeer and the mountain hares were important fur-bearing species. After reindeer the horse was the most commonly hunted Late Glacial animal in Britain, as I have already discussed. But there is some variability between sites, as with the hares at Creswell Crags. Interestingly, Roger Jacobi believes that herds of reindeer could have migrated across the North Sea Plains to Britain during the spring to the safer highland birthing grounds in the Pennines. Indeed, the North Sea Plains could well have been their summer grazing lands. The evidence from Stellmoor in Germany, which provided a kind of natural bottleneck concentrating reindeer herds, shows that they were intercepted and hunted there in the autumn when they were migrating down from the mountains. Reindeer would pass through the area on their way to the south of the contemporary tree line to overwinter. Places like Creswell might have served a similar function to intercept seasonal migrations of reindeer and horses, perhaps even utilising the gorge as a confined kill-zone.

Other animals common during the Late Glacial and probably hunted in varying numbers were lynx (*Lynx lynx*), brown bear (*Ursus arctos*) and wolf (*Canis lupus*). In parts of the south of England and southern Ireland elks (*Alces alces*) were known to have lived; also the eponymous Irish elk, or more correctly Giant Deer (*Megalocerous giganteus*), first known from a number of Irish sites such as Killuragh Cave, the Edenvale Caves and Ballybetagh, as well as from a number of sites on the Isle of Man (i.e. Glen Balleria) and from Kirkhead Cave, Cumbria. This giant deer (resembling most closely a giant fallow deer), possessed of outlandishly large antlers, began to die out during the short-lived cold-snap of the Younger Dryas stadial. It is not known if hunting played a significant part in their extinction but it is suspected that it contributed to it.

Humans and animal migrations in the Late Upper Palaeolithic

Cro-Magnons travelled great distances following the herds of game, particularly during the Magdalenian, in the Late Upper Palaeolithic. This, in part, might have been because of a special relationship that they had with horses. It is not impossible that this relationship was perhaps based upon a loose concept of, or a form of ownership of particular herds of horses. It is possible also that this is what is reflected in the parietal and mobile art of the Upper Palaeolithic. The next chapter explores this relationship in more detail but in essence the proliferation of 'horse art' and related symbolic behaviours, which in much of Europe seems to be far in excess of their importance as a food animal, was based upon a simple herding and hunting strategy that might be broadly reflective of the later prehistoric horse cultures of the East. In other words, this relationship may show some similarities with the Kazak and Mongol horse cultures of the Eurasian Steppes today but which we know has its roots in the early Bronze Age (more accurately Copper Age) of the region. Upper

Palaeolithic cultures may not have ridden the horses or even used them as pack animals, but they were valued perhaps as a status symbol, or as a means of displaying wealth and negotiating or facilitating access (via status and wealth conferred by 'owning' large numbers of horses) to large territories as they followed or controlled the migrations of their horses throughout Europe. The Kazak horse culture of today works along similar lines – again this cultural trait has a deep history. Such a thing is possible by training the lead mares so that they will respond to certain humans, recognising them as dominant. As dominant mares, in a family group lead mares will lead the group wherever she indicates.

In Britain during the Magdalenian there was a 're-colonisation' of our islands (not forgetting at this time we were connected to Europe by Doggerland, now the North Sea), which occurred around 16,000 BP. This was part of the ebb and flow of people that came and went as the ice associated with each stadial or glacial receded. This re-colonisation followed the Late Glacial Maximum around 18,000 years ago. At this time ice covered all of Scotland and much of northern England to a depth of around 1300–1400m. Only the south of England was ice-free during the LGM. A significant rise in temperature occurred 15,000 years ago in north-west Europe and gave rise to a period of accelerated deglaciation between 15,000 and 13,000 years ago; but there then followed a short-lived period of climatic deterioration known as the Younger Dryas stadial between 13,000 and 11,500 years ago, which led to the formation of ice-fields in the western Highlands of Scotland and small glaciers in eastern and northern Scottish Highlands. Cirque glaciers formed in the lakes and mountains of North and South Wales. This was the last time glaciers could be found on mainland Britain.

During this time Magdalenian people were migrating north and south within Britain and probably even further afield, perhaps between the south of England and the Midlands and the Paris Basin. There are researchers who would disagree with calling these re-colonisers of Britain 'Magdalenian'. The flint tool evidence found at Creswell Crags gave rise to a tool tradition labelled 'Creswellian' by Dorothy Garrod in the 1920s, who first described it. It was subsequently also found at Gough's Cave in Cheddar Gorge (separate to the local flint type known as 'Cheddar Points' first discovered here), and other places. The Creswellian industry has for a long time defined a British element of the Continental tool and cultural traditions of the late Upper Palaeolithic. However, the tool assemblages and other cultural traits, such as the cave art discovered at Church Hole Cave in Creswell Crags, are certainly similar enough to the continental Magdalenian tradition to warrant classifying it as such.

Sites like Creswell Crags, which would have been a highly important hunting site both for its useful gorge into which animals could have been driven, and for the shelter it provides to human inhabitants, were also likely to have had cultural significance as aggregation locales, a point I touched upon earlier. These were places, in an otherwise stark and hostile environment of steppe tundra, where people would have naturally gravitated to. They were real landmarks. It is likely that Creswell Crags and sites like it, such as Cheddar Gorge, became important aggregation locales, places

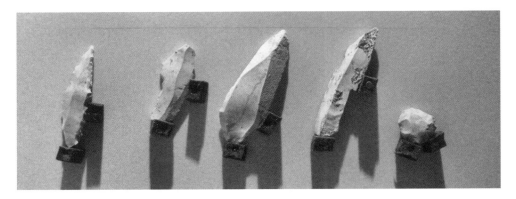

15 Late Upper Palaeolithic flints, Creswellian. (Barry Lewis – photographed courtesy of Creswell Crags Heritage Trust)

where people of different family groups or clans would meet, negotiate marriages, make art, practise religion, hunt and feast. These activities were crucial in the Ice Age, especially where resources were scarce in the tundra landscapes. Interestingly, there was little evidence of occupation in Church Hole Cave, where rock-art was made, yet opposite, on the north side of the gorge, occupation evidence in Robin Hood's Cave was abundant. Similar patterns are seen in the French Pyrenees with Niaux Cave having plenty of parietal art and little occupation, and the caves opposite having much evidence. Contact with other groups offered chances for trade, perhaps in the instance of Creswell Crags, furs could have been traded for ivory, flint nodules or the right to encroach upon the territories of others to take deer or horses. Places like Creswell or Cheddar were set apart and not subject to the normal rules of territorial and social contact. Their 'specialness' meant that at predetermined times groups may have been able to come together without fear of conflict or recrimination and negotiate peaceably for the things that would ensure their clans' survival in the coming months.

The use of such places as aggregation locales would require ready access to game for feasting activities. Sometimes this might necessitate feasting on 'special' meat, perhaps horse. For example, Gough's Cave at Cheddar Gorge, Somerset, provides ample evidence of horse hunting. At Gough's the body parts of hunted horses of all ages were represented, meaning that the horses were killed close by. Evidence from South Germany at Brudertal, a Magdalenian cave site in Petersfels near Engen, shows a rich abundance of tools and faunal remains pointing to open air camps and kill sites contemporary with the cave. Here the activities were not just confined to the caves but also out in the open, close to the cave. This is a category of evidence that is lost from Cheddar Gorge due to natural and human modification within the gorge. If such evidence were ever there it could point to aggregation and feasting activities in the cave and gorge. Above Gough's Cave the gorge narrows and horses could have been driven into a natural cul-de-sac and slaughtered. Dogs were probably used

16 Cheddar Gorge.
(George Nash)

in these hunts aiding the humans in these activities – the earliest evidence of their appearance and use in Britain (covered in more detail in the next chapter). There was also evidence of other more domestic activities taking place there, including making glues by removing horses' hooves, hide manufacture evidenced by the use-wear on flint scrapers and flint manufacturing provided by discarded cores. Bone tallies were also found, as were a collection of Amber pebbles perhaps sourced from Doggerland. So we have feasting on horseflesh and the creation of ornaments taking place here. In general, the artefact and activity evidence from here points to some ostentation and display, some domestic activity and extended gatherings. Gough's Cave, it is clear from the evidence, was an aggregation site, a place where human groups came together to meet and negotiate access to resources, hold ceremonies, build alliances through marriages and similar mechanisms.

On more than one occasion so far I have raised the suggestion that Magdalenian groups that were occupying the Paris Basin and the Ardennes region of Belgium were the same ones that used the caves at Cheddar Gorge and Creswell Crags.

There is some tentative evidence for this in the particular ways flint tools were worked and subsequently deposited at these sites. It has even been suggested that the same groups, even individuals, were responsible for the manufacture of the flint implements found at some of these sites. This then points to these Magdalenian clans covering distances of up to 600km in a seasonal migratory round. If this is the case then these people would clearly have had some form of contact with groups living in what is now Germany and the Czech Republic. Hence the domestic dog could easily have spread into Britain from these interactions. Dogs we have seen had a role to play in horse hunting at Cheddar.

Much as we are aware of climate change today, so too were the people living in Britain at this time. Remembering that we are dealing with people much more attuned to their ancestral pasts and commemorating those ancestors, they undoubtedly had a rich oral tradition; they were also fundamentally more aware of their landscapes than we are. Changes that affected their environments would have been as obvious to them as they are to us today. Even without the benefit of long meteorological records or scientific data from ice cores, oral history and a deep sense of ancestral past would have provided them with the stories of what the world they inhabited was like many generations back; even into a mythological past of strange beasts, perhaps grazing forested landscapes where neither existed during their time. Indeed, it is entirely possible that climate change was as rapid at the end of the Ice Age as it is now and that the changes were manifest within a human lifetime. Such changes will naturally have an effect upon vegetation, weather and the animals that they hunted. This meant that the landscape these people inhabited was changing too, along with their concepts of territoriality. Coastlines were changing, the Doggerland Plains were vanishing, threatening to cut off their linkages with kin in what is now France and Belgium. In the era that followed, the Mesolithic, a time of boreal forests, the nature of human subsistence, especially around the coast, had changed – as had their concepts of land tenure and territoriality – both of which were intertwined with hunting. I will talk more about this in a later chapter.

4

Human-Animal Relationships

At this point it is pertinent to look at human-animal relationships, given the context provided by the preceding chapters; it is fundamental to the story of hunting as we go forwards through time into the Mesolithic and on even to the modern era. The focus of this chapter is our relationship with horses and dogs, animals that depending where in time you stood were either food or partners in hunting, or even both.

Horses and dogs: from prey to symbiosis

Here I shall look at two of the most critical human-animal relationships in hunting: the relationship between humans and dogs, and humans and horses. Horses, dogs and hunting together are iconoclastic of how we would perceive hunting in modern Britain. To those who have been involved in the world of sport hunting in the last two or three millennia, horses, dogs and prey would arguably be the Holy Trinity of the perfect hunt. The scholastic study of these human-animal relationships has a complex history. Much has been said on the issue of the domestication of wolves, the creation or emergence of the domestic dog and how this happened. Likewise, the history of herding and of the domestication and bridling of horses is long, contentious and complex. Here I will explore some of these issues for they are important to how we look at the use of horses and dogs in hunting today. Much of the chapter will focus on these relationships since the Upper Palaeolithic, but a brief section will look at horses and early humans of the Middle Palaeolithic because this will provide some background to the nature of human/horse relationships in later times.

Certainly the horse was food long before it was ever a 'useful mount' for the hunt, and even when it was ridden it was, for a long time, still viewed as food. Even the dog was sometimes an important food source in British prehistory. When the Romans came it is likely there was already a well-established culture in Britain of using horses

17 Huntsmen, horses and dogs; the classic image of hunting and symbolic of the human-animal relationship

and dogs in hunting. They then continued and certainly refined this tradition, introducing ideas and fashions to hunting that were familiar even in more recent centuries. By the medieval period it was absolutely *de rigueur* in elite and royal hunting to use dogs and horses. All through these periods dogs and horses were selectively bred to produce types and breeds to hunt all manner of prey. Dogs were bred to hunt bear, stags and even big cats, whilst the evolution of the mounted horse led to the creation of the Medieval great horse, favoured in battle and ultimately leading, in more recent centuries, to the Irish hunter (an Irish draft and thoroughbred cross) – a type of horse that was strong and ideally suited to a long day in the saddle, and able to jump fences and hedges during a modern foxhunt and, after the ban, drag hunting. Alongside Irish hunters ran foxhounds, staghounds, beagles and bloodhounds, all dogs that were bred for the hunt.

The idea of the early (Palaeolithic) domestication of dogs has, since the nineteenth century, enjoyed something of a chequered history. Dog domestication was nearly always perceived to be linked, in one way or another, with the hunting of horses or reindeer. Early French researchers into the Upper Palaeolithic fell into two broad camps on the issue of the domestication of animals during this time: the one camp believed there was a way of discerning evidence of the proto-domestication of animals such as reindeer from the butchery evidence; whilst another camp, firmly opposed to this view, argued that if any animals were ever domesticated at this time then it was the dog. The argument went that if reindeer or any herd animals were domesticated then evidence of dog domestication would be apparent, because it was the dogs that would be the guardians of the herds. But since no such dog remains were (during the mid-nineteenth century) found, then there was no domestication until the Neolithic. This was based upon observations of the use of dogs in the northern European cultures of Lapp, Ostyak and Samoyed reindeer breeding. In these cultures using dogs seemed to be critical. However, and quite critically, what was ignored (or only just at this time being ethnologically described and therefore perhaps missed) was that there were remote cultures, namely the Chukchee and Tungus, who bred and herded reindeer without the benefit of dogs. Where all this leads us is down a brambly path where argument and counter-argument has, from time to time, reignited and flared up surrounding the thorny issues of corralling, husbandry, herding and indeed restraining and harnessing animals, including horses.

Archaeologist and Palaeolithic rock-art specialist Paul Bahn cautions against using terminology like domestication, which implies a level of control, and husbandry, that might not have existed for many millennia afterwards, but does advocate other terms that suggest a certain degree of control of horses, for example. Terms like corralling, herding, restraining, even husbandry are all usable in this nomenclature. The reasoning for this comes from data at a number of Continental Palaeolithic sites, where there is a limited body of evidence including faunal remains, mobile art and rock-art pointing to the assumption that such activities were going on. Paul Bahn suggested that some form of herding or corralling was happening even as far back as the Middle Palaeolithic; from the site of La Quina, a Mousterian site, there is evidence of wear on horse teeth consistent with crib-biting, something that usually only ever happens to horses that are either kept tethered or stabled for prolonged periods. At this time there had been no studies that pointed to crib-biting in wild herds. Indeed, the whole issue of crib-biting still has not been systematically studied. The La Quina evidence seems to point to bark stripping rather than actual crib-biting but, again, the lack of systematic study makes the drawing of conclusions problematic either way. There are other horse remains from a number of Upper Palaeolithic sites that show crib-biting evidence and these shall be looked at in a little more detail later in the chapter – along with the recent controversy and discussion created by Bahn's work since the 1970s.

In the Magdalenian (at the end of the Pleistocene *c.*12,000 to 9,000 years ago), and touched upon in the last chapter, there is good evidence to suggest that there were domestic dogs in Europe and even in Britain. The central European evidence which put people on the right track came from sites in the Czech Republic and Germany, where the remains of 'wolves' were subjected to oesteological analysis that found physical traits similar to those found in domestic dogs, such as overall limb size measurements and a reduction in size of the mandible. Figure 18 shows *Canis lupus* and *Canis familiaris* skulls side by side, and the right skull shows a shorter snout on the *familiaris* (domestic dog). This evidence also showed that the speed of the appearance of these 'domestic' traits was rapid. Also of interest was a study of the Mitochondrial DNA of dogs done by an international team led by Carlos Villa in 1997, which suggested that genes of domestic dogs diverged naturally perhaps as far back as 135,000 years ago. The Czech and German oesteological evidence was examined by Czech researcher Rudolf Musil, who had analysed the variations within a number of wolf/dog skeletons. This variation in the faunal remains of wolves can be seen as the beginning of a long process of domestication that led to the many varieties and breeds of dogs that we have today. At these sites there was an emphasis on horse hunting and an implication

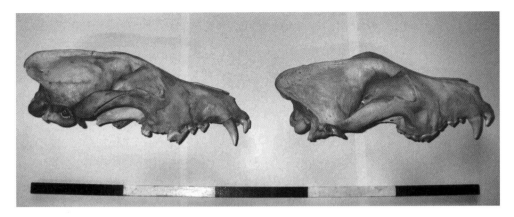

18 Wolf (*Canis lupus*) on the left and dog (*Canis familiaris*) on the right. (Barry Lewis – photographed courtesy of Creswell Crags Heritage Trust)

that the domestication of wolves, their willingness to identify a pack-leader, even a human one, and their natural instinct for hunting, improved the strategies and methods during horse hunts. This benefit to Magdalenian hunters was the beginning of a human/animal symbiosis that led to a process of selective breeding in dogs to maximise useful traits. However, Villa and his team showed that the nature of the genetic evidence suggests that the genes of the earliest 'domestic dog' were more like those of the coyote – a new divergent species. The coyote began its divergence from wolves around 1 million years ago. The earliest types of 'domestic dog', it is thought by some researchers, are likely to be a natural divergence that started over 100,000 years ago, and that humans later began to selectively breed from these during the Magdalenian. Perhaps of most interest in this study was that the great variations between breeds in dogs were achieved by cross-breeding back with wolves. Precisely when humans started to selectively breed and truly domesticate dogs has yet to be pinned down but it could be in excess of 15,000 years ago – perhaps significantly more.

Interestingly, and as we saw earlier at Gough's Cave in Cheddar Gorge, recently reassessed evidence, which suggests that horses were hunted there using dogs in the Magdalenian, was published by Roger Jacobi of the British Museum. A number of skeletons, initially assumed to be those of wolves, were re-examined and found to be domestic dogs – this, in conjunction with Musil's work in the Czech Republic and his archaeological observations of dogs being used in horse hunting, combined with the great number of horse remains found at Gough's Cave, prompted Jacobi to make this reinterpretation of the evidence.

So dogs really are likely to be the very beginning of true domestication. Theories about the need to domesticate, and the role of domestication, during the Late Glacial and early post-glacial periods, suggest that dogs fitted the pace of our lifestyles and were useful in hunting activities at a point when we were able to sustain that kind of symbiosis in our developmental and technological stage at that time.

It has been suggested that reindeer, for example, would have been far easier to domesticate than the wolf, but our technology and consequently our social development were probably not sufficiently advanced to keep and harness them in any useful way, due to the constraints imposed upon us by the hostility of the environment and the migratory mode of living. The same was probably true with horses to some extent too. Dogs, however, supported us, were relatively low maintenance and asked little of us in return – perfect for humans in the Ice Age.

The mechanism by which the first wolves were domesticated was probably fairly simple. It is likely that humans and wolves had loose interaction centred around the hunting of herd animals, such as deer or horses, perhaps each utilising the skills of the other to maximise the chances of a kill or capture without ever formally interacting for millennia. For example, humans might have understood from the visible movements and audible calls of wolves across the expanses of tundra that a hunt might

19 Wolf. (Retron)

well be under way. Wolves, likewise, probably sussed human hunting methods, such as the driving of game into kill zones (like gorges) resulting in the odd injured or disoriented escapee that would be easy prey for them to pick off. Or it may have been by the campfire where discarded bones brought the odd scavenging wolf into contact with humans. Stories of this nature abound in the pioneering days of Frontier America, making it even more likely in the Ice Age that this kind of interaction happened. Eventually it may have been the discovery of a clutch of pups that were then hand-reared that finally created the start of this critical symbiotic relationship. Humans, regardless of their omnivorous natures, have a tendency to take in and care for sick or orphaned animals – children in particular do this. This may have been the start of a perceived 'ownership' of animals. People who hunted the tundra were undoubtedly familiar with the wolf and its lifecycle, its pack behaviours and its skill as a hunter. It is this knowledge and the observations of those hunters that would have made the domestication of the wolf a fairly straightforward process, whatever mechanism was employed to do it.

Domesticated wolves became extra ears for humans, bringing them further protection from carnivores and hostile human groups. Knowing the wolves' natural predisposition for protecting their 'pack' meant that this relationship would quickly develop and spread throughout human society. This and the advantages they brought to the hunt: better sight, hearing and most importantly scenting. All of these features were most advantageous to people and ensured the huge success of this relationship right down to the present.

Dogs, as most people know, have a natural aptitude or instinct for hunting and it was this that was useful to hunters; harnessing this was a good way for Ice Age hunters to up their game and improve their kill rate. Over time, favoured dogs with particular aptitudes for hunting would have been preferentially selected for breeding; perhaps as much for their physical characteristics, defining them in some way as better hunters, as for their personalities. It was not necessarily their skills in running down deer and bringing them to the ground that was sought after, it was more likely their skill to herd and control, and for listening to and obeying commands that were important. The whole package, much like the desirable traits sought in a modern working sheepdog, was needed. For example, a collie may be excellent at rounding up and herding sheep but if it is no good at obeying commands most of the time, or shows aggression to sheep or humans, it would be discounted as a decent sort. Favoured hunting dogs then, like those in more recent times, had a higher intrinsic value, making it beneficial to ensure that at least some of those favoured traits were passed on to the next generation. Living a nomadic existence at the end of the Pleistocene, relying upon the abilities of one's dogs, watching their behaviours, identifying which dog mated with which bitch, and doubtless noticing that some of the key traits of the better hunting dogs were being passed to the next generation, these hunters would have soon learned the benefits of selective breeding. Hence those 'domestic' traits appearing in a short space of time in those bone assemblages examined in the Czech Republic and Germany by Musil.

It is no accident, therefore, that the hunting of animals during the late Upper Palaeolithic reaches its zenith. One of the key differences being that at this time medium and small animals are hunted rather than the large game of the preceding periods. Typically, the game species represented in faunal assemblages at this time are reindeer, horses, hares and foxes. There are a number of reasons for this change in prey size, which are discussed elsewhere in the book, but here it is important to note that dogs are most suited to aid the hunting of these smaller, faster game species.

The human-horse relationship started as a hunter/prey one and remained so for a long time. Somewhere along the way the relationship changed and something approaching domestication took place. This story was not a structured continuous evolutionary one; rather it can be described as a sporadic and complex narrative that took many twists and turns. The story is further complicated by the difficulties in interpreting the various classes of evidence; this was seen as a problem in the nineteenth century and it is a situation that looks set to continue for the time being. As we have already seen, there are many debates about when and how horses were domesticated and what 'domestication' is in the context of the arguments proffered.

So it is against this hazy and confusing background that the story is told. One of the key protagonists is Paul Bahn, who in 1978 wrote *The 'Unacceptable Face' of the West European Upper Palaeolithic*, published in Antiquity, which reassessed the debates of the nineteenth century and examined more up-to-date evidence and arguments. One aspect was examining the symbolism of the horse and the way it was used in parietal and mobile art. This paper stimulated a heated debate, which continues to smoulder to this day. Firstly, it is useful to address some of the genetic studies as background to the discussion of the human-horse relationship before returning to the contentious debate stimulated by Bahn.

It has been frequently noted that dogs have a greater in-built genetic variation, far more than cats do for example, which arises from a deep time depth of domestication and from breeding back with wolves from time to time (at first this may not always have been intentional!). Whilst accepting that there might be genetic reasons

20 La Chaire à Calvin (Calvin's Pulpit), near Mouthiers sur Boëme, Charente, France. Taken from a cast in the Musée National de Prehistorie, Les Eyzies. (Barry Lewis – object photographed courtesy of Musée National de Prehistorie, Les Eyzies, France)

for this, it is too coincidental to accept that all of this is due to unusual genetic traits manifesting over time thereby creating so many breeds. Human intervention in selectively breeding dogs from early prehistory is no doubt critical in this. The differences between a Chihuahua and a Great Dane are obviously very great indeed. There is a similar variation in equines, with the marked differences between breeds being equally startling – compare the Shetland with a Shire horse for example. Whilst one is obviously a pony and the other a horse, it again serves to highlight the high variation rates within both dogs and horses. It is important to note that fossil and (frozen) carcass evidence for late Pleistocene horses do show that there exists a marked variation in sizes between horses across great distances, which are indicative of different species geographically. Accepting this baseline of high genetic variability, this still points to dogs being the earliest domesticated and selectively bred animals. With horses the evidence of anything like early domestication is not quite so clear cut.

Another genetic study by an international team, again led by Carlos Villa, and again with some of the researchers who were involved with the dog study, found that horses were domesticated in multiple places at differing times: '… modern horses suggests the utilisation of wild horses from a large number of populations as founders of the domestic horse. A single geographically restricted population would not suffice as founding stock.' (Carlos Villa *et al*, 2001 – see Select Reading List.) The genetic traits passed down the female bloodline (mtDNA) shows that there were at least 77 ancestral mares, grouped into 17 phylogenetic branches, which account for the genetic variability in modern populations. The male aspect of modern horse DNA, passed on by the Y chromosome from sire to colt, shows such remarkable homogeneity that there is (genetically speaking at least) only a single Stallion – a Y-Chromosome Adam!

Therefore, all modern horses are descended from many and varied wild mares and very few stallions. The reason for this is that the majority of stallions are truculent and difficult to handle and consequently only those few considered to have a good disposition were selected and bred from. This point about selecting stallions was put succinctly by David Anthony: 'From the horse's perspective, humans were the only way he could get a girl. From the human's perspective, he was the only sire they wanted.'

In the period following the end of the Pleistocene wild horse populations began to dwindle. This was due to changing environment and habitats, resulting from a warming climate and perhaps over-hunting by growing human populations being squeezed by the same forces at the same time exacerbating this decline. By the Iron Age in much of Western Europe the wild horse populations had greatly declined. Whilst in contrast to this in Kazakhstan, domestic horse remains became an increasingly familiar feature of the archaeological record from around 6,000 years ago. Also at this time there is good evidence of bit-wear on the teeth, indicating that they were ridden. In this region, at least since 6,000 years ago, human interference has manipulated horse genes by selective breeding and produced an increasingly large variety of breeds and types. In other parts of Europe it is likely that horses were being domesticated from local wild stocks later on, with perhaps some bloodstock coming from the east from time to time to speed up the process.

It is conceivable that the capturing of horses for meat, milk and hides began in the Magdalenian (12,000 to 9,000 years ago), as indicated by Bahn's work. However, the sensing of the evidence for this in the archaeological record is fraught with problems. Even the evidence we have for the domestication of dogs dating to the late Ice Age is very sparse. Searching for comparable evidence is even more difficult with horses. This is partly due to minimal archaeological evidence and, in some areas, lack of real research, such as into widespread studies of crib-biting, which remains an area where only cursory studies have been conducted. So far, it also seems there has been no systematic study, nor any methodical assessment, of equine faunal remains for the presence of deciduous teeth shed by captured stock, a strong indicator of domestication. It should be mentioned now that all of what is talked about in relation to early domestication and horses almost equally applies to reindeer, an animal that in some sites and areas was of comparable importance to the horse (though lacking a comparable symbolic assemblage as is devoted to the equines at this time). Horses are discussed here because of their overall relevance to hunting and this book, as well as the overarching symbolic importance that they command over all other prey animals in the Upper Palaeolithic. Domestication has been marginally easier to describe in dogs, as discussed above, than it has in horses, as we shall see below.

The Lower to Middle Palaeolithic: wild horses and early humans

Pleistocene fossil horse remains have been found in Siberia, the Czech Republic, France, the Iberian Peninsula and England. So far, the evidence suggests that they did not get into Ireland, perhaps at that time the Pennines, and the braided glacial melt-water rivers of the lowlands, of what is now the Irish Sea, was a barrier to their penetration to the west. In England there is a single possible parietal engraving at Church Hole, Creswell Crags, dating to the late Upper Palaeolithic. The number of horse remains discovered suggests that the Eurasian horse population was high throughout the climatically favourable periods of the Pleistocene. Discoveries of horse remains found thawing from permafrost in Siberia suggests that there were at least three species, all of which were similar to the wild Asiatic horse (*Equus przewalskii*) or Tarpan, found today in Mongolia, where it was recently reintroduced. In stature, choice of habitat and general appearance the Pleistocene European horses were potentially very much like the wild Asiatic. They stand at 12–14 hands (1.23–1.43m) at the withers and are distinguished by their large heavy heads, straight profile, broad forehead, long ears and smallish almond-shaped eyes. Generally, their colouration is palomino, or yellow dun, and they also have mealy coloured muzzles, a broad, fairly short neck with a bristly mane. Sometimes Przewalskii horses bear zebra markings on their legs, no doubt a trait harking back to their even more ancient predecessors. Representations of these horses can be found at rock-art sites such as Naiux and Cap Blanc, France, and Las Monedas, Spain.

Closer to home, mobile art at Creswell Crags, Derbyshire, bears a figurative engraving of a horse head on a piece of rib discovered in Robin Hood Cave in 1876. Palaeolithic portable art is rare in Britain, if indeed it is from Creswell Crags, for it has been suggested that this may have been a 'plant', which had its origins in France (see Colour plate 8). As mentioned above, there is a single faint engraving at Church Hole on the ceiling of the cave, and visible just in the daylight zone is the back line, neck, mane and foreleg of an identifiable horse that at first glance seems to be missing its head. After a closer look, however, the eye can detect the presence of faint natural undulations in the rock surface that could have represented a small head, perhaps now somewhat eroded by weathering processes. If this is the case then the small size relative to body is a classic feature of late Upper Palaeolithic European cave art. Aside from the slight but unrelated issue of the provenance problem of the engraved rib from Creswell Crags, in all instances the resemblance of these images to Przewalskii horses is very strong. Sometimes horse remains were the canvass for decoration, such as in the instance of a horse jaw from Kendrick's Cave, Llandudno, Wales. This jaw was one of a number of significant items discovered there in the 1800s and was initially thought to be of Neolithic date, until it was purchased by the British Museum and its similarity to Continental Upper Palaeolithic art was noted. The jaw was subsequently dated by radio carbon dating and was shown to date around 10,000 BP (see Colour plate 9).

The human-horse relationship is as old as the history of human occupation in Europe in the Pleistocene – at least from a hunter/prey point of view. The possible

21 Reconstruction of a Pleistocene horse bearing zebra-type markings

but highly contentious evidence of crib-biting in horses has already been mentioned from the Middle Palaeolithic, but there was certainly evidence of scavenging of horse carcasses by *Homo s. neanderthalensis* in the earlier portion of the Middle Palaeolithic (*c.*125–35,000 BP). Horse skulls in Italy were found in Middle Palaeolithic sites cracked open by stone tools, a job other carnivores could not do. This allowed Neanderthals to expand their range of foods from edible plants and small mammals, as discussed earlier. By the latter part of the Middle Palaeolithic, around 55,000 years ago, other bones, like limbs, ribs and vertebrae, were appearing in rock shelters and caves representing animals of prime reproductive age, indicating a crucial shift from scavenging to hunting of large game including bison, aurochs, reindeer, ibex, mammoth and antelope. It is important to remember that there is no technological revolution taking place at this time that accounts for this shift. Only a suggestion that new strategies were implemented, making food sources more reliable, therefore leading to increases in population providing further manpower to communal hunting. Communal hunts could control the direction of herds into kill zones and was instrumental in increasing success. Sometimes communal hunting was responsible for killing many dozens of horses, mammoths or deer in a single event. Sites such as La Cotte de Saint Brelade in Jersey show us how the Neanderthals achieved this. At Solutré there is evidence that broadly similar methods were employed in the Middle Palaeolithic to kill horses. This suggests one method for the hunting of horses, although it is debatable that large numbers of horses could be forced to leap from rocky precipices in this manner; an argument that we shall return to later when discussing hunting in the Solutrean period, by modern humans. Other methods could have been employed, including forcing numbers of horses into corral-like kill or capture zones.

Evidence for Middle Palaeolithic horse butchery from the Continent at this time shows that hunted horse remains were jointed, suggesting a dividing of the hunted carcass amongst participants from within the community. The evidence for this comes from cut marks on the bones, and experimental butchery replicating this has shown that the carcass was skinned and gutted, with little waste. Also, it was noted that the tongue, a valued piece of meat, was cut out. In parts of the Upper Danube, Germany, the horse was the most frequently hunted animal, despite the fact that there were other, admittedly more difficult to hunt, larger prey, such as mammoth available. Here at least, the remains of horses were far more common than reindeer, which tends to be the most commonly hunted animal. It seems there was variation in horse populations from place to place but that wherever they existed they were usually one of the favoured game animals. Whether this is due to ease of kill or a general preference for horsemeat is not clear. Certainly a single mammoth kill at any of these sites would have contributed considerably more meat than a number of horses. So the effort to hunt a mammoth, no matter how difficult, must always be worthwhile and probably more worthwhile than hunting fleet and nimble horses. A clear choice is being made by selecting and hunting horse that goes beyond the economic. There may be symbolic or quasi-religious reasons for this preference. Remember, we are dealing with hominids that buried their dead in a ritualistic fashion and created some art.

Although the development of stone projectile points were about 20,000 years away at this point in time, it is not to say that spears were not used. Spears, we have seen, were discovered dating to *c.*400 KYA in 1995 at a Pleistocene site in Schöningen, Germany – a very rare survival. They were made resembling the modern javelin, with long tapering ends and a sharpened thicker, heavier distal end. Their lengths varied from 1.70m to 3.2m and could, due to the presence of grooves possibly for inserting flint flakes, be the earliest known composite weapons. However, until proven, they are believed to be simple wooden thrusting spears. This discovery forced a rethink of our understanding of just how sophisticated *Homo neanderthalsis* were as hunters if their ancestors *Homo heidelbergensis* were already using these weapons. These spears were found in conjunction with many flint implements and the remains of a number of butchered horses, amongst many other species. What this important discovery highlighted was just how little is known about the use of organic materials during these periods and the class of evidence they represent. Had it not been for this discovery and another similar one of a single thrusting spear found in the 1940s in Lehringen, Lower Saxony, Germany, dating to 125,000 years BP, we would have very little evidence for their sophisticated hunting methods. A spear tip made of yew was found in Pleistocene levels in Clacton-on-Sea and dates to 410,000 years BP.

In Britain there is evidence that Neanderthals were here at the same time as horses. In Pin Hole Cave at Creswell Crags, horse remains were found of *Equus ferus* (wild horse) that were radio carbon dated to 44,900+/2800 years. These remains, although not in this instance showing signs of butchery, correspond with a number of Mousterian stone tools. More unequivocal evidence for hunting of horses at an earlier time comes from Boxgrove (*c.*500,000 years ago). Here a controversial piece of evidence points to spear usage at a time that predates the German and Clacton-on-Sea discoveries by around 100,000 years. A horse shoulder blade that has a semi-circular hole through it, according to the pathologist Bernard Knight, is highly consistent with a high-speed impact from a weapon such as a spear. Experiments confirmed that the wound was consistent with this type of high-speed impact with a penetrative sharpened wooden implement. Horses were also butchered at Boxgrove, and again the evidence for this was unequivocal, with the carnivore damage to the bones coming after the butchery by humans. We can infer from this evidence and that discussed from the Continent that Neanderthals were likely to have been hunting and butchering horses in Britain during the Middle Palaeolithic. The direct evidence for Neanderthals, and what they hunted and where, is quite sparse in Britain because 160,000 to 60,000 years ago was defined by a harsh and unforgiving cold stage that led to the abandonment of these isles along with much of northern Europe. This gives only a small window of opportunity when perhaps relatively small numbers of Neanderthals reached Britain for a period of around 20,000 years before they were then assimilated or usurped by modern humans.

Controversially, Paul Bahn in 1978 argued that there is evidence of crib-biting at La Quina, France, which dates to the Middle Palaeolithic and, he argued, offers the best evidence for a form of horse domestication in the Palaeolithic known up to that point. As we shall see later there are a number of problems with the evidence, but some of the points he raises on the issue of a form of domestication in the Upper Palaeolithic are at least worth considering for a number of reasons.

The Upper Palaeolithic: horses and modern humans

In the early Upper Palaeolithic, which is mainly dominated by the presence of modern humans in northern Europe, the human relationship with horses began to change. Symbolic behaviours began to appear and the methods of hunting horses were more efficient but, perhaps most critically, humans may have learned the skills of corralling horses and possibly, as Bahn has suggested, harnessing horses. This may have heralded a key change in human behaviour or at least an important conceptual shift at this time – a possible concept of animal ownership. In Solutré, near Mâcon, east-central France, the remains of an estimated minimum 40,000 individual horses were discovered from an area excavated in the nineteenth century. Much of the evidence at this site dates mainly to the Solutrean period (Solutré is the site type for this period, dating to *c.*32,000 BP) but also up to the beginning of the late Upper Palaeolithic – from 32,000 to 12,000 years ago. The weapon of choice at this time was the flint stone point and split-based antler or bone spear point, hafted onto a wooden spear shaft and thrown using an atlatl (spear-thrower).

Indeed, Bahn has argued that evidence he reviewed in his controversial paper of 1978 suggests that the activity seen at Solutré is in fact more indicative of domestication than of hunting. The faunal assemblage, when it was excavated and examined in the 1870s, stood out as an unusual assemblage. Henri Toussaint examined the remains of the 40,000 horses found there and concluded, on the basis of a prevailing theory relating to certain osteological elements such as vertebrae, scapula and ribs being present indicating on-site butchery, that this was indicative of domestication. One of the chief objectors was a researcher named Piétrement, a proponent of the butchery theory, which until this instance had been used to argue against any kind of domestication in the Palaeolithic. He added his weight to Arcelin's theory that this was a kill site utilising the topography, in much the same way as La Cotte de Saint Brelade, to drive large numbers of horses over a cliff. Bahn (1978: 185) stated: 'Charles Piétrement … lent his support to Adrien Arcelin's startling theory that the horses were driven over the nearby precipice, a hypothesis which could not be taken seriously by anyone familiar with the topography of the site.'

As it turned out it seems that Toussaint and Bahn were almost right – the horses were not driven over a precipice. It was found they were actually 'corralled' by taking advantage of the local topography. The horse herds favoured migration routes between summer and winter feeding grounds and would pass close by, and the hunters would separate off groups from the main herd into an artificially narrowed drive route that led into a natural cul-de-sac defined along one side by cliffs. The hunters, armed with spears, probably formed a human barrier, perhaps utilising rough fencing panels or a simple spiked palisade, or even a crude stone wall or similar structure to ensure that as few as possible escaped. Such barriers could be easily constructed and be of interrupted, rather than continuous construction, as even this would cause horses to continue forwards. Confined this way the hunters could then attack, ensuring that as few horses as possible escaped. The age of the butchered horses, how they were butchered and the season of kill, combined with topographical studies and choice of weapons point to this being the most effective method employed here. Evidence from studies of thin sections of teeth cementation (cementum) layers shows that the horses were killed between spring and autumn. Prime adult horses were killed indicating that young horses were either taken and killed and butchered elsewhere or that they were released to maintain populations. There was no evidence to support the earlier theory that horses were driven over the cliffs.

Recent work suggests that the kill site at Solutré and the way the horses were killed was more opportunistic. The suggestion is that people simply laid in wait and that the horses, following their ancient migratory route, passed close by and were simply ambushed. In my own experience of horses, their sensitivity to areas where predators might lurk and general dislike of closed-in places offering ambush opportunities, makes this an unlikely proposition. I think many others would agree.

Plains Indians in the United States employed similar methods envisaged at Solutré, including building brushwood palisades and sometimes using cairn-like piles of stones constructed a few metres apart that eventually converged into two lines. This worked because animals will take the line of least resistance and avoid dodging between closely spaced obstacles, favouring the open route in front of them. Any evidence at Solutré for the construction of these cairns, which might well be expected to survive down to the present day, could have been eradicated by stone robbing to build houses over the last thousand years or so.

Suddenly, evidence from Gough's Cave makes some sense. Here, perhaps, was a site that could have been used in a similar way. Horses could be driven into the gorge and against a steep, hard slope or cliff wall and killed or captured using dogs. Certainly Creswell Crags could have been used in this way too. Given the likely use of Cheddar and Creswell as aggregation sites it is possible that horses were hunted when sufficient numbers of people were gathered, perhaps from a number of clans gathering for ceremonies. This would allow a large hunt to take place. It is possible that the horse was a feasting food, reserved for special occasions – hence their greater symbolic importance.

Like most highly successful methods of hunting the one at Solutré persisted for many thousands of years – in fact nearly 20,000 years. It is almost inconceivable that throughout the time these successful methods were employed the hunters did not figure out a method for capturing and restraining live horses – either for breeding, milk or for later killing and consumption. The skeletal evidence, it was pointed out, may represent a form of control or selection if some of the prime horses were released. Indeed, in the Ariége and in Charante at La Placard, during the Upper

Palaeolithic, there is some evidence of crib-biting. At Solutré the sheer volume of horses killed over time has been taken to be indicative of not just hunting but herding; that it implied a relationship with horses verging on domestication, where at least parts of the herds of captured horses were perhaps in some way controlled. H. Toussaint in 1873, based upon the estimated remains of the huge numbers of horses recovered from just one part of the site at Solutré, said this was proof of Upper Palaeolithic domestication of the horse. And as we saw earlier, this was a position that found little favour at that time and when recently resurrected by Bahn still meets with considerable resistance today.

Humans did not settle at Solutré for any period of time, except during the latest phases of hunting at the site. Rather it was a temporary camp where people came during the summer months to hunt and went away during the winter. This, combined with the lack of young horse remains, might indicate that at least some of the young horses were captured, kept and taken away elsewhere to use as food during the winter. Is it possible that the young horses might have been captured and taken away with a view to breeding? Or to improve already captured herds elsewhere? Certainly, the genetic evidence supports the idea that domestic horses originated from multiple captured populations in widely scattered places, at least in later prehistory. Parallels might be drawn with the Kazak nomads of the Eurasian Steppes, whose nomadic lifestyles and relationship with horses revolves around an individual or family's wealth being tied to the size of the herd in their possession, and the control they have over sizeable winter grazing areas. The migration of Kazak horses will affect the migration of people, and in the nineteenth century some seasonal routes were known to be in excess of 1,000km. This kind of transhumance, dictated by the seasons and migrations of animals, fitted with what is known archaeologically of Upper Palaeolithic people. This might be a theory too far, but the evidence is at least *suggestive* of such a symbiosis between humans and horses based purely on food and possibly of a form of perceived wealth. Future research into this topic might concentrate upon, for example, the rock-art of the Upper Palaeolithic, which might yield clues about the basis and nature of the relationship that humans and horses had at this time. The tracing of the use of 'secondary products' from animals, as outlined in Andrew Sherrat's *The Secondary Products Revolution*, may prove to be a useful line of future research. *The Secondary Products Revolution* is a model that is used to chart the chronology, spread and development of a broad package of diversified 'other' uses for animals and of animal products, such as traction, riding or transport, milk and wool. Developed by Andrew Sherratt (in 1981), the model particularly applies to the Neolithic and the effects that the model had upon early agricultural societies.

In the Eurasian Steppes the drinking of koumiss, a fermented drink of mares' milk, was an important reason for the capturing and corralling of horses since at least the Bronze Age. The drinking of koumiss was important and prevalent throughout the Near East, including Turkey (where it was known as kimiz), and into Eastern Europe including Hungary. Mares' milk contains more sugar than cow or goat milk and the fermenting of it means that it has a mild alcohol content. Precisely when the making of koumiss started remains unknown, but the evidence for collecting milk generally comes from residues in ceramic vessels dated to the early Neolithic in Europe and Asia Minor. This, and other matters relating to the chronology and spread as modelled by *The Secondary Products Revolution*, needs further research and scrutiny, but represents an area of considerable future research.

Palaeolithic art and the horse

In the Upper Palaeolithic the importance of the horse was reflected in the cave paintings and engravings and the portable art of the time. This provides a good body of evidence about the huge importance of this human-animal relationship. In Germany, where butchered horse remains outnumber those of all other animals that were hunted in the Upper Palaeolithic, there is, unfortunately, no rock-art. It is unclear if this is due to poor survival conditions in the more temperate north or if it simply has not been discovered yet. Britain has one possible example on the roof of Church Hole Cave at Creswell Crags, showing a fairly clear outline of a horse body and leg, but which may have utilised the natural features of the rock surface to create a small head, since eroded. However, in France, Spain, Portugal and Italy, as well as one or two other places within Eurasia, there exists an extensive and important body of rock-art. Researchers Pat Rice and Ann Paterson have compared faunal remains for the numbers and species that occur in sites across France and Spain, with the numbers of those animals that occur in all cave art and mobile art, and came up with some interesting data; the most interesting element being that although horse skeletal remains were less common than deer, in art horses outnumbered every other group of animal. The implications of this are, as already made clear, that in some way and for some reason, horses assume a greater symbolic importance. Speculations as to why this might be the case are discussed in the next section, but some clues might be garnered from what has been written above. It seems likely that there was probably a form of totemic symbolism associated with food exclusion centred upon horses in many sites throughout Europe in the Upper Palaeolithic. Could it be that one was centred upon eating horseflesh only at aggregation and feasting occasions?

At sites like Peche-Merle, Lascaux in France, and Chuffin and Altamira in Spain, horses were depicted alongside other animals such as bison, deer, mammoth and aurochs to name but a few. Abstract designs, such as dots or 'signs', were also created, as were hand stencils and bas-relief engravings of animals that utilised some of the natural features of the rock surfaces. Mobile art consists of incised drawings on antlers and bones, sometimes of very high quality, such as those that appear on bâton de commandements, or shaft straighteners, like that discovered at La Madeleine, France. Also, spear throwers made of antler were carved to resemble animals, as were pieces of limestone, again reassembling animals and large women, the so-called Venus figures. But it is the horse that predominates in all this art.

1 Creswell Crags. (Barry Lewis)

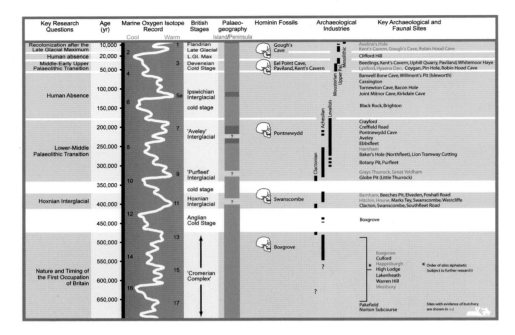

2 Time Chart of the human occupation of Britain during the Pleistocene.
(Reproduced with permission of the AHOB Project)

3 Reconstruction of mammoths, woolly rhinoceros and horses, and other animals of the
Ice Age in the Siberian tundra. (Source: http://www.livescience.com/; artist: Mauricio
Anton)

4 The remains of at least two hunted aurochs discovered during a watching brief at Bleasby Quarry, Nottinghamshire. A small number of Mesolithic microliths were discovered in close association with the vertebrae of one of these animals. It appears they may have been driven into a palaeochannel, perhaps to escape pursuit whilst injured

©Barry Lewis

Opposite above: 5 Red deer (*Cervus elaphus*) depicted in rock–art discovered in 2003 in Church Hole Cave, Creswell Crags. (Photographed courtesy of Creswell Crags Heritage Trust)

Opposite below: 6 Giant Deer (or Irish elk), in a reconstruction of its environment during the Ice Age. (Deer model photographed courtesy of Musée National de Prehistorie, Les Eyzies, France)

7 Cheddar Gorge and Gough's Cave, an important aggregation locale in the Upper Palaeolithic. (George Nash)

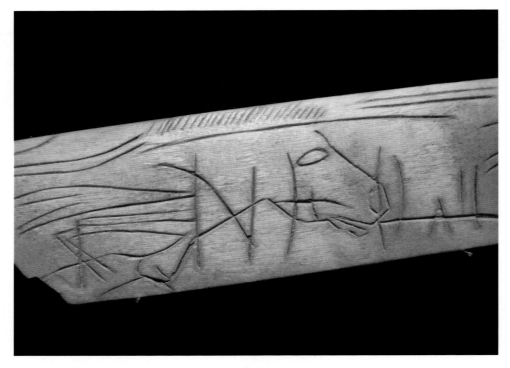

8 Rib with engraving of a horse discovered in Robin Hood's Cave, Creswell Crags, Derbyshire. (Photographed courtesy of Creswell Crags Heritage Trust)

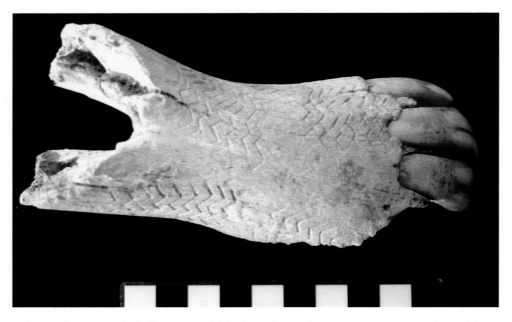

9 Incised horse mandible from Kendrick's Cave, Gwynedd, Wales. Late Upper Palaeolithic. (George Nash)

10 Burnt mound at Girton Quarry, North Nottinghamshire. (Trent & Peak Archaeology)

11 A hunt scene

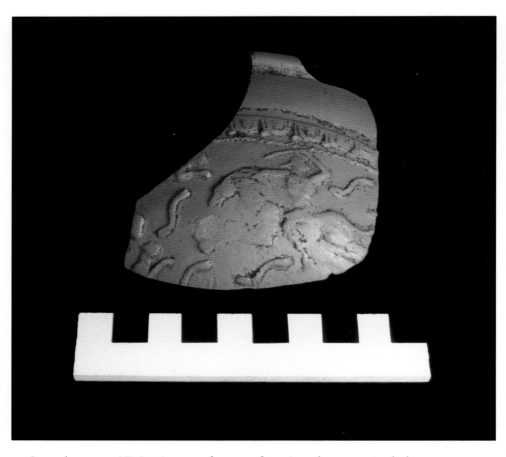

12 Second-century AD Samian ware fragment featuring a hunt or animal-chase scene. Found at Tiln Quarry, Nottinghamshire. (Trent & Peak Archaeology)

13 Aberlemno roadside, Tayside, Scotland. Pictish symbol stone featuring a hunt scene, including dogs chasing down deer and mounted huntsmen. (Lloyd Laing)

14 Barrow-upon-Trent, South Derbyshire; Anglo-Saxon fish weir (fish-trap) during excavation. Note the wattle panels that were supported along the sides by lines of posts

15 Dotard oaks, Chatsworth Park, Derbyshire, to the south of the house in the Old Deer Park

16 Peveril Castle, Castleton, in Derbyshire's Peak District

17 St Helens Church, Darley Dale, in the Peak Forest; medieval foresters' grave slabs

18 The Stand at Chatsworth, Derbyshire, constructed *c.*1570 and designed to, amongst other things, encompass views of the surrounding countryside and for watching deer

19 The stables at Chatsworth, Derbyshire

20 Avelines Hole, Cheddar Gorge, Somerset. (George Nash)

21 Small leaf-shaped arrowhead, probably early Neolithic, recovered on a high spot overlooking the western vale near Creswell Crags, Derbyshire. (Trent & Peak Archaeology)

CURRENT AFFAIRS
MAGAZINE OF THE YEAR   £2.95

THE SPECTATOR

ENGLAND RIDES AGAIN

St George's Day special issue

ROD LIDDLE, JOAN COLLINS,
BERYL BAINBRIDGE, ANDREW NEIL,
ALEX JAMES AND CHARLES MOORE

22 19 April 2008 cover of *The Spectator* using an image of hunting to define 'Englishness'. (Courtesy of Amanda Lockhart and *The Spectator* magazine)

23 A huntsman clearing a hedge

22 Decorative carved bovid atlatl (spear thrower) end. (Barry Lewis – object photographed courtesy of Musée National de Prehistorie, Les Eyzies, France)

At Lascaux, for example, horses dominate in terms of numbers of depictions in pigment and especially engraved forms, but it is the paintings of bovids, powerful bulls, spilling across the walls in The Hall of the Bulls, magnificent imagery that captures the imagination. This suggests that the people who created the art had a totemic linkage to the horse but found power in the bovids. Alternatively, superimpositions or the overwhelming size of the bovids may suggest dominance of the cattle clan over the horse clan. Interestingly, Paul Taçon of Griffith University, Queensland, notes that the horse was important in Aboriginal rock-art in the post-colonial period in Australia too, being the most widely depicted post-contact motif. The fascination surrounding horses at this time was the almost inconceivable idea that the Europeans were riding these animals. This fascination persisted for some time in Australia, and as the colonists spread around the country so too did the depictions of horses, dominating the contact period rock-art throughout Australia. The important consideration here is that unlike the introduced cattle (which also figures quite prominently in contact art), the horse had a special relationship with humans and that centred upon them being ridden. The concept of riding horses created a very special connection, which had considerable symbolic power for Aborigines who soon became highly proficient

23 Drawing of Les Combarelles engravings (after the Abbé Breuil *et al.*, 1902), showing the superimposition of a horse onto earlier bison figures.

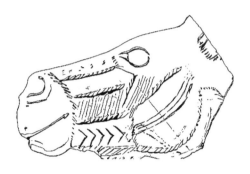

24 Horse head engraving from Saint-Michel d'Arundy, France, which shows the lines interpreted by Bahn as being a possible rope halter or bridle, whilst others interpreted this as stylised apportioning of the muscles in the horse's head. (After Randall White 1989)

horsemen themselves, often excelling as stockmen on the cattle stations. In many Aboriginal communities horses and riding are still very important, even today.

Of the predominance of the horse in the Palaeolithic parietal and mobile art, Paul Bahn had this to say:

> It is certain that the horse was of tremendous cultural importance to people in Western Europe during the Upper Palaeolithic – horse teeth and bones have been found carefully placed in Magdalenian hearths in a number of deep Pyrenean caves such as Labastide and Erberua, as well as near hearths at the Magdalenian open-air camp of Pincevent near Paris (despite the fact that reindeer account for almost 100 per cent of this site's faunal remains). At Duruthy (Landes), the carved horses were found in a kind of 'horse sanctuary' dated to the twelfth millennium BC; the biggest, a kneeling sandstone figure, rested against two horse skulls and on fragments of horse-jaw, while three horse-head pendants were in close proximity.
>
> (*Journey Through the Ice Age* by Paul Bahn and Jean Vertut, p. 142)

Generally, in cave art horses are sometimes depicted in small groupings, such as at Peche-Merle and Lascaux. At Lascaux and Chauvet Cave horses are also painted in panels alongside other animals such as bison, aurochs and rhinos. In some instances horses are shown displaying behaviour, such as trotting or, as at La Chaire á Calvin, Charente, France, in an attitude of cantering or galloping (see Fig. 20). At other sites there are indications of horses having distinct 'M'-shaped markings on their withers or sides, which mark the change from the darker hide to the lighter underbelly, a feature still clearly visible on some modern animals from time to time. At Lascaux, there were numerous engraved horses that outnumbered the pigment ones. Les Combarelles also contains many examples of engraved horses, outnumbering any other animal.

Some of the mobile art, such as the carving of a horse head from Saint-Michel d'Arundy, France, shows lines that seem to divide up the facial elements of the horse into its muzzle and the natural musculature and bony contours of the face. These lines were interpreted by Paul Bahn as representing a bridle. Examining a whole range of other evidence for the possible domestication of horses in the Palaeolithic he argued that the *bâton de commandement* were cheek pieces for a bridle, based on their similarity to known ones made of antler in later prehistory (Bronze Age). Bahn also argued that the spotted horses depicted in Peche-Merle represented piebald coats, known only in domestic animals, even though the spots extend outside the outline of the horse bodies. Bahn had also presented the evidence for tooth damage in Upper Palaeolithic horses as evidence of crib-biting, but this was denounced due to similar damage having been found on horses dating to the Middle Pleistocene in North America (but see later). It is fair to say that the jury is very much still out where some of these claims are concerned. Hopefully, future research might concentrate on and test some of the issues concerning crib-biting, such as the very specific types of pathologies that would be seen in tethered horses, and properly test the hypothesis that only tethered or corralled horses crib-bite. There is some suggestion that some wild horses bite bark on trees, for example, and this may create a fairly specific form of pathology. Such research would go a long way towards resolving some of these key issues.

Can we see Palaeolithic proto-domestication of horses?

This is a controversial issue and is likely to remain one for some time. The evidence, in my opinion at this moment in time, appears to favour some form of at least very minimal control. However, it is impossible to say unequivocally that this is a form of proto-domestication of horses we see happening in the Upper Palaeolithic period. Bahn has suggested that some form of horse domestication may have its roots in the Middle Palaeolithic. The evidence, at first glance, is quite compelling, especially if one looks at the fairly broad range of evidence that Bahn presents. Taking a holistic approach to the evidence I offer my own speculative theory of how some form of control of horses might have worked:

Firstly, the importance of the horse, as demonstrated in parietal and mobile art, far outweighs its importance as food in the faunal record, particularly in southern

25 Broken end of a bâton de commandment; the resemblance of these to Bronze Age horse cheek pieces was noted by Bahn and other researchers. (George Nash)

and Western Europe. In Germany, where there are no parietal depictions of horses currently known, the evidence for the importance of the horse in the diet as reflected in the faunal assemblages is much greater than that for other animals. There is supporting evidence from the mobile art of the period, particularly from Gonnersdorf, Germany; here, plaquettes of slate show engravings of horses, and from Vogelherd a small carved ivory horse was found. In the Upper Palaeolithic we know that humans were highly mobile, perhaps travelling great distances, maybe in excess of 1000 km over time in a seasonal round following herds of animals. This suggests two possible relationships with horses: one, that groups of humans may well have been seasonally following specific herds of horses between parts of Germany to southern Europe and the western seaboard of the Continent; and two, that the method of transhumance practised was at least very broadly similar to that of later Kazak people, whose notions of wealth and prestige was based upon a form of 'ownership' of horses, the origins of which could be very ancient.

In the rock-art, particularly from Peche-Merle, we know that there are some unusual anomalies like the dots on the horses that have been interpreted by Bahn as representing piebald coats – a feature only found on domesticated horses. Whilst this interpretation may be incorrect in this instance, because these dots are also found outside the horse body outline, it might perhaps represent a tally of some description by the people occupying the cave. There is compelling evidence that the use of dots in some instances relate to the depiction of driving lanes, and that at the end of these lanes enigmatic rectangular motifs might represent enclosures or corrals where the horses were captured and held. At Solutré such drive lanes, consisting of piles of stones or palisades, might, as we have already seen, have been a method employed in horse hunting. Might simple corrals have been used too? Corrals were perhaps not the only method for controlling horses. Hobbling, a method whereby the legs are tied together, could have been another method employed to stop horses wandering too far. It is also a simple method, still used in the Steppes, but would leave very little or no trace in the archaeological record – except in very rare circumstances where preservation conditions are favourable.

The genetic and archaeological evidence can make a compelling case for domestication of sorts, beginning in the late Pleistocene with wild horse populations being captured over wide geographical areas. But this evidence should be used carefully. The genetic studies so far carried out highlight the difficulties of tying down a particular place and a particular time for the domestication of horses. Rather the evidence suggests that there were multiple foci for it throughout Europe and Eurasia. In other words, the story of when and where for the domestication of horses is far more complex than it is for cattle or sheep.

This may suggest that human populations in different places domesticated from local wild stock at different times; perhaps in Eurasia humans engaged in a form of horse culture based upon meat, milk and hides. This culture might be based upon the capturing, breeding and releasing of horses. It is possible that this early horse culture became the precursor for the Kazak horse culture, and the centre for what can closely be described as true horse domestication, over 6000 years ago. Slightly later, and elsewhere in Eurasia and Asia, horses were being domesticated too. Pinpointing precisely when this happened is challenging. Looking at the same evidence (i.e. mtDNA) for cattle, sheep and water buffalo, for example, there are a few locations around 10,000 to 8000 years ago where this is likely to have taken place. With horses the evidence is much more difficult firstly, to ascertain, and secondly, to interpret. As I discussed earlier there were many locations, many mares and few stallions that account for the domestication of modern horses. Chronologically this is all difficult to tie down. All we can go on is the other bodies of evidence that point to a time and place for the most likely location for where horses were domesticated. So far the evidence points to the Eurasian Steppes, where David Anthony and others' work on bit-wear evidence, and the archaeological material and linguistic evidence, ties it to that location. However, there is still considerable latitude for the emergence of new evidence and a re-examination of current evidence in light of it to show that horse domestication may have taken place elsewhere and at an earlier date.

The Upper Palaeolithic and earlier evidence from horse mandibles proposed by Bahn for crib-biting, a nervous condition known mainly in horses that have been tethered or confined, was supposedly exploded by oesteological evidence from North America, from a period before people had arrived on the Continent. From the United States there is evidence of fossil wild horse incisors showing signs of crib-biting from deposits dating to the early to middle Pleistocene. However, most other studies, albeit small-scale ones, have generally shown that this wear pattern on teeth is in the vast majority of cases peculiar only to tethered horses and rarely to non-tethered ones. The American evidence may come under future scrutiny due to the growing body of evidence that suggest that there might well have been humans in the Americas for a considerable time prior to 16,000 years ago. As a class of evidence, what is often not considered is the psychological nature of crib-biting, both in terms of the types of wear they could produce and the extent of the visible pathologies in horse populations and how these might be discriminated. It is still the case, as we have seen, that crib-biting and its apparent pathologies are poorly understood phenomena in terms of its usefulness as a method of identifying domestication in horses, but neither can it be ruled out.

Crucially, the domestic dog had a role to play in all of this because herding and hunting would have required the assistance of a speedy animal capable of these activities. It is arguable that the proto-domestication of the horse (and of course reindeer) and the domestication of the wolf went hand in hand. The usefulness of the dog as a hunter, a herder and possibly even as a food source in hard times, outlived the relationship that horses and humans had at the end of the Pleistocene and the start of the Holocene in Western and northern Europe. Dogs were our constant companion, but our relationship with horses was perhaps more fickle for the reasons I am about to describe.

In the late Upper Palaeolithic, people were migrating great distances, probably hundreds of kilometres a year, from the Paris Basin and the Ardennes Region of Belgium to places in Britain, such as Cheddar Gorge in Somerset and Creswell Crags on the Nottinghamshire/Derbyshire border. The evidence from Cheddar Gorge tells us that they were using dogs to hunt horses, and that in places like Cheddar and Creswell Crags they were meeting with other groups, aggregating at these key locations, interacting and negotiating access to resources, and feasting – primarily on horsemeat. Did these important gatherings at these critical aggregation locales revolve around a horse culture? Were these special feasts, where horsemeat was conspicuously consumed as displays of wealth and power and hunting prowess?

It has been said that if horses were herded, bred and domesticated in the Palaeolithic then why was there a decline in horse populations after the close of the Ice Age? This can be answered by the widespread warming associated with the end of the final glacial phase, reaching its maxima 18,000 years ago (the Late Glacial Maximum or LGM) and cooling again 11,500 years ago (the Younger Dryas stadial), bringing with it a subsequent and rapid change in environment. Following this, increasing human populations, combined, possibly, with over-hunting, lead to a subsequent change in the human-horse relationship dynamic. Also, the afforestation of much of Europe in the early Holocene led to the large reduction of the vast steppe-tundra ranges of land required for the large horse herds that had previously been seen in northern and Western Europe. Boreal conditions prevailed at this time and with it came aurochs, deer and other animals of the forest. Yet the genetic evidence suggests that there may have been at least small pockets of horse populations in many areas, perhaps under some form of human control and from which, much later, domestic horses sprang regionally.

It has been stated by others that a long-term dependence on domesticated horses requires horse-riding to manage the herds. What I am arguing for in the late Upper Palaeolithic is a more short-term strategy of occasional horse herd control for hunting, and the capture and corralling of mares, perhaps for breeding and consequently milk. Using dogs to hunt and to herd was a critical part of these strategies. A good model to compare this to might be the Lapp reindeer culture – perhaps even less evolved than that. The human-horse relationship could be reflective of the type of hunting that came much, much later; a form of elite hunting, which had restrictions over who could hunt and eat particular types of game. It is possible that only the most senior members of certain clans could hunt and eat the horseflesh. Eating horsemeat was perhaps also subject to a form of totemic food exclusion, something we suspect that happened in prehistory and that anthropologists know about today from indigenous societies in various parts of the world, including amongst Australian Aborigines. This is, of course, largely speculation but who knows where future research could take this subject. Clearly the horse was important in the Upper Palaeolithic, and what is needed is more work to discover how important, and what the nature of this relationship was.

An Upper Palaeolithic horse culture of some kind seems to be, based on the evidence, a distinct possibility. However, that has to be tempered by saying that there are still many problems understanding and interpreting the evidence. Such a horse culture in the Upper Palaeolithic can only be tentatively suggested. It may not have been a horse culture based upon riding or using them as pack animals necessarily, but they might well have been marked or branded showing they belonged to specific human groups. Some of whom may have migrated vast distances across Europe to follow them, in much the same way North American Indians seasonally followed bison herds.

The reasons for capturing and keeping horses may have been for meat, milk and hides. We have seen in a previous chapter that Upper Palaeolithic people who were in the Paris Basin could have been the same groups who visited Creswell Crags and Cheddar Gorge. We have seen that the widespread importance of the horse in art and society in the Upper Palaeolithic points to a special relationship, a co-dependence perhaps based upon a perceived wealth of ownership of horses; perhaps this was based upon totemic rights. The basis of this relationship was probably about the control of territory too. The ownership of herds may have bestowed upon the group the rights to greater ranges of territory that the horses required. This is reflected in the modern Kazak horse culture. This relationship perhaps began to break down in Europe during the height of the final Devensian Glaciation, as territories and suitable environments became squeezed and human populations lived in ever-closer proximity and denser groupings. Following the end of the Ice Age much of Europe became afforested, and this sort of land was largely unsuitable for this way of life. New prey replaced the horse, such as red deer, elk and aurochsen, which could be hunted in the forests across

Europe. Ultimately, it may have been because humans had not yet learnt to bridle and ride the horse that led to its decline. It was during this time that there was a huge decline in horse numbers in Western Europe, probably as a result of over-hunting and changing environment. From this time a new horse culture may have begun to flourish further to the east, where eventually the horse increased in importance because humans had learned to bridle and ride the horse in the vast Steppes of Eurasia, as it declined in the west. David Anthony's book (see Select Reading List) discusses the careful experimental work on bits that he had undertaken, trying out materials like rope, leather, bone and metal. The dating work undertaken upon sites he excavated showed evidence of the first ridden horse and dating them to 3700 BC. It seems that at this time horses were used to hunt horses at Botai in northern Kazakhstan. It would be a while before a fully fledged domestic horse returned to the West.

A summary of Bahn's arguments for and against Palaeolithic domestication

Threaded throughout the recent chapters are references to arguments for or against domestication, particularly the domestication of reindeer and the horse in the Palaeolithic. In reality, this argument started in the first half of the nineteenth century and continued in the third decade of the twentieth century before quieting down. Central to the argument against domestication at this time was that dogs needed to have been domesticated first before the large herbivores could be controlled, and since there was no evidence of this then herbivores could not have been. The other major component of this anti-Palaeolithic domestication argument was that the prevailing 'butchery theory' held that there was no evidence of certain osteological elements such as scapula, ribs and vertebrae at occupation sites, indicating that animals were hunted and butchered elsewhere and only the larger meat bearing joints were brought to camp.

Then, in 1978, Paul Bahn reignited the debate with his paper 'The "Unacceptable Face" of the West European Upper Palaeolithic' in the journal *Antiquity*, in which he argued that the personalities and research agendas of particular French workers in the nineteenth century turned the tide away from the acceptance of Palaeolithic domestication, or more accurately semi-domestication, as being the prevailing dominant orthodoxy that would perhaps still be with us today. Instead, the prevailing orthodoxy, he argues, sees the possibility of any form of domestication as near impossible in the Palaeolithic. Also, Bahn published in 1980 a paper that considered crib-biting as being a distinct possibility during the Palaeolithic, and arguing that one of the best sites that may show Palaeolithic tethering of horses, and therefore domestication, was a Middle Palaeolithic site – La Quina. In 1978 Bahn had argued that the agendas of particular researchers during this time had perhaps clouded the whole issue and the legacy of this still remains with us. He argued that dogs were not critical to the argument and that a number of contemporary researchers had demonstrated this, and the butchery theory did not hold true even by the standards of that time – Solutré was a case in point with the theory actually being used to demonstrate semi-domestication at that site. Bahn saw the modern era as a time to look at these arguments afresh, and reassess the evidence for at least a form of semi-domestication in the Palaeolithic. His efforts were not well received.

During the 1980s and 1990s a number of papers were published by researchers who were vociferously opposed to Bahn's argument, including a paper by Randall White in *Current Anthropology*, which encourages printed debates within the journal, allowing for responses from other researchers, in this instance Bahn himself (as his earlier papers were being challenged), and others including Jean Clottes. In this particular part of the debate the main assertion of Bahn's being challenged was that there is evidence within assemblages of European art mobilier of the Upper Palaeolithic showing horses wearing rope bridles or halters (see Fig. 23). Bahn's detractors argued that what could be seen was merely apportioning of the muscle groups of the head and face. Peter Rowley-Conwy joined the debate later and challenged Bahn on mainly osteological grounds, arguing that the evidence of Palaeolithic crib-biting by horses was unproven because there was evidence that wild or un-tethered horses demonstrated the same pathologies. Also, such pathologies were not sufficiently tested to be identifiable as either evidence of crib-biting or strap wear. Bahn had noted that a reindeer bone from the Palaeolithic site of Isturitz, which showed a healed fracture, indicated control and care by humans, particularly in an environment where there was a high number of predators. Rowley-Conwy argued that on the basis of recent examinations of the pathologies of deer in the New Forest killed in road accidents and showing signs of surviving earlier injuries, including one that had survived a severed metacarpal (lower fore-limb), this was not always proof of care by humans. This particular injury had healed and the deer subsequently went on to be in foal before being killed. To be fair to Bahn, there is not an abundance of large predators in the New Forest today.

Some of these papers provoked acerbic responses from Bahn. He wrote a particularly cutting reply to White's paper, and later to the rest of the comments made by the other contributors to that paper, in *Motes and Beams: A Further Response to White on the Upper Palaeolithic* (1990). Since that time there has been little further debate on these issues. Interestingly, since then there has been a general acceptance of the Upper Palaeolithic domestication of the dog, both in central Europe and more recently in Britain, at Cheddar Gorge. Recent studies into horse and dog DNA, and the discovery of the relatively early domestication of horses in the Eurasian Steppes, perhaps makes it timely to once again re-examine the evidence for Palaeolithic semi-domestication.

Later Prehistory horses and the dogs

The domestication and breaking of horses for riding is likely to have arisen in the Eurasian Steppes, that is Kazakhstan, southern Ukraine and Mongolia around

6000 years ago. Analysis of bit-wear on equid teeth seems to suggest that the phenomena began in Kazakhstan at about 3500 BC, and as a major innovation in land transport, this predates the wheel. Other classes of evidence have included antler tines with perforations that show wear from cord being threaded through them and used as possible cheek pieces dating to 4000 to 3500 BC, and found at Sredni Stog culture sites in the Ukrainian Steppes. Later these came to be found in pairs in later burial contexts dating to about 2000–1500 BC in the Ukraine and eastern Germany. Stone maces of the exotic material porphyry, carved into horse head effigies with indications of bridles used to symbolise military power. Finally, the whole cultural package shown in the archaeological record of the Ukrainian Steppes between 3500 and 4000 BC shows changes that were probably due to the adoption of horse riding. Recently, an international team, including Dr Alan Outram of Exeter University, discovered solid evidence of domestication in Kazakhstan, which included morphological changes to the lower limb bones of the horses, markedly different from local wild populations of the time; bit-wear showing harnessing and probably riding; and fat residues on pottery vessels belonging specifically to horse milk. This shows that they were also making koumiss at this time. This critical development played a key part in central Asian pastoralism and the diaspora of ideas, and the Indo-European language. Eventually the benefits spread throughout Bronze Age Europe, and the invention of the wheel and development of the chariot ushered in the age of horsemen from the Eurasian Steppes. Although the focus here is on British evidence for when the first ridden horse may have arrived here, and what developments and advances in hunting they ushered in, these are difficult things to tie down. There has been woefully little work done on these sorts of questions.

One clue as to the importance of the horse in the late Bronze Age or early Iron Age can be found on the Berkshire Downs in Oxfordshire: the Uffington Horse, a 110m-long hill figure created by removing the turf from the underlying chalk. More importantly is the clue it could give us in terms of understanding the nature and depth of the relationship between horses, people and the landscape. The Vale of the White Horse as it is known is overlooked by this huge figure, indicating some religious or magical reason for it being there. The figure resembles coinage designs dating from the Roman Period that depicts horses, and it has been known as the 'White Horse' since the eleventh century AD. The site itself is within a landscape of prehistoric significance, with Wayland's Smithy, a Neolithic long barrow, just 2km to the west. It has been suggested that the White Horse is on the border of two territories and that this symbol faces the neighbouring or opposing territory, a symbol of the groups' power. In this way, might the White Horse be a group's totemic symbol? If this is the case then there is a thread going back through time to the Upper Palaeolithic groups, an ancient linkage and an ancient symbol of power represented by the horse that is tied to long-remembered connections and ancestry that has an almost unimaginable time depth. It could be that through these remembered connections to long dead ancestors in a world full of extinct, fantastical creatures that were hunted by them, these stories were so old they were legend passed from an age of hunting and honoured hunters, intact, down to the present.

Horses arrived in Britain sometime during the later Bronze Age and undoubtedly had a huge impact upon transport, communication, warfare and hunting. However, the impact of the horse on British society and culture during this period is a little discussed facet of archaeological debate in this country. In terms of what the horse represented when it arrived in Britain, both symbolically and culturally, is poorly understood, not I suspect due to any lack of material evidence but due to a lack of realisation of the transformative role that the horse had on British society and culture at this time. Only recently has the debate about the Bronze Age Kazak horsemen and their role in transmitting language, culture and riding throughout the ancient world begun to infiltrate into the mainstream of archaeological thought. Yet these influences and skills were also transmitted to the British Isles too. Nobody could deny that the horse was of great symbolic importance by the late Bronze Age/early Iron Age; the Uffington horse confirms that. The use of the horse in decorative metalwork is also a feature of the period. There is little doubt that the horse revolutionised communications in the British Isles in a way that would not be seen again until the wheel arrived, and yet there is little discourse about the horse's role and importance in human development and societal culture change.

Human-animal relationships in British Later Prehistory

Unlike central and southern Europe there is, unfortunately, little information to go on about the place and role of horses and dogs in hunting in the British Isles during prehistory, and what little evidence is gleaned from archaeological sites tends to largely ignore the importance of these animals in prehistoric society. Our first historical mention of either horses or dogs in Britain comes from the Romans, who merely describe Iron Age Britons as using horses and dogs to hunt. So from this we can glean that by the later Iron Age horses were ridden here. We can also say that the Romans were impressed both by the hunting prowess of the Britons and by the quality of their horses and dogs. Dogs seen by the Romans in their early encounters with the British would be recognisable even today, dogs such as mastiffs.

A ruler of a group of Britons, Cassivelaunus, in around 54 BC, used his 4000 charioteers, which would mean 8000 chariot horses – a large number of horses to train, feed and keep on the move – to harass Julius Caesar's army and mounted cavalry as they marched for the Thames. The technique employed by Cassivelaunus and the charioteers was to drive madly in all directions whilst throwing javelins, using the noise of galloping horses and wheels over the ground to disorient the enemy. He was finally defeated after a rival tribe, the Trinovantes of southern Britain, took Caesar's side in the ensuing skirmishes. The level of organisation required to produce, train and pull chariots in battle meant that the horse must have been a very significant part of the British way of life, and yet in mainstream texts on the history and archaeology of the later Iron Age and the early Romano-British people they get little mention – just passing, almost throw-away references such as the example just mentioned. The sight of 4000 chariots and 8000 horses must have been truly spectacular, and no doubt the Romans thought so too.

The horse was undoubtedly important in the domestic sphere of life in Iron Age Britain. A particular feature of the Iron Age was the preferential and deliberate burial of horse, dog and raven remains in disused grain storage pits and at the terminuses of ditches, probably for ritual purposes. Burial of horse remains in ditches and pits continued into the Romano-British period in some places such as Besthorpe, Nottinghamshire, in the Trent Valley. Certainly when the assemblages of bones from various late Bronze Age/early Iron Age sites in the Trent Valley, such as Gonalston, are examined, and despite the relatively poor preservation of bone material, horse remains are often recovered in significant quantities, including in burnt mound deposits. Burnt mounds are perhaps best described as social and ritual kitchens and were a relatively long-lived feature in Trent Valley prehistory, stretching from the Neolithic and into the early Iron Age, although it has been noted that they are often imprecisely dated and that a significant investment in scientific dating is required. Colour plate 10 shows one prior to excavation at Girton Quarry in the Trent Valley.

Artefacts perhaps give us the best indication for the importance of the horse in Iron Age Britain, particularly the rich metalwork items, such as strap ends and rings used for bridles, often found in association with La Téne chariot burials in East Yorkshire, as we shall see shortly. These large formal cemeteries included the horse, cart or chariot and associated equipment, and had strong similarities with burials in the Champagne region of France. The La Téne cultural package was evident in Britain from around 600 BC to 50 BC, which with the Hallstatt Culture leads some to consider that the British Iron Age belonged to a wider pan-European Celtic Iron Age cultural package. Certainly linked with the Swiss La Téne style were high-quality gold items such as torcs and brooches, and weapons and personal items, including swords, shields and ornate horse harnesses. In Britain, particularly southern Britain, the Midlands and the Trent Valley, it is interesting to note that the progression from the earlier open pattern of landscape of the late Bronze Age, to the early enclosure phase of the earlier Iron Age, is associated with small but significant quantities of La Téne pottery wares. By the middle and later Iron Age the occurrence of La Téne wares is much more common.

The horse in the Iron Age is significant symbolically as well as domestically, and the culturally symbolic aspects of horses were likely influenced by the La Téne cultural package. As we have seen, the White Horse at Uffington, near the Ridgeway and Uffington 'Castle' hill fort, attests to the powerful symbolism associated with the horse in the late Bronze Age and into the Iron Age. Horses as bloodstock or ridden animals were certainly traded in Britain, and work by Robin Bendry on strontium isotope ratios from the analysis of horse teeth suggests that a horse discovered at an Iron Age settlement site in Rooksdown, Hampshire, might have come from Continental Europe. Previously, analysis of horse bones had indicated that on some sites, such as Gussage All Saints in Dorset, the absence of young horse bones had suggested they had been bred else-where. The high proportion of stallions noted at Danebury and the Gussage evidence had pointed to horses being captured from wild herds and being broken for riding. Earlier I made reference to the late Iron Age British tribal leader Cassivelaunus; his not insignificant 8000 chariot horses has led some researchers, including Peter Reynolds, to infer that there were significant horse breeding operations working in the south of England during this time. Bendry's work also indicated that the Rooksdown horse may have been traded between Hampshire and the Winchester area, or Scotland, Wales or the south-west of England.

Horses were clearly important in Britain as a ridden or traction animal during the Iron Age, most especially for the role they played in warfare. Horses were probably first ridden here at the turn of the second millennium BC and there are harness fittings appearing at the beginning of the first millennium BC. When the wheel appeared in Britain is uncertain, but throughout most of this time the roads were too poor or non-existent to use carts as a prime method of transporting goods and people, and it seems unlikely that any wheeled vehicles would have been used for anything other than show or in occasional warfare. Chariot burials did follow later at places like Wetwang Slack, Humberside, where a number of them were revealed in the 1980s; others had been found elsewhere in earlier excavations (all in East Yorkshire). These burials, resembling the La Téne burials on the Continent, involved the intern-ment of a man (sometimes a woman) with grave goods, which in the case of men consisted of swords, spears and shields, and above all this was placed the pole of the chariot, horse harnesses and the chassis of the vehicle. This tradition may have been a Continental culture whose artefacts suggest a link with the Rhineland and east France. Is it possible that these vehicles were used in some form of hunting? Warfare was not necessarily a constant theme in Iron Age society and hunting has always been used as a way of training for warfare.

For dogs we can say that during the Iron Age and Romano-British periods British dogs were highly valued on the Continent, and that the breed types we were famous for then are still recognised today. Mastiffs, for example, were highly prized as hunting dogs used for hunting bear and lions by the Romans and in the amphitheatre. Other than that, our knowledge about dogs during this period is unfortunately woefully inadequate.

The Roman horse

Roman horses were selectively bred for three main spheres of work: for use in the Sacred Games, racing, hunting and war. The literature of the time, which is quite extensive on this subject, describing the points of conformation, would be recognised today as being close to the ideal for horses in these types of work. Literary Romans such as the poets Virgil and Oppian, the geographer Strabo and gentlemen farmers

Varro and Columella, to name but a few, are the source of much information about horses, their breeding and uses. Horses in the Roman world, according to Columella, were divided into three classes of stock, each of which had varying types of control of when and how they were bred and their monetary value. Noble stock were used in the circle or Sacred Games, whilst next down were the breeding mules, whose foals could command prices as high as good noble stock, and finally the common stock, horses which were used for producing ordinary horses. It has to be recognised that whilst horses were important in the Roman world, they were more so for sports, hunting and as pack animals and, perhaps surprisingly, less important in warfare – essentially the Romans preferred to fight on their feet. The conformation of the Roman horse as described by these authors is close to two main breeds we recognise, the Quarter Horse and the Arab. Roman horses, it seems, were around a maximum of 15 hands high (hh), perhaps excluding some taller warhorses. A sloping shoulder was considered important, as this indicates a good endurance horse, as was a dark colouring. The reason for selecting dark colouring was (and still is) quite sound, as darker coloured horses, blacks, bays and some chestnuts tend to have black or dark hooves, which are stronger and less brittle than lighter coloured ones. This was especially important in Roman times because much of the Empire was stony ground and horses were not shod.

In the Roman world the favoured horse was the Libyan. Ann Hyland of the Carnegie Museum, who has written extensively on the subject of horses in the classical and Roman world, notes that references made to Libyan, Numidian and African horses mean that they can generally be categorised as 'Libyan', and are close in size and conformation to the modern Arabian horse. Indeed, horse remains unearthed in the early twentieth century at the important Roman fort at Newstead, Scotland, on the Roman Frontier were around 14hh, and a skull recovered, when compared to a known Arabian example at the British Museum, was almost identical. The Romans, however, were not master breeders of horses; nomadic peoples in Africa and in Asiatic regions just to the east of south-east Europe were better. But the Romans did breed horses that were fit for purpose. That said Romans also valued the aesthetic of horses as well as good conformation, and for this reason they would have valued the Libyan horses, which, even by modern standards, horsemen would still recognise as a pleasing horse. More importantly perhaps is that horses of this type of conformation, that is typical Arabian, would be hardy, tough and intelligent, and for their size were reasonable weight carriers.

All forms of mounted hunting was an occupation of the rich, but hunting hares with hounds at this time, excepting some small differences, was remarkably similar to foxhunting of recent centuries. A pair of leashed hounds was set upon the fleeing hare on open ground and hunted by a number of men on horseback according to strict rules of conduct. Like modern fox-hunters before the ban, many Romans disagreed with the digging out of a hare after it had gone to ground or undergrowth and allowed the creature its escape. The horses recommended for use were Scythian or Illyrian horses, not considered lookers but were rangy horses capable of

26 Roman
horseman
in combat

chasing down a stag to the end of a hard day before it was captured or dispatched. Scythian and Illyrian horses were produced by nomadic people from the region of Iran (Persia) and the western Asian region. Perhaps influenced by the Libyan horses they were considered to be highly effective hunters, recommended for stag hunting particularly, according to Arrian, because of their ability to chase and wear it down.

Oppian advised the use of stallions over mares because of their greater speed, except in hunts where there might be a number of mares to distract it and cause it to neigh and prance, which would scare away the prey. Gallic horses were the horses of Celtic Europe, and this probably included Britain. No descriptions of these horses have survived down to today, which suggests that it was not a fine looking animal – Romans only tended to describe those horses that were pleasing to their eyes. However, we do know that the Gaullish Cavalry were, in the early Empire, adept horsemen. Indeed, Strabo indicates that they were the best cavalry force the Romans had. No doubt the Romano-British horses were descended from Gallic-type horses, with infusions of better blood from time to time to improve the breed. The horses of the Iron Age British people were probably a Gallic-type horse and were probably the same types as the 8000 chariot horses used by the British tribal leader Cassivelaunus to harass Caesar's army on its march to the Thames. So breeding for points of conformation, hardiness and the right qualities were as important and understood in Britain as they were on the Continent. Only the by then old-fashioned use of chariots, although deployed quite effectively, let down the British warriors. There can be little doubt that Cassivelaunus's horses were as fit for purpose as Roman military horses. The so-called Celtic ponies (*Equus celticus*), derived from the Northlands ponies and related to a number of still surviving ancient breeds across northern Europe, are the likely progenitors of the modern Fell and Dales ponies of the Pennines. The Exmoor pony particularly shows signs of having an ancient lineage with its characteristic mealy markings being indicative of its antiquity. These breeds of pony became important in the establishment of many later breeds of ridden pony, not just in Britain but also throughout the world.

All this gives us at least a sense of the types and uses of horses in Roman Britain. Horses were important in Roman life as a means of transport, militarily and in hunting. Excavations in the Trent Valley, particularly at Besthorpe near Collingham, Nottinghamshire, recovered the badly preserved bones of several horses. The locations of these bones and the nature and form of the enclosure ditches of these farmstead settlements suggested that horses were kept closer to home than other forms of live-stock. There may also have been deliberate placements of horses or parts of their bodies within some of these ditches, which may be for ritual reasons that harked back to earlier times. Horses are high-maintenance creatures, requiring more care and investment of time to keeping, rearing and training them. The burial of horse remains in ditches might represent some form of ritual offering behaviour that was aimed at attempting to win protection from the gods. Certainly this kind of practice was common enough in the Iron Age.

The study of horses and horsemanship in Roman Britain is a hugely understudied area considering the importance and centrality of the creatures in the lives of the Romano-British people. They were also symbolic as objects of wealth and status in the Roman world, and numbers of horses owned and one's skills in horsemanship were highly regarded, again something often overlooked in the archaeological inter-pretation of the many rural sites that have been excavated. Certainly horse remains are not as common as other livestock such as cattle or sheep, but they were an important component of the rural and urban economy – although it is stressed that depending upon the type and context, horses were rarely used as beasts of burden because they were far too valuable. Ploughing and general lesser tasks were the domain of beasts of burden like oxen. Although the Romans did recognise the Friesian, in its home range of the Netherlands, as being a powerful working horse, they regarded it as ugly. The Friesian still exists today but as a much improved animal, and because the Romans favoured it and used it here in Britain it has since influenced Fell and Dales ponies, via the English Great Horse, the Shire. Besthorpe seems to show a slightly unusual number of horses, which was perhaps reflective of the use of the site as a possible cattle centre, attracting people to buy, sell and ship cattle close to the banks of the River Trent; or it may be that it was a horse breeding and rearing farmstead taking advantage of its trading position.

Horses in Medieval Britain

There is a great deal of literature on medieval horses and horsemanship, particularity related to warfare and hunting, and some of these aspects have been touched upon in other chapters in this book. Therefore, I will confine myself here to the archaeological evidence for horses at several places in Britain and describe some aspects of medieval horse breeds and their development to flesh out the bigger picture of how and what types of horses were used in hunting during this period.

Familiar to most people will be the Great Horse, the medieval charger used in jousting. The Great Horse, more a type than a breed, was derived from the draft horses of northern Europe, such as the Friesian, and crossed with oriental types and breeds. This selection to get the best morphological traits of the various breeds of horses has, as we have seen, a long history. Modern Shires are the descendants of the Great Horse, and were improved by infusions of other breeds such as the Arab, Barb and the Andalucian. The Shire is a far bigger horse than the Great Horse was however.

The aim of developing the Great Horse, and it is still an obvious trait in the Shire, was to allow it to be able to carry a knight in full armour for the joust and in warfare — and it owed much of its development as a type to the efforts of Henry VIII (1491–1547). A soldier in full armour could weigh in excess of 200kg by Henry's time and the requirement for a horse to carry a soldier and his armour was critical. The formation of the Great Horse owed a lot to the efforts of Henry VIII to increase its size for use in battle; this was done by decreeing larger landowners to keep two or more mares over 13hh or over, plus, stallions of under 15hh could not be grazed on common land in the Midlands. This was because the strength, size and stamina of the horses of the time were not able to keep up with the heavier modern armours being developed. This was seen as being a weakness in English medieval warfare that was in need of urgent correction. Carefully chosen horses were imported from the Continent, particularly from Spain, Hungary, Denmark and Sweden, selected for their greater size and strength. The end result was a horse that by today's standards would still be fairly small. Indeed, the Great Horse probably resembled the Friesian in many aspects of conformation and height at around 15hh (*c*.1.52m). Osteological evidence has shown that most medieval horses would be around 14hh, or a little more, and not exceeding 15 hands, fitting the size and physical proportions and conformation of a Friesian. Around a century after Henry VIII, Oliver Cromwell gave the Great Horse the title the 'English Black', which was continuously improved and was still being ridden by the King's Household Cavalry during the reign of Charles II (1630–85). Just how useful some of these larger physical attributes would have been in a ridden hunt is debatable.

In hunting the Great Horse was probably not used too often in a ridden hunt because a horse with stamina and a fast turn of speed was sometimes required, and smaller, lighter horses were better suited to this job than the Great Horse was — although hunting provided training for horses in war, and in some types of hunt, such as deer coursing, it was probably suitable to use the Great Horse over that type of ground. Coursing required a long, straight, fairly treeless belt of land. In the right sorts of conditions a Great Horse could also be used in boar hunting. For hunting in wooded parks or rougher ground, or where greater turns of speed were needed, smaller and quicker horses were required. Something like the ancient breed of the Welsh Mountain pony, which at only 12hh (*c.*1.22m), and very sturdy and tough, was ideal. Crossings of this with other breeds or types could have produced a slightly bigger horse useful for this type of hunting.

In archaeological terms the numbers of horses and remains gathered on site are not usually very high; for example from Stafford Castle, just outside the town of Stafford, excavations revealed a low number of individuals for each of the six phases examined, relative to all other domesticated species, such as cow, pig and sheep. This is perhaps not surprising because the contexts usually reflect food consumption. Maybe more telling are the number of game species in each of the six periods, particularly red deer, which in periods two and three show roughly the same number of individual specimens as cattle and sheep, and we can expect that at least some of these would have been hunted on horseback. Also, a relatively high number of items of horse furniture and horseshoes were discovered in parts of the site during the excavations. The furniture included harness and bridle fittings, bits, buckles and pieces of curry combs. Many of the horseshoes that were identifiable and datable belonged to the period of the eleventh to thirteenth centuries and the fifteenth century – identification difficulties notwithstanding.

What happened to horses once they had outlived their useful lives, especially in the context of somewhere like Stafford Castle, is that they were often fed to the hunting hounds, excepting in those instances where the horse was deemed special enough to warrant a more dignified end, such as a burial. Most of them it seems were disposed of by the knackerman. Sometimes, but rarely, they were eaten by people – usually only in times of stress, such as during the Civil War (1644–46) sieges at Banbury, Carlisle and Chester. In the medieval period the sense is given that horsemeat was not usually for human consumption. The treatment of horses used for farm and domestic work was probably quite different from those used in warfare and hunting. Often the domestic horse was described as 'old and worn out' and 'is but caryen' (carrion). Certainly horse remains from Dudley Castle showed signs of a hard life, with wear and tear consistent with long hardworking lives. Documentary sources show that the use of horseflesh to feed hunting dogs was a common practice; but whilst the archaeological record supports this, it shows that it was mainly a rural feature with horse bones from urban contexts showing few signs of butchery.

Post-Medieval horses and dogs

The importance and usefulness of horses to daily life in areas such as agriculture, transport (especially coach horses), sport (such as steeple chasing and flat racing) and of course hunting was huge. It is often difficult to convey just how important horses were in daily life and just what an investment of time, effort and fiscal resources they required. In much the same way we take for granted the presence, usefulness, impact on the economy and expense of motor vehicles, so we have taken for granted the existence of the horse in daily life prior to the age of the automobile. What we have singularly failed to grasp is the importance, the expense and the physical presence of the horse and its impact upon the economy of the time. For example, in urban excavations of domestic settlements dating to any age prior to the existence of motor vehicles, there are very few references to the presence of stables. Where they are considered, little attention is paid to how many horses may have been stabled or for what purpose they were used, or their relative importance to the people living there or their likely economic impact within the locality.

More often than not, the horse during this period is usually most considered by historians and archaeologists in military terms, especially in the context of barracks (archaeology and architectural history), or their role in wars (history). Yet horses were much more than just mounts for soldiers; they were the lifeblood of rural economies, used to transport grain to the mills and flour to the towns and cities that by the eighteenth and nineteenth centuries were the centres of the Industrial Revolution. In the urban areas, and only with the emergence and rapid rise of the canals and railways, did the horse begin to be superseded as the primary means of moving goods and people between cities, towns and ports. Eventually, even in rural areas the horse was starting to be replaced by the rapidly expanding rail network but it was still a vital asset in more remote areas.

On the land the horse would remain important for ploughing, and specialised breeds such as the Shire horse were developed to provide the necessary pulling power for the new ploughs and seed-drilling machines that the industrial age had brought. For the clay-lands of the south-east of England (Suffolk and Anglia) and the Scottish Lowlands, breeds such as the Suffolk Punch and the Clydesdale were developed, both having less feathering around the feet – a distinct advantage on clay soils. Stud books were developed in the eighteenth and particularly in the nineteenth century to ensure that the quality and purity of these animals were maintained, something which has contributed to their survival into the post-industrial age. Steam-powered traction engines began to replace the horse on the land in the latter half of the nineteenth century, and the pace of mechanisation gathered in the first half of the twentieth century with the motor-powered tractor – the little grey Fergie (Massey Ferguson) leading the way.

In parts of the country the management of semi-wild herds of horses, such as the ponies of the New Forest, Dartmoor and Exmoor, continued in much the same way as they always had, whilst always seeking to improve the stock. This is particularly true in the New Forest, and since the proclamation by King Cnut of Forest Law in 1016, when he won the English Kingdom, there have been efforts to improve the stock. There is documentary evidence of the use of Welsh pony mares turned out into the Forest in 1205 in an attempt to improve the stock, and in the eighteenth century a famed thoroughbred stallion named Marske was used to serve Forest mares. Even Queen Victoria had a hand in the improvement of the Forest ponies by loaning Arab and Barb stallions from her own stables. However, it was the Lords Lucas and Cecil who were most influential in creating the Forest pony type we

27 The Andalucian horse – an important and ancient breed used to improve many types of British horse. (Kat Lewis)

28 A thoroughbred – another important breed used to improve horses

recognise today – between them they introduced blood from Highland, Fell, Dale, Welsh, Dartmoor and Exmoor ponies. When Lord Cecil returned from the Boer War he brought back a Basuto pony, which was added to the mix as well.

Human intervention in the breeding process, or selective breeding, has had a radical effect upon the conformation, size and colouring of horses over time. This process has been going on in multiple locations at different times, which accounts for the variation in the results of genetic studies of horse populations around the world. Unlike most other domesticated animals (dogs being the other exception), it has not been possible to tie down to a single location or timeframe when the horse was domesticated. Human requirements for the horse, whether it is for riding, pack transport, ploughing, food, or a combination of these reasons, has led to a wide variety of breeds and types, representing a considerable investment of time, knowledge and resources to achieve the end result.

One such example of a British light draught horse is the Cleveland Bay. There has been a bay-coloured packhorse in the Yorkshire Riding since the Middle Ages, and these were known as the Chapman Horses. The Chapmen were travelling merchants who plied their wares throughout the country. In the seventeenth century, in the north-east of England, there was a considerable stock of Spanish Horses, such as the Andalucian and the Barb, and these were used to improve the Chapman Horse so that by, certainly the eighteenth century, the breed we recognise as the Cleveland Bay appeared. The Cleveland was used to plough clay soils and haul loads and, because it was a notable jumper, carry heavy men out hunting. The Cleveland Bay was, until the time of George II, considered the best coach horse and was in use in the Royal Stables for this purpose. Only after the creation of the tarmacadam roads (which the Cleveland was considered too slow for) was the thoroughbred put to the Cleveland to create the Yorkshire Coach horse, which effectively became extinct in 1936, leaving only the Cleveland, now a rare breed horse which still has a place in the Royal Stables and still pulls coaches on State occasions. Thoroughbreds were often used to improve many types of horse.

The Irish hunter

Into the post-medieval period hunting on horseback required the right horse for the work, and the creation of the Irish hunter, by crossbreeding the versatile Irish draught and the English thoroughbred, fitted the bill. The nature of the hunt during these times, and the evolution of the foxhunt into quite a different sport than had been seen in earlier periods, meant that the type of ground and the landscape it covered was quite different from the 'Chase' of the medieval period. The enclosure of the British landscape, which happened on a piecemeal basis from the twelfth century, peaking between 1450–1640 and 1750–1860, meant changing the large common pastures into privately owned enclosures. The resulting landscape was broadly similar to that seen today, particularly in the English Midlands. The hedged landscape was

29 A rider clearing a fence in a hunt. (Amanda Lockhart)

managed as much for the hunt as for agriculture, and hedges were maintained to ensure that horses would not be injured when jumping the fences in pursuit of the fox or hind. The Irish hunter had the stamina and speed to withstand a long day in the field and the big scopey jump to clear ditches, gates, fences and hedges. It also had the strength to carry a weighty rider, which given the dietary excesses of the aristocracy of the time was an important requirement. Also, this crossbreeding produced a horse that was not only of the right 'stamp' but looked to be of quality stock, which was equally important to their usefulness. Horses, particularly thoroughbreds, were the ferraris of their day – indeed, the Irish hunter is still highly regarded as a good-looking competition horse, particularly for cross-country.

The Irish had a love of the hunt, and the Irish Draught was already a horse capable of jumping formidable obstacles and had in its own lineage Spanish Andalucian horses. Prior to these improving additions it owed much of its size and strength to Flemish and French heavy horses imported into Ireland in the twelfth century. From medieval times the improvement of horses was very much an international business and up until the Industrial Revolution the contribution of foreign stock was enormous. Even today the movement of competition horses and thoroughbreds for breeding purposes around the globe is big business. A modern twist in the bloodstock business is, of course, the transport of frozen sperm from prized stallions to fertilise mares thousands of miles away.

5

The Landscape of the Hunter

The Post-Glacial landscape of hunting

In this chapter I shall be reviewing a broad range of evidence from a wide subject area, and touching upon the emergence of Neolithic monumentality and associated theories. I will also encompass discussions about the emergence and spread of the Neolithic and agriculture, as well as the Neolithic and Mesolithic transition. I shall try to slot in a discussion of how hunting fits into all this and the implications this has on these areas of study and on landscape archaeology generally. These of course are large areas of knowledge to bring into a new discussion and so the reader will have to forgive me if it seems I am only addressing some of these topics, theories and discussions in a superficial fashion; it is unavoidable and I make no apology for it. Time and more research and discussion will ultimately bring greater satisfaction.

There is a belief amongst some archaeologists that the dawning of the Neolithic brought with it the end of, or at least the serious decline of, hunting – this was not so. It could not be so because whilst people spent time perfecting the science of farming and husbandry, from time to time they failed to raise successful crops due to diseases or bad weather. Raising livestock could also fail for any number of reasons, so hunting and gathering had to be what people fell back on to survive. In order to do this it was important to retain the knowledge of the skills required for hunting and gathering.

We know that hunting eventually became an elite sport. But how did this happen? When did this happen? The clearest route for these circumstances is via two mechanisms. These two mechanisms, whilst in some ways are mutually exclusive, are in many others complimentary, with each leading to the other as conceptual frameworks for elitism in hunting, becoming responsible for turning the act of hunting into a specialised sport of the nobility. Beginning in prehistory, the story can be told in relation to other archaeological stories that relate to monumentality and the emerging new social order of the Neolithic, and eventually the changing social order of the Bronze Age. Indeed, it is fair to say the story that can be told is a reinterpretation of this evidence that relies not on farming or the Neolithisation of people, but instead relies on hunting as the catalyst for these great societal changes as they become manifest in the British landscape and archaeological record.

Dealing with the hunting directly: in many societies around the world hunting is viewed as a male role, with the status of the male being very much tied to his prowess as a hunter. It is often a group event, with 'competition' between males within the group being very evident; skills are honed through training and practice and from time to time displayed to others in the group or to impress the women of the tribe or clan. There is little doubt that hunting was a key component in daily life and that such skills would have been held in high regard. Therefore, when the Neolithic gradually crept up on British people they, as everywhere else, no doubt embraced it, but they also hung on to the hunting tradition with some ferocity too, particularly because of the role hunting could play in these communities not just in terms of supplying valuable food in lean times but as a social mechanism for display and intergroup cohesion. As more and more individuals within these communities were, over time, required to develop their skills as farmers rather than hunters, it becomes possible to see that eventually only certain people had the time and the inclination to hunt. It is possible that these people were likely to be the ruling class. Such skills would still have been held in high regard and might well have sharpened social divisions within clans and groups. This split within communities might well have been used to the advantage of the elite tier to set themselves apart and promote self-aggrandisement through the controlled participation of hunting. In the contact between groups and clans, the skills of hunting were probably mechanisms by which elite groups enacted certain rituals relating to hunting that facilitated social exchange between them. Over a greater span of time, such mechanisms and control over hunting, seen as being beneficial to the elite because of the way it elevated status through participation and control of land, may have ultimately led, millennia later, to the creation of forests and deer parks.

This is because there is a gradual mechanism that has everything to do with land tenure and how this was perceived, and how it changed over time linked to the gentrification of hunting. Much stock is placed in the changes wrought upon landscape by the adoption of agriculture over that of a hunter–gather–fisher lifestyle and what this meant in terms of human interactions with the world around them, almost to the complete exclusion of the continuing role that hunting must have played in landscape, land tenure and the human perception of these things. This chapter argues that concepts of land tenure, perceptions of landscapes, largely discoursed as elements of agriculturally defined lifestyles, and political constructs are also inextricably tied to more ancient traditions and concepts of what might be loosely defined as 'hunting-related land tenure', stretching far back into the Mesolithic and probably beyond.

30 Map of some of the sites discussed in this chapter

In the early Neolithic and subsequent periods land tenure, its meaning and its importance had changed considerably. This led to a revolution in which relatively widespread but often localised clearances in the early Neolithic began, then accelerated, with the at first piecemeal enclosure of the later Bronze Age landscapes, followed by the broader subdivision of landscapes in the Iron Age and Romano-British period; also, the infield–outfield farming that typified the Saxon and medieval periods, along with the creation of forests (both Royal and not, also as an economic entity, not just as a hunting forest) and parks, until very recent centuries in Britain, which saw the enclosures and the growth of the sport of hunting with hounds and the management of the countryside to benefit this sport.

These marked shifts in concepts of land tenure highlighted the importance of laying claim to land, firstly collectively as demonstrated in the Neolithic by the building of communal monuments, particularly chambered tombs: for example, Minninglow, Derbyshire, and Carn Ingli in Pembrokeshire, which were also reflective of their importance as already ancient special places and were imbued with changing meaning so that by the Bronze Age and into the Iron Age the nature of monumentality took on a more individual, more elite-focused aspect, leading to new classes of monuments and ostentatious displays of power, and changed social structures and ideas of land tenure. The creation of larger capital building projects, such as the later phases of Stonehenge, Avebury, and particularly Silbury Hill, to name but a few, indicate the presence of an elite class in the landscape. In the Iron Age the hill forts of Hengistbury and Mam Tor continued to show that the power of the elite was capable of organising society sufficiently to feed itself and have energy surplus to complete these huge projects.

There seems to be a general acceptance that during these periods the hunted landscapes, such as Britain's highlands, were too marginal for agriculture and therefore became less important. The assumption was that any concept of tenure could only be loosely applied to these landscapes. I want to argue that in these agriculturally and sometimes politically uncertain times, particularly in the early Neolithic, a key nexus point between perceptions of land tenure, agriculture and hunting, land use and tenure of 'marginal' landscapes was more important – not less. The critical agenda in this period was the control of land by certain people and finding a mechanism by which to control this resource – hunting, and its by now elitist associations and growing perception of it as an elite pastime, provided that mechanism.

Certain landscapes, namely the highland zones of Britain, even down to today are, in some ways, disputed land resources, as they have been since prehistory. Recent decades have seen controversy over the right to roam, bringing landowners into conflict with walkers and ramblers, and at the heart of this has been the perceived disturbance to game birds reared for shooting. The conservatism of hunting, and its links to the nature of land tenure associated with it, seems passively perceived; it is almost as if people are not aware of the nature of this strong link, the origins of which must have emerged in prehistory. This link is taken for granted and yet the strength of that link has coloured the views of people where land tenure is concerned, particularly

31 Mam Tor, late Bronze Age/early Iron Age hilltop fort in the Peak District, Derbyshire

landowners, well into recent decades. As a concept the argument I make here is not 'new'; Oliver Rackham in *The History of the Countryside* has already explored the depth of history visible in Britain's countryside and argued that some of the types of landscape visible during the medieval period and even today had their origins in prehistory, for example wood pasture. Cognitive and post-processual archaeological thought has also grappled with this issue, in works by Chris Tilley in a *Phenomenology of Landscape* published in 1994, and more recently by George Nash in several papers, notably *Settlement Dynamics and the Territoriality during the Late South Scandinavian Mesolithic* (2003). In these works the issues of Mesolithic hunting and landscapes associated with hunting, as continuing activity or with reference to past hunting, are touched upon as aspects of the reasoning behind Neolithic monumentality.

Mesolithic

At the end of the Mesolithic people were more settled due to the more complex hunter-gatherer lifestyles they led. This was particularly true of the coastal Mesolithic communities with fairly stable renewable resources to exploit. Work by R. Shulting and M. Richards, in Brittany, France, at the sites of Téviec and Hoëdic, firstly determined by stable isotope analysis (which can determine differences between marine and terrestrial proteins) that there were dietary differences between coastal Hoëdic and Téviec, which is inland; with a mainly marine bias at Hoëdic. Secondly, their work used AMS dating to provide ages for burials earlier recovered from the two sites, which contained a number of elaborate cist graves with single, double and multiple interments. There was also evidence for the reuse of these graves after some centuries at these sites – a characteristic of Neolithic passage graves. Interestingly, the effect of a mainly marine diet, as at Hoëdic, can skew the calibration and therefore the results of AMS dating, making them up to 400 years too early. That being allowed for, the results of this study showed that there was, despite the nearness of the two sites, considerable continuity of settlement at the end of the Mesolithic, meaning that the two groups remained distinct for a very long time. Certainly there were links between the two groups with things like ochre being exchanged, and flint being sourced from the beach was used in microlith production, which again showed some differences in production style. Also there was evidence of intermarriage, with women from the hinterland probably marrying into the coastal Hoëdic population, showing that there was at least some cohesion between the coastal dwellers and some inland groups. It has been hypothesised that coastal complex hunter-gatherer groups were further apart than their inland counterparts, due to the more restrictive range of resources they exploited. At these sites the bones of large mammals, such as red deer and boar, and a range of smaller mammals, such as beaver and 15 bird species, were recovered from sea-eroded middens (these were much further from the sea during the Mesolithic/Neolithic transition). In addition to this, a single tooth of a sheep/goat and the suspected fragments of a cattle bone indicate a possible pastoral element to the local economy. The dates recovered from the Téviec remains were 5200 calBC and this suggests that the emergence of the cist burial phenomena may be contemporary with the arrival of Neolithic influences. However, the continuation of the Mesolithic economy, world view and reuse of earlier cemeteries and some burial practices, plus the lack of any attendant pottery evidence, suggests that the complex and highly conservative hunter-gatherer lifestyle hung in for longer here than in most other parts of the European Atlantic seaboard, including Scotland. There is considerable data from Denmark which highlights a rapid shift from a coastal marine, complex hunter-gatherer-fisher lifestyle, which had a particularly heavy dependency upon fish more so than on shellfish, to a Neolithic agricultural one – it is envisaged that this pattern may apply to Britain.

In Scotland the pattern and nature of Mesolithic life is hard to describe for the country as a whole due to the paucity of evidence, which has been subjected to the erosive forces of agriculture, clearance, drainage, time and environmental change. Many of the sites occupied between 9000 and 5000 BC were inundated by rising sea-levels. A project, Scotland's First Settlers (SFS), has been addressing this lack of evidence by looking at the Inner Sound, a stretch of water between the Isle of Skye and the mainland. Prior to this the evidence for Mesolithic sites suggests that the occupation of sites, such as at Kinloch on the Hebridean island of Rum, involved temporary shelters built of skins and timber, with occasional 'base-camps' where longer periods of time might be spent before moving on. The SFS has highlighted the great importance in Scotland of marine resources, with seasonal migration routes incorporating the sea into the round, along with the lochs and the rivers – mainly because these provided useful highways of communication. The rocky, forested hinterland was difficult to negotiate. The raw material bloodstone, for the stone tools used here, was procured from Rum, which is some 30km to the south; while baked mudstone and siliceous chalcedony came from Staffin on Skye, 10km to the west. Locally procured chert and quartz were also used.

Mammals, including red deer, wild pigs and cattle and many species of bird, showed that the diets of the inhabitants of the area were not restricted to just marine resources. During the excavation and study of these sites it was noted that the sea-level during the late glacial was higher even than today. This was due to the great weight of ice from the Ice Age pressing down on the north of Britain. This left the land mass considerably lower than it is today. Once the weight was removed the land mass was able to rise, a process known as isostasy, which causes the south-east of Britain to dip towards the sea – hence London is sinking. This gave rise to features known as raised beaches in Scotland and the north-west of England; beaches that are considerably higher than they were during the Ice Age.

During the Neolithic in Scotland, the placement of chambered monuments and long cairns favoured a relationship with rivers, particularly in south-west Scotland (Dumfries, Galloway and southern Ayrshire). While being located on average at 165m AOD, many of the higher ones are on what is today moorland. Leaving aside the possibility of attrition to this assemblage of monuments by agriculture or wilful destruction by people, these fairly substantial memorials survive in ploughed fields, thick forestry or areas of intensive grazing, which suggests a reasonable level of survival, perhaps highly representative of the original quantity of monuments built. The monuments here were impacted upon by their position in the prehistoric world, with influences from Ireland, the Isle of Man and by the people and styles to the east of them.

What Vicki Cumming showed in her work was that the monument types could be classified by their relationship to landscape and, to some extent, to the contemporary influences their builders were subjected to. Of interest here are the differences that they marked out within the landscapes they occupied. The relationship between the monuments and the sea was not a particularly obvious feature of the structures; they showed more apparent affinities with the rivers and seem to mark out the division between the higher ground and the more fertile valleys. However, Cumming's analysis demonstrated that things were not quite so clear cut, and that the relationships were as much about transitional monument styles, influenced by distinctive groups, as they were by the landscape. The relationship with the landscape was also about making obvious, or marking out, these regional differences. Cummings said of this relationship: 'It was this landscape, of mountains and sea, that added significance to the monuments of south-west Scotland.' However, there is a clear relationship between the rock-art of the region and the sea. What is not clear as yet is if there is a relationship between rock-art and the monuments of the region.

This is an area of considerable further study, as George Nash has shown in western England, Wales and Anglesey. He has shown that if concerted efforts are made to look for rock-art within or just around these monuments it will invariably be found. So far his investigations have discovered a previously unknown cup and ring motif on the chambered tomb of Garn Turne, Pembrokeshire, adding to a corpus of known embellished monuments that include Pentre Ifan, Pembrokeshire; Bryn Celli Ddu; and Barclodiad y Gawres, Anglesey. A number of sites were known to be embellished by rock-art in Wales, the Welsh Borders and Anglesey, but since the 1990s that number has risen to more than 50 sites. These monuments are usually marked on their capstones, sometimes inside or on the uprights, but it is not clear if these markings are contemporary with the construction of these monuments or date to its later use, or even if they were made after they were disused. Traditionally the dating of this type of rock-art is considered to be of late Neolithic or early Bronze Age date, but this is far from clear. It is even the case that some were reused stones from other forms of monument. There is a fairly widespread tradition of doing this; for example, in the Gulf of Morbihan, Brittany, a single standing stone was broken and incorporated into two passage graves.

We know of the obvious Irish examples of rock-art being part of the monument, such as at Newgrange; and in Argyle, Scotland, we have North Cairn, Nether Largie, which interestingly has a grave cover-slab with cup marks and axe-head engravings. In this instance a decorated standing stone was probably reused as a cist cover. So here we have another form of marking places and spaces, or making statements that speak of people's relationships with places and resources, marking out in some way the connection between people and landscape, people and the past, and people and the present and future. By building monuments and by making rock-art they are defining the form of tenure for the future, a form of tenure that is very much based upon the past way of life of their ancestors – the hunter-gatherer forefathers who held the land and territories before them. Defining them for the future by making reference to the lifestyles and tenure of the past legitimises their claims and rights for the future. There is a clear association or connection between rock-art, death and burial. Possibly they played a role in the ritual activities that took place at these sites.

Another area where Nash and I have some parity is on the issue of hunting and territoriality during the Mesolithic. During the 1990s and into the first years of the twenty-first century (in a paper published in 2003), Nash looked at these issues in the south Scandinavian Mesolithic. He concluded that against a background of complex and social political change and changing population there was a 'need to consolidate prime hunting, fishing and gathering territories'. The mechanisms he saw as working during this period favoured ways of creating intergroup cohesion, developing contacts and exchanging with neighbouring groups. Part and parcel of all this was

32 Rock-art at the monument of
Barclodiad y Gawres, Anglesey, Wales.
(George Nash)

exploring new ideas and technologies including agriculture and pottery making, and
making and utilising static and mobile art were important parts of this package of
behaviours. These were viewed as adaptations in the face of increasing population
pressures and socio-political difficulties.

Britain in the Mesolithic was undergoing similar processes, albeit differing in
nature and complexity depending where in the British Isles people happened to
be living and exploiting. The nub of the matter is that in the British Neolithic,
the dissemination of ideas and cultural traits peculiar to Neolithic groups spread
and acculturated Mesolithic peoples. Some of the complex hunter-gatherers were
more receptive to these influences; some were less so no doubt. Hunting continued to be practised as evidenced by the range of arrowheads etc. found in
the archaeological record from the Neolithic and into the Bronze Age. Alasdair
Whittle draws attention to the mobility of Neolithic communities, which was
perhaps based upon seasonal camps and their relationship with pathways and
route ways within the landscape. The extent of this 'mobility' was regionally vari-
able and perhaps reflected the nature of the mobility of preceding Mesolithic
communities. Marking rocks, special places and route ways using rock-art was
one way of linking back to the hunter-gatherer ancestral landscapes of symbolically charged places; certainly a phenomenon visible throughout the British Isles,

such as we just saw in Argyle, for example. These places had to be recognised and in order to do this they were mythologised and consequently they continued to be so into the Neolithic. Understanding the limits, boundaries and relationships with hunted spaces belonging to a particular community was important as this resource was likely coming under increasing pressure by growing populations and sedentism. Beyond the stock enclosures the landscape was still fairly wooded or afforested, and we can see this in the pollen records which show considerable oak and elm woodland (the elm decline notwithstanding). Shepherds and stockmen would have taken their livestock into these areas from time to time, so they were important for their contribution in this way into the new agricultural age. There can be little doubt that these areas were considered 'wild' and were still important as hunting landscapes.

Areas close to the settlements at this time, particularly those areas that were very marginal yet still influenced by human activities, such as hay meadows seasonally used for grazing fringing the wilder areas, are likely to have been especially replete with game (in its broadest sense as the range of animals hunted was far wider than we would consider hunting and eating today). So the perception of the wild was more acute than we would think of today; its value perhaps taken more for granted than we might, but its importance was no doubt recognised both as a ready source of food in times of scarcity and a place to expand into in times of plenty, prosperity and community growth. It is worth making the point at this juncture that as humans became increasingly sedentary, and more divorced from wild places, it is likely that even as wild places shrank the human concept of 'wildness' and what it represented increased.

The Neolithic onwards

Recent work by Cummings and Whittle, published in 2003, has shown that some monuments were purposefully placed in wooded environments and that this might be intended as an aspect of their sitting within the landscape. Reference is made to a very much non-agricultural aspect of the landscape, and one that is much more centred upon a relationship with hunting – here described more as a relationship or a throwback to the Mesolithic past. Tilley has shown us that in south-west Wales there is a complimentary pattern between Mesolithic sites and early Neolithic monuments. A point made by others is that there is a link between Mesolithic cultures and Neolithic communities that either overlap (Mark Edmonds made this point in 1999 in *Prehistory in the Peak*) or are to be found side by side, as at Grotte du Gardon in the upper Rhone Valley. Evidence of the Neolithisation of Mesolithic cultures is fraught with problems, with the fine detail of these interactions yet to be fully understood, but it does highlight that the Mesolithic and all the cultural baggage of that era did not stop, die and wither away and then the bright new Neolithic age suddenly start, with all that went before being suddenly forgotten. The sedentary hunter-gatherer lifestyle of the late Mesolithic, I would argue, was highly conservative. In the Linearbandkeramic (LBK) of northern Europe, it was argued by Whittle in 1996, hunting and gathering was not important, but the evidence suggests that there was variability of hunting in this period that responded to settlement, with a predominantly arable focus where they occurred in densely forested areas that had less reliance upon cattle and sheep husbandry. This, it seems, is interpreted as an adaptation or a slant on the Neolithic by a predominantly Mesolithic population by Amy Bogaard in *Neolithic Farming in Central Europe*. In Britain a similar argument can be constructed at least for the uplands, but probably in sparsely settled forested lowland areas too. The watersheds of the North Pennines are marked out by rock-art on grit-stone boulders and the placement of burial cairns that were considered by some researchers to separate the wild landscape from the domestic one, or the hunted from the agricultural landscapes. The same patterning could be noted more generally for the East Moors of the Peak District. Yet here there is a relationship between Bronze Age settlement, cairn fields and field systems in the uplands that make that relationship in many ways less distinct as we move into later prehistory. The reason for this, as well as being climatic, with warmer more favourable conditions existing in the Bronze Age, is also tied to tenure. The expansion of settlement into the margins of former hunting grounds was desirable due to population pressures, as well as the elite seeing personal benefits of this expansion of 'ownership', plus benefits to the community. Critical to this is the idea of these hunting spaces, beyond the watersheds, or what would be termed in the medieval period as 'wastes' and 'commons', being used and operated primarily as elite hunting grounds, controlled, protected and administered as a commodity under the management of the chief and the lead family, ostensibly for the benefit of the whole community. In actuality, and certainly as time passes, this is increasingly a patent illusion.

In the Trent Valley, in Nottinghamshire particularly, the palaeoenvironmental evidence during the later Mesolithic suggests a fairly densely wooded environment within the floodplain and higher ground; lime trees were also present on the margins with damp grasslands within the understory of the canopy. Within this forest there was a significant amount of human activity, particularly on the higher, drier ground

33 Rock-art typical of the watersheds of northern England. This is from Ashover, Derbyshire

where significant numbers of late Mesolithic flint artefact scatters have been recorded. Here, as on the Magnesian Limestone escarpment near Elmton, Derbyshire, there is a trend towards increasing later Mesolithic activity, which might be accounted for by greater mobility of later Mesolithic groups, or more speculatively by sustained population increases. However, it is noted that there are a number of problematic factors in trying to argue for this.

By the beginning of the fourth millennium BC there was a widespread forest cover of oak woodland, termed 'wildwood', over much (but not necessarily all) of the Trent Valley. In the south Pennines, piecemeal burning may have been used as a tool to create clearings that encouraged herbivores such as red deer into them for hunting and the growth of edible plants. Later, in the Neolithic and Bronze Age, this expanded into the growing of cereals and the clearing, both by using stone axes and burning, became much more widespread, this time to facilitate wholesale land clearance. The Trent Valley remained a fairly wooded environment and Neolithic settlement and activity went on within the wildwood; it was only by the Bronze Age that it could be argued that significant open stretches existed within this region. However, evidence in the form of redeposited trees within the reworked gravels of the Trent, at two locations in the lower and middle reaches at Colwick and Langford, indicate that some clearance was taking place from the early Neolithic, and the palaeoenvironmental evidence shows that this was probably sufficient to cause erosion of the newly exposed forest soils. In places within the Trent Valley there is scope for the continuation of at least some elements of the hunting and gathering tradition that typified the Mesolithic way of life to have continued well into the Neolithic. Arguably, an earlier form of land tenure centred upon hunting prevailed too.

Traditionally, the placement of monuments upon the edges and ridges of the high ground in the uplands is viewed as laying claim, on behalf of a community, to agricultural and settlement grounds in the valleys below, and the more marginal 'liminal zones' above. Equally, and not often considered, this activity could be representative of maintaining ancestral ties to ancient and well-known hunting grounds – these would be a vital resource if the crops failed or the livestock was destroyed by disease or natural disaster. Even as people became more experienced and better at farming, this reasoning would still be a difficult concept to shake off, and maintaining linkages to these landscapes in this way would continue to have been important for millennia. Interestingly, the work by Cummings and Whittle on Neolithic monument locales found in wooded landscapes clearly shows that these monuments were not always intended to be visible, as had previously been suggested by Tilley, who said that the main point of locating chambered tombs was to be visible, or at least intervisible, between each other. This leaves open the possibility that monuments were sited in wild places for laying claim not just to the settled agricultural territories of people, but for maintaining and negotiating access to the hunting resources of the wider landscape, perhaps defined and consolidated by using familial and clan linkages, even with other groups and communities. This could be supported by the types of interment at these early tombs, which favoured communal burials, expressing the commonality of settlement and these places, and representing the prevailing attitude towards land tenure.

Work by Ian Hodder, published in 1990, has highlighted the role of monuments with hunting and concepts of 'wild' and 'domestic' spaces. For example, he notes that within the relatively well-preserved Neolithic houses of Çatal Hüyük, Turkey, burials of men are associated with hunting points, whilst wall paintings and symbolism generally concerns the wild and hunting. Another point noted about these burials was their relationship with the rear, inner part of the house, which was associated with the wild and death, and that this relationship could arguably be made with Wessex long-barrows, for example, where the disarticulated remains of males were deposited deep within the inner parts of the tombs – arguably reflecting a similar world view. We can take from this that hunting was not only still relevant in the Neolithic but critical to the way society was stratified and organised, playing a key role (via the interment of the dead, creating a linkage with the wild and with hunting, in highly visible monuments at key locales) in organising society and orchestrating interactions between individuals and groups. More contemporary hunter–gatherer communities (see, for example, Val Attenbrow's book *Sydney's Aboriginal Past: Investigating the Archaeological and Historical Records* for enthohistorical descriptions of various ceremonies in the Sydney region of New South Wales, Australia) are known to share access to resources by negotiation of that access through various mechanisms, not least through the use of aggregation locales such as bora (initiation) grounds. Hunting played a very important part in these ceremonies, which brought people from distant lands who were linked to people at these places by totemic affiliations. Such ceremonies were relatively infrequent and were themselves negotiated between groups, who in most circumstances would hold a small bora to initiate young men into manhood, but occasionally the elders of various groups would decide that a larger event was required and all the boys could be initiated in a larger ceremony at a proscribed place. Moiety linkages meant that one group would host the event within another group's territory, and food sufficient to feed this large gathering, which sometimes lasted for days, had to be obtainable in the vicinity of the bora ground. Dances and rituals were performed that highlighted the role of hunting in manhood and these played a key role in the ceremony.

Beyond the role of initiating young men into adulthood the ceremony had a wider function, which was to negotiate access to resources in other territories and to seek marriage arrangements that might facilitate this and ensure their survival until such time that these groups might again meet peaceably. Whilst there is little to dispute that the use of monuments in the early Neolithic had an intrinsic link to territoriality, sedentism, expressions of power etc., they might equally be viewed as a response to sedentism, settlement and the creation of human space, or as a response to a perceived threat to the hunting resources so long relied upon. They could therefore be viewed as a way of renegotiating their relationship with nature, the landscape and each other ('other' here defined as other human groups). It is perhaps a response to the uncertainty that undoubtedly was part of early agriculture in those few millennia after humans started to farm; monuments responded to the uncertainty of things, such as failing crops, disease, prolonged bad weather and a narrowing of one's resource base and a changed relationship with other people.

At the heart of the hunter-gatherer-fisher lifestyle is cooperation and sharing and the negotiation of rights of access to other areas for hunting and gathering, whether that means crossing the territory or range of another group to get to places where certain seasonal game or plant foods might be found, or to join with other groups to hunt migrating game that seasonally passes through certain places. Studies of land use and social territories in Italy by Robb and Van Hove, published in 2003, noted the importance of hunted and forged resources as a back-up to agriculture; furthermore, they argued in their model that demographic pressure upon resources was not the driving force responsible for the spread of the Neolithic, given that communities throughout Europe combined hunted and foraged resources with garden agriculture. A key element in this study highlighted that the areas of hunting and foraging zones around them decided the locating and spacing of settlement. Also, and more interestingly, there were likely to have been overlap zones in these wild areas, and I suggest that in Britain these were perhaps viewed as being 'in common' with other settlements and communities, in other words the concept of the 'commons' that we are familiar with in rural Britain but having their roots in prehistory. In essence, the work by Robb and Van Hove argues that the choice of location for settlement and mode of subsistence, be it more agriculturally focused, or hunting and foraging focused, was a social choice and not so much a response to need. There is no reason why this mode of land tenure should not have been widespread in the Neolithic, even in Britain.

This type of tenure makes more sense as a model during the spread of agriculture as an adaptive approach to the way the land was exploited and used in earlier times – it also explains why monumental tombs emerged in the Neolithic. Another class of monument that may have fulfilled this role, and one that I would suggest might have a closer association with initiation ceremonies, is the fairly common burnt mounds of Lowland Britain. Often interpreted as possible saunas, the residues of industrial processes or locations for social gatherings and feastings, burnt mounds and the activities associated with them, closely fit the pattern of usage for an aggregation locale; suggesting these were places where inter-tribal groups would come together. In the Trent Valley these monuments seem to span (better dating notwithstanding) the period from the late Neolithic well into the earlier Iron Age. Like the monuments of the uplands, these places seem to occupy the edges of territories, having a close association with river channels, and are often away from contemporary settlement.

In this scenario, access to common wild food resources, or shared human resources to access wild foods and game, might have been perceived to be under some sort of threat, or that for various reasons certain places and spaces needed to be marked out and encoded. Therefore, as a response to this, monuments were built. It is perhaps no coincidence that there is a complementary pattern of Mesolithic sites and early Neolithic monuments in south-west Wales, as

Tilley noted in *A Phenomenology of Landscape*. Or that the placement of tombs within the wildwood tree cover at certain locales was important and articulated a relationship between people and landscapes. Other theories suggest that the placement of monuments, and sometimes rock-art at the watersheds of the uplands, such as in the North Pennines, correspond to 'liminal' zones marking the distinction or a break between the wild and domestic landscapes; and life and death. These are places defining not just the locations where people lived and farmed, but also where they hunted and foraged, occupying the space at the edges of territories on the fringes of overlaps with other territories, creating a shared but negotiated space perhaps best described in our modern terminology as 'commons'. This makes the relationship between the wider unsettled landscape and the settlements complex. We know that references to wood-commons existed in Anglo-Saxon charters, and that in prehistory, even as early as the late Mesolithic/early Neolithic, the concept of and presence of wood-pasture is likely to have existed in Britain – at least in some form. That being the case, this may give us a direct link into the prehistoric past to a concept of commons.

Amy Bogaard notes that the 'permanence of cultivation plots may have implications for tenurial claims on land and on social ranking' (2004: 53). Clearly, cultivation has implications at least for the nature of tenure, and how it was perceived and who may have had control of it, including groups and communities that might have had some investment in the perception of that tenure. Critically, there must have been some crossovers with the way land tenure worked in the earlier hunted landscapes, and these may well have set the parameters for how that tenure worked once the land was cultivated, and time and a sense of permanence was invested in. In other words, the earlier type of tenure and how it was perceived could well have set the ground rules for agricultural landscapes. Mark Edmonds describes vividly the nature of garden cultivation that may have taken place in the forests of the late Mesolithic and early Neolithic, as groups cleared trees, settled, moved on and perhaps returned years later Neolithisised, and eventually cultivated areas – always drawn back to remembered or significant places. Under this kind of social regime tenure would probably tend towards communal ownership, aligned towards a Mesolithic structure of perceived tenure based upon moving around the landscape with reference to mythologically significant places, and having its roots reaching far back into prehistory; in other words, the social and political tenurial structure of a hunting and gathering landscape.

The notion of Common Land, which continued into the modern age, albeit in a radically truncated form thanks to the enclosure of the commons, starting in the twelfth century and gathering pace between 1450–1640 and between 1750–1860, is perhaps a relic of a concept that long ago was about open and free hunting grounds for the community, becoming transformed and reworked into a tenure that became associated with grazing in later millennia. The enclosure of parks and forests invariably encroached upon manorial wastes, woods and commons, and in doing so they eradicated the rights of usufruct and tenants who had exercised their common rights on this land. Even neighbours lost their rights. The enclosures were only halted when the Enclosures of the Commons Act, 1876 came into being thanks to the efforts and campaigns of the Commons Preservation Society. This became one of the first environmental protection measures enacted by law. Commons always were privately owned, usually by wealthy landowners. They became places that were controlled by a social elite; they probably always were and the mechanisms open to the elite like, for example, the law, has in more modern times been used to control such land. It is by mechanisms such as this that the relationship between people and places changed. Change was wrought by social elites using whatever mechanisms were open to them at the time to create or retrench common land as and when it was needed or was politically savvy to do so. Human consciousness has land tenure perceived as owned or at least a controlled commodity, and even where it may not be, as can be the case with common land, it is still perceived today as a resource that can be retaken either by law or an act of compulsory purchase if it was required for some other purpose by the landowner. For much of history, commons only remained so because the elite found it advantageous to allow the existence of such places, perhaps to keep the peace or maintain control amongst the population; the mechanism of creating 'rights' consolidated the perception of the existence of common land.

During the medieval period, particularly in the twelfth century, as virtually whole counties became defined as hunting forests, and areas within were enclosed as parks for the raising and hunting of deer, all the settlements within and around the forests became subject to Forest Law, and commons and wastes were encroached upon. Commons were important places that the largely rural population relied upon for grazing their stock (right to pasture); and they had other important rights such as the right to catch fish (piscary) or to estovers, the right to take fallen wood and small trees sufficient to meet the commoners needs. Even the person who had the rights was defined, having only the status if he or she lived within a specified area and was called a 'commoner'. The ownership, management and control of the commons by the aristocracy in the medieval period and through to the post-medieval period was arguably the culmination of a shift in emphasis; that is to say, controlling and managing what had previously been a resource for the benefit of the many, taking it for the benefit of the few.

However, this process did not begin in the medieval period; it is likely to have started far earlier. The process of creating the concept of common land was advantageous to social elites far back into prehistory. It is pertinent to point out that although I use the term 'common land' here, perhaps overly so, it is an appropriate term due to its familiarity, even though the precise parameters of the type of land tenure I am trying to describe can really only be guessed at in prehistory. The term 'common land' is nonetheless perhaps the closest fit. The ownership of places, in this instance land, that is favoured for hunting either for sport or for the purposes of accumulating wealth by the few, began with the emerging social elite of the Bronze Age and, perhaps in some areas, in the earlier Neolithic. The creation of this type of tenure was advantageous to the elite because it allowed, through their ownership, the administration and control of places that provided both game and sport – food and prestige. Controlling this may have allowed the illusion of shared management with a community, including the control of types of game hunted and when and where the wider community hunted them. The mechanism of at least promoting the perception of some form of idea of common land may have served to maintain the control of the ruling family over the land resource in various ways, whilst keeping the community on side. Later, perhaps generations later, when land was needed for agriculture or settlement, the right to, and nature of tenure to the land was renegotiated between the chief and his community and his followers. Land could be annexed, taken out of common, parcelled and boundaries created which brought the resource effectively under his total ownership and control, perhaps allowing him and his family, by right of descent, to a proportion of the produce grown or raised upon it: taxation. The mechanism that allowed him to do this was the type of tenure that was in existence when this was a hunted landscape and established deep in the mists of time to prevent things like over-hunting or conflict with neighbouring groups. The idea of sacred landscapes, aggregation locales, watersheds and various other ritualised landscape phenomena, formed a part of this package of behaviours and ideologies that made up land tenure as a concept into recent prehistory (Neolithic onwards), lead to the creation of monuments such as chambered tombs, cursus monuments, and barrows. All these phenomena served a purpose – to continue the form of the hunting-related land tenure prevalent in earlier prehistory (Mesolithic and earlier) into later prehistory, where it underwent a series of transformations dictated by societal change, even down to the present.

Part of the suite of changes evident in later prehistory was perhaps due to a perceived change in emphasis brought about by time and developments in agriculture, technology and social and religious life, which whilst not necessarily undermining the importance of hunting, made it possible to rationalise clearances and encroachments into previously important hunting territory. A description of how and why this could have worked is necessary: the emerging social elite of the Bronze Age, and the accompanying social structures, may have recognised that there were benefits to be had in controlling hunting and the places that were hunted for sport (maybe), particularly with reference to 'specialising' certain game animals, perhaps for exclusive consumption by certain tiers of society (much as we witnessed until recent centuries with deer and, arguably, more recently with swan). However, there was a much more significant gain by controlling access to hunting, and using certain food taboos. The elite ultimately controlled ownership of the land, not only physically but also the perceived rights of that ownership through exercising and managing control of the hunted resource.

The nature of Bronze Age enclosure and division of the landscape (see, for example, work on the Dartmoor Reaves by Andrew Flemming, 1979), which while varying in density and intensity took place broadly throughout Britain, following extensive clearances and expansion of settlement, and saw the creation of two well-defined landscape spaces: the wild and the domestic. Terminal reaves, for example, defined the edge of the unenclosed moorland, perhaps marking the edge of the hunted landscape, distinguishing them from the grazing spaces. As we have seen, defining these spaces marked out the differences between the wild hunted landscapes, making it distinct from the domestic sphere of existence. It required considerable manpower to mark out and construct these features, and local elites were clearly capable of organising this work. Their rationale for doing so was that alongside exercising seasonal control of grazing in those areas, the elite could also control access to hunted resources. Elites were perhaps able to control the species of game that could be hunted, perhaps through the continued use, or through long traditions of food taboos, even modifying them to ensure that favoured game was not widely hunted – extending the idea that such taboos are a socially created mechanism, reinforced by religious dictates that acted to preserve the numbers of certain types of game. This is probably why humans managed to avoid hunting most species of deer to total extinction, as the forests and woods shrank and agriculture expanded.

In the Iron Age, a period characterised by extensive woodland clearance and fairly extensive settlement, the pace of tenure must have changed radically in tandem with societal change. The nature and structure of the upper segments of society no doubt had a big impact upon these changes, and vice versa. In the later Bronze Age, in some parts of Britain, such as the Trent and the Derwent Valleys, larger-scale landscape division in the lowlands sometimes took the form of pit alignments. These were pits, regularly spaced, such as those seen at the site of Derby Racecourse, which probably incorporated an interrupted line of posts that stretched sometimes for several kilometres through the landscape. These porous lines probably allowed people and animals to pass through them, but were a visual statement of a new type of land tenure and the emergence of different societal attitudes to landscape, and the position of people and animals within it.

By the Iron Age there is clear evidence of the intensification of pastoral and arable production, increased land clearance and claimed ownership of land, and with this came societal change and a shift towards the compartmentalising of landscape using boundaries. Yet considerable expanses of the countryside must have remained 'wild' and continued to be favoured hunting places, both by the elite and probably by the general populace. It is unlikely that these places remained 'un-owned'; such places were certainly part of territories belonging to a tribe or clan and, de facto, to its chieftain. We know that when the Romans arrived in Britain hunting was important here from the fleeting references made in the literature. To what extent these wild places were truly controlled is unknowable, but reference to the territories of the earlier periods, marked out by barrows and rock-art in the landscape built and made by the ancestors, were remembered by people who were descended from them. These landscapes of memory and genealogy were no doubt important in maintaining a group's claim to land during times of upheaval and great societal change. We can be certain that the depth of oral tradition and remembered genealogy was in the Iron Age far deeper than it is today. This conservatism was embedded in the perception of land tenure and transmission through each successive generation, almost certainly

34 Pit-alignment at Derby racecourse; the figure in the background shows the direction of this boundary feature. (Trent & Peak Archaeology)

ensuring the continuation of these traditions into this period, despite the societal changes that were being wrought.

As discussed earlier, the Vale of the White Horse is overlooked by this large, prehistoric figure, which has been known as the 'White Horse' since the eleventh century AD. The site itself is within a landscape of considerable prehistoric significance. The White Horse probably borders two territories with this symbol facing the neighbouring or opposing territory. In this way might the White Horse might be a group's totemic symbol? If this is the case then there is a link going back through time to the Upper Palaeolithic groups who held the horse up as a totemic symbol, a symbol of power as we have seen at Lascaux and possibly even at Creswell Crags. Through such remembered connections to long dead ancestors in a world of fantastical creatures hunted in ancient legendary stories, the understood rules of tenure were communicated down to the present.

The role, standing and initiation of men into the community was likely to have been closely tied to hunting, as it is today in some pre-industrialised societies. This makes it likely that continuing the tradition of hunting would have been an important feature of past agricultural groups. The tradition and skills of hunting are highly conservative, and are unlikely to have changed much over time. Technologically speaking much has changed in hunting over the last six centuries, with the introduction of firearms and the use of motor vehicles, for example; but in essence much remains the same. Yet in many ways these last six centuries were the least conservative; conservatism in hunting is likely to have been far greater in prehistory. At the beginning of the Mesolithic, the biggest development was perhaps the use of the bow and arrow; prior to that would have been the introduction of dogs and the invention of the spear thrower. Somewhere between the bow and arrow and the gun was the introduction and use of the horse in hunting. The most fundamental change, however, was the introduction of agriculture and with it new plant foods that required large amounts of land, sedentism, investment of considerable community time and effort and a very different rhythm and type of life. New animals were introduced too and these needed care, rearing, space and enclosures, some protection from predators such as wolves and again, a great investment of time. With all of this came the opportunity for creating wealth by creating surplus and by exchanging that surplus for prestige goods and power – hunting had a new role in all of this because it became as much a pastime as a necessity. Predators such as wolves and bears, now threats to reared livestock, were hunted more for sport but also necessity because of the threat that they posed. Conservatism in hunting was maintained against a broadly identical technological background, and whilst some of society's values had changed in the early centuries of the Neolithic, the landscape was recognisably similar and still wild. Wild resources certainly continued to be important during the Neolithic and Bronze Age – despite the assertion by some researchers that hunting became far less important, even almost nonexistent. I would argue that into the Iron Age the concepts of land tenure were still tied to those earlier ones that emerged from the time when hunting and gathering was the primary mode of subsistence and still prevailed.

Changes in numbers and types of prey are perhaps discernable in the archaeological record, offering evidence for the proportion of game hunted and consumed in the diet – such evidence might elucidate patterns that show which communities were using game resources more frequently and why. For example, a community may be blighted by repeated poor crops forcing them to hunt and exploit more game – wetland or wetland fringe areas may offer more evidence of this type of response. One such peculiarity in faunal assemblages that has been noticed and reported by Ian Hodder, is that the remains of wild pigs, used perhaps in feasting, have been found in chambered tombs in the highland zones of Britain, whereas the reverse is true for settlements. The use of hunted animals in these contexts may be significant, marking a further distinction with the domestic landscape, reinforcing the wild association of the monuments, place within the landscape and their connection with the ancestors. Perhaps the use of these animals in feasting marks out the activities taking place there as special and requiring the higher status value now assigned to hunted game.

After Prehistory

Throughout a period of prehistory, spanning from the Neolithic to at least the late Bronze Age, those territories that were considered wild would have dwindled, a fact that was perhaps not lost upon the contemporary population. Possibly, this increased the concept of 'wildness'. Over time, livestock-rearing and crop-growing took precedence over hunting as the prime method of ensuring contemporaneity of lifestyle and food supply whilst increasing population. Conspicuous consumption was perhaps centred around feasting upon cattle rather than game, at least in some circumstances, but the evidence from the monuments of the British uplands, and in some burnt mounds in the lowlands, shows that in those places considered to be marginal, game species, particularly the dangerous boar, were still the preferred food choice – perhaps out of deference to their ancestors who were hunters, or as part of some display of male hunting skill and bravery. Whatever the reasoning for this choice it is likely to have been considered a show of status, perhaps consumed only by elite group members at the feast or for the benefit of showing generous hospitality at inter-group feasting. Later, perhaps, there might have been a reversal in this trend, with domesticated animals taking precedence over game during feasting occasions. Managing the wild, even in the face of growing agricultural dependency, was most probably being practised well into the Bronze Age and into the Iron Age. As I have explained, there were advantages to doing this if you were the elite. Later, when the Romans arrived, as we shall see in the next chapter, they brought with them a concept of *saltus* or un-owned land outside of the settlements that consisted of forest, marshes and unsettled land that belonged to the state. *Saltus* was hunting grounds, the precursor of the forests we are familiar with in the medieval period.

Agriculture is all too often put under the microscope as the key catalyst for various aspects of change within these areas of archaeological debate and discussion, yet there is more than enough evidence that hunting, its role in the management of landscape and its undoubted continuing importance throughout prehistory and even into the last two millennia, must take some of the blame. Yet in these crucial debates hunting continues to have only a fleeting mention, if it gets mentioned at all. More often than not it is entirely missing as a component in these discussions. For much of human existence hunting has been practised as the key means of human survival; it did not stop being important once domesticated plants and animals appeared, indeed hunting may have become the key means by which the elite appropriated land since the Neolithic by a process of gentrification, for lack of a better word, and elevating hunting to a prestige pastime. By doing this, and using political savvy, the elite ensured that they controlled vast areas of land to reproduce their wealth throughout succeeding generations. Much later, after the Norman Conquest, this led to the creation of formalised hunting, the expansion and then the creation of Royal Forests and Parks in the early medieval period; before this, the Anglo-Saxons, as will be examined later, had their formalised hunting too, and even the Romans brought formal hunting with them to the British Isles. Again, this formalised hunting, and the whole complex arrangement of land tenure that was associated with it, did not spontaneously emerge and nor was it purely the product of agricultural ideas and forms of land tenure. They no doubt brought with them similarly aligned tenurial ideas and concepts. The structures used for the control of hunting, via mechanisms such as forests and parks, is in evidence in the Saxon and medieval periods, and hunting, in part, was the medium used to justify the application of these forms of tenure. More significantly, was it the extension of the ideas behind this type of elite land tenure, which had, in earlier periods, been used to appropriate and own land by the few, which has survived down to recent centuries and is responsible for the appearance and nature of the British landscape? Is it possible that, blinded as we are to the role of hunting in land tenure and its deep time depth, in favour of the long-held prevailing wisdom that tells us that agriculture is the primary driving force behind tenure, we have largely failed to see this connection?

On this subject I can only add this observation: when we consider history we take a point in time, discuss it and describe it, then examine how this affects us today by looking forward from that distant date all the way to the present. When we examine a technological innovation, such as the invention of the automobile, the car, we look at what went before to see why we call it a 'car' (horseless carriage), and look at why we measure the power of engines in 'horsepower' (obviously because they were the measure of traction before the car). Yet when we look at land tenure and monumentality in archaeology, we more often than not look back from a post-agriculturally defined world (the one we are in) to attempt to describe these phenomena – not by looking before agriculture and describing monumentality and particularly tenure from that viewpoint all the way to the present.

What I have discussed here should open a debate about the role that hunting is likely to have played in the nature of land tenure and clearance, monumentality, landscape enclosure and its pace and extent over the millennia. These discussions, as well as the mechanisms that they gave to prehistoric social elites to control, alter and of course 'own' land throughout the long time depth of prehistory, are curiously missing in the discourses of these topics. The resulting explanations of some of these issues are, in my opinion, monosemic. Consequently, they are one-dimensional and do not take into account the sum of human experience in landscape and land tenure before agriculture, which must have evolved throughout the long course of human experience as it related to the essential art and craft of hunting.

6

Elite Hunting: Roman to Post-Medieval Periods

This chapter looks at hunting from the Romano-British times to the end of the medieval period. Hunting as a sport, as we perceive it to be from sources such as the media, of red-coated men, women and sometimes children mounted on horseback with a pack of dogs speeding ahead, began to truly evolve during the periods I will discuss in this chapter. During these periods hunting became more formalised and ritualised, hence the wearing of red coats, or pinks that we see today. This was in part due to the elitist origins of sport hunting, something that by now has become perceived as a part of the tradition of sport hunting. The appearance of an elite hunting class beginning in the Roman period can be tracked through an almost unbroken archaeological and documentary record through history, down to modern times. The limited written sources that survived from the Roman period allow a sketchy picture of hunting to be built during this time. However, this information, combined with archaeology and other studies, can add to that picture; studies such as examinations of Samian ware pottery decoration, for example, which sometimes show hunting scenes.

During the Dark Ages there are only a few references to elite hunting, but the sport makes a strong appearance after the Norman Conquest in Britain. The hunting elite were always there, despite their seemingly minimal presence in the contemporary literature, and we can find some evidence of them and their activities in the archaeology. We can glean from records, such as Domesday, that the Normans replaced a feudal system and estate system, including woodland hunting grounds and hunting preserves or parks, that was not entirely dissimilar to the system that they introduced. By the end of the medieval period elite hunting, with its rules, etiquettes and formality, was shaping the foxhunts and deer hunts that would eventually supersede them from around the seventeenth century.

The scholar and author Richard Almond pointed out that until his book, *Medieval Hunting*, there was little written about hunting in the medieval period due, in part, to the scholarly focus which considered hunting to be of little social and economic benefit in the medieval world – in other words, a cruel and unnecessary 'frivolity' of the elite classes and not worthy of study. What Almond pointed out was that there were invisible aspects of the cultural and social life of all classes missed by not considering the importance of hunting in the later Middle Ages (the period focused upon in his book). If this is the case in the later Middle Ages then it is certainly the same picture we see for the earlier medieval period, where even less work has been done on the subject of hunting. One wonders whether such blinkered thinking has been responsible for undervaluing the role of hunting and anything associated with it: like the role and importance of dogs and horses through all these periods.

The issue of hunting in archaeology, and hunting for just about any period after the start of the Neolithic, has been politicised. Sometimes it seems only acceptable to discuss hunting throughout the Pleistocene and early Holocene in any detail. One gets the sense that when the Neolithic arrived and agriculture takes hold we must begin to view the world differently, and that we humans must have surely begun to turn our backs on the barbarity of hunting wild animals; therefore, the whole issue of hunting and its attendant cultural baggage throughout prehistory and, as Almond tells us, even into the later medieval period, should be viewed as a marginal issue. Only the inconvenience of there being a documentary element to the later periods (Roman onwards) seems to make researchers consider the subject at all, which is a great shame as I suspect that the disciplines of history and archaeology are at best impoverished and at worst largely built on incomplete information for significant sub-disciplines of them.

Hunting in Roman Britain

There has been woefully little work done on hunting during this period, and what little has been written had to be gleaned from sources far and wide. Roman hunting is very much a composite picture, built of fragments and scraps of literature, art and even pottery. It goes without saying that hunting at this time was important – it is just that this has been largely overlooked in favour of other aspects of Roman life and history. The Roman settlement of towns, the presence of the military in town and country, the mosaic pattern of rural settlement, its relationship to the preceding Iron Age settlement patterns, the growth of the Roman Villa, and the road network and other engineering and industrial feats at this time, tend to be the focus of study in Britain. Hunting rarely gets a passing mention. Yet, like in all preceding periods, and all periods subsequent to the Romans, hunting can be shown to be of great importance. Again, a whole useful class of important evidence is missing for the Romano-British period, which should surely mean that what we understand of the social and cultural life of the people at this time is very deficient. Can one venture to say it is so deficient that we could re-examine the whole of the period, with hunting as one of the core tenets of Romano-British cultural life, and show a very different Britain at this time?

In Britain, as in much of Europe, we have the Romans to thank for the early emergence of that economic entity, the Royal Forest, which came during the medieval period. The idea of 'Forest' existed here and on the Continent during the Anglo-Saxon period, and emerged out of the Roman concept of *tractus* or *saltus*, which are terms that applied to all uncultivated lands. These included forests, marshes, pastures, steppe, and indeed just about any land that was sparsely populated or uncultivated and were deemed to have no owner. It was very much like that Australian concept of *terra nullius*, which meant that all seemingly unused land in Australia belonged to the Crown. In effect, that is roughly what *saltus* meant: land having no perceived owner and therefore belonging to the state.

At that time, Roman settlement and farming was confined to lands fringing the Mediterranean, where the regular pattern of Roman roads and field systems, created at right angles to the roads, could be found extending deep into northern and Western Europe. Even up the Thames valley this pattern of fields and roads was probably recognisably Roman. Throughout the rest of Britain, much of it had been cleared, settled and farmed by the Iron Age inhabitants, who readily (in most instances) accepted the Roman way of life, becoming Romanised — hence we know them as the Romano-British people. Over much of Britain, where Iron Age people were settled and cultivating land inside their sometimes huge enclosures, which eventually became the settlements of the Romano-British people, there followed the superimposition of a more regular grid-like pattern of fields and roads upon the landscape. However, outside of these areas, and the Roman estates, much of the land was *saltus* and belonged to the state. Arguably, I would say that this followed an earlier pattern of ownership whereby such land belonged to whatever elite family could call that territory theirs (see previous chapter).

Roman Villa estates are a difficult thing to nail down in terms of size and function, either archaeologically or from the few contemporary documents or inscriptions that exist. It is clear though that in some instances they were in effect large country estates, not unlike those to be found in Britain many centuries later, possessing farms that were tenanted and no doubt tracts of land used for hunting. At least, if the gentry of the time were also in the employ of, or favoured by Rome, then the permitted use of the *saltus* would provide ideal hunting grounds for deer and boar. We know that Roman soldiers, garrisoned at forts up and down the country, were able to hunt and often did so both for sport and for food; and on the Continent they did so sometimes within the units' *vivarium* (effectively a park). R.W. Davies, who in 1971 looked at the diet of the Roman military, claimed that around a third of the faunal remains he examined throughout Europe at military camps were of hunted game, including red deer, roe deer, boar and hare (which was most commonly hunted for sport, as was the boar). Other animals like fox, badger, wolf and beaver were also hunted, most likely for sport.

Exciting recent research by Naomi Sykes, Judith White, Tina Hayes and Martin Palmer, analysing strontium isotopes in the teeth of deer, has shown that Romans introduced fallow deer into Britain; certainly at Fishbourne Roman Palace, in the first century AD, and probably elsewhere. This is important for a number of reasons and not least because it implies, along with other supporting evidence, that there was a park or *vivarium* there, the only known example in Britain. Fallow deer had been found at other sites, but in some instances these remains could have represented traded body parts, such as their antlers for craftwork or foot bones for offerings. At Monkton, Kent, the meat-bearing remains of fallow deer were excavated but were of body parts that could be interpreted as being joints of preserved imported venison. At Fishbourne the evidence for their presence was much more conclusive. After analysis of the strontium in their teeth it was concluded that they were reared locally. We know from Italian classical texts, and from excavations there, that 'preserves' or *vivarium* were a common feature of Roman estates and that the keeping of wild animals was a display of status. Having a *vivarium* and owning exotic animals, thus implying travel and having a degree of control over nature, enhanced the social standing and ranking of the individual concerned. This was similar to what would in later centuries be known as a 'cabinet of curiosities'; an expression of one's status and knowledge of the world expressed by owning and displaying objects or 'curiosities'. It was also a way of displaying one's wealth by possessing and displaying the exotic and the rare. At Fishbourne it could be that the original fallow deer were gifts from a high-ranking official of Rome to the owners of the palace. An area was emparked and the deer were allowed to breed, and their offspring were raised for capture and consumption. What precise form the capture took is not clear, but for these important symbolic beasts of the Roman world, it would surely be fitting that it was perhaps hunted. The fallow deer was emblematic of the Roman Empire, and this discovery and research at Fishbourne now requires a reassessment of how we view Romano-British landscapes and hunting. Until fairly recently it was assumed that parks were a Norman import, but research has put these features back into Britain's Anglo-Saxon landscape, and now as far back as the first century AD.

As was noted in Chapter 4, when the Romans arrived in Britain there was already a strong native hunting tradition, plus Britain was famous for its hunting dogs. There were many types and breeds of dogs by the time the Romans arrived, including mastiffs and greyhound-types. At Tiln on the River Idle in North Nottinghamshire a fragment of Samian ware was recovered (see Colour plate 12), that shows an animal-chase scene, probably a hunt. These scenes are not uncommon on Samian vessels, which themselves are high-status items of pottery and tell us this was not only a high-status activity but an activity to which people aspired.

Horseback hunting was already a well evolved sport in the Celtic world; the horse was an important symbolic animal at this time. Pottery vessels from the Colchester and Water Newton areas have been given the name of Hunt Cup because of the illustrations of hunting scenes on these decorative wares. Most depictions involve hounds chasing deer. Wild boar would also have provided excellent sport for the Romano-British people and an altar found on Bollihope Common, County Durham, records the successful hunt of a 'boar of remarkable fineness which many of my predecessors had been unable to bag'. This boar was captured by prefect G. Tetius

Veturius Micianus, of a cavalry regiment stationed in Lancaster, who was visiting the prefect of Binchester Fort, near Bollihope, who invited him to hunt.

The most ubiquitous form of hunting at this time was hare coursing. It has been suggested that the brown hare (*Lepus capensis*) was introduced into Britain from the Continent to provide sport. There are a number of depictions of hare coursing from pottery and glassware, and a sculpture relief from Bath illustrates a hare which has just been put up and a dog which is about to be unleashed. A fourth-century glass bowl from Wint Hill, Somerset, shows a hunter on horseback using hounds to drive a hare into a long-net. It is interesting that in this period the use of hounds, long-nets and horses seems to us a familiar image of hunting in the British countryside of recent centuries.

Pheasants were also probably introduced to Britain by the Romans, who would have used the bow and arrow, or nets and bird-lime to hunt them and other birds. Weapons found in a domestic context on archaeological sites point to the use of the bow and arrow in hunting; as in contemporary law, it was one of the few instances a man might appear in public armed. Therefore, hunting played an important role in wider society, with even the general population able to go hunting too. These sorts of freedoms were to continue into the following period but perhaps in a more restricted manner than was allowed under Roman rule. Bear-baiting for the amphitheatre tells us that bears were hunted and captured for the purpose of public entertainment – no doubt using mastiffs for the purpose.

Dark Age Britain

Before the Norman Conquest the picture of what hunting was like for either the peasant or the aristocracy was a difficult one to glean from historical records. The mentions of hunting and what was hunted and where are few and far between. There are a few scrappy references here and there that manage to shed a little light on the subject. For example, it seems clear that there were mentions in King Cnut's (*c.*994–1035) laws, dating to around the end of the tenth to early eleventh century, to his preserves where hunting was restricted. However, it seems that hunting elsewhere by all levels of society on their own land was tolerated – much as it seemed to be in the preceding period under the Romans. Hunting was, it seems, a little more egalitarian than it was to become in the Norman period, or had been previously. Perhaps what is most obviously known about Anglo-Saxon hunting is the close relationship between hunting and warfare. Much of what is known form the epic literature of the time, such as *Beowulf*; this great Anglo-Saxon classic, inspired from Celtic sources and events in Scandinavia, was thought to have been written in East Anglia or Northumbria. The relationship between war and hunting was one that was mirrored in the post-Conquest period and even in the Roman period, because to hunt was to practise the art of war, to develop and practise one's killing skills and maintain fitness and war-readiness.

In the Anglo-Saxon period, armour, such as boar-crested helmets and cuts of the animals themselves, would often end up in burial contexts along with the accoutrements of the hunt. Hunting certainly extended beyond the acquisition of food; it was demonstrating status and power. Hunting was a symbolic show of one's social standing and prowess as a warrior. Aspects of this, we shall see, become even more focused in the post-Conquest era.

We know from studies of the Anglo-Saxon Royal Estates that hunting lodges were built on the orders of Harold in 1065 at Porteskewett in Wales. There is certainly evidence that Anglo-Saxon kings took part in hunting, and arguably in specified places such as parks. Cnut, as we shall see later, had a hand in the early creation of what we understand as Forest Law as early as the eleventh century, but it was the demonstration of power that could be shown through the act of hunting that was most interesting to Saxon kings. The danger of hunting was part of the excitement of it as a public sport. Alfred the Great (b.849; King of Wessex 871–899) was a keen huntsman, as we know from the account given from Asser's *Life* where it was said of him that 'in every branch of hunting … no one else could approach him in skill and success'. There are some reasonable grounds to assume that these acts of hunting, witnessed and described as they were by courtiers in this way, were public spectacles. The public nature of royal hunting events is again attested to in the account given of the close brush with death of King Edmund (b.*c*.921; r.939–46) during a hunt in Cheddar Gorge, Somerset. Going back to Harold and his lodge in Porteskewett, here we had in the year before he became king, in 1066, a thegne who, to impress and perhaps upstage the current King Edward the Confessor, King of the English (b.*c*.1005; r.1042–66), used the understood rules of high-status display to attempt to show himself as an equal of the king.

In these hunts the king used his huntsmen, independently acting men whose job it was to provide high-status meat for the kings table, to make the kills of deer and boar. However, the king's participation in the chase was important, as no doubt this provided the public spectacle of skill, bravery and power. The job of the huntsmen was usually to ensure the sustainability of stocks of deer and boar in parks, preserves and royal hunting grounds. Although not formally defined as Royal Forests until after 1066, these hunting grounds were nonetheless in existence, and Fig. 35 displays the twelfth-century forests and chases alongside the Hampshire and Dorset night's farm manors, showing the correlation between pre-Conquest preserves and hunting grounds and the Royal Forests, Chases and Parks and Warrens that followed it.

One very useful line of evidence for the importance of hunting in northern Britain for this time can be gleaned from Pictish symbol stones. These show quite vivid scenes of hunting amongst their subject matter, such as Meigle 2. Symbol stones, therefore, become an important record, particularly of the significance of elite hunting during this period. Indeed, the subject of hunting in the symbolism shown on these stones is the most common theme. This is important because work by Lloyd Laing, of Nottingham University, shows that these stones were commissioned

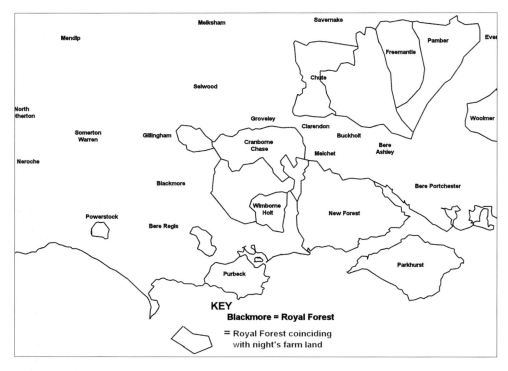

35 Twelfth-century forests and chases in Dorset and Hampshire's night's farm manors. (After Ryan Lavelle, 2007)

and erected not just by the Church or for religious reasons, but most were secular sculptures commissioned and placed by important individuals, and were done so as a form of aggrandisement. The symbol stones can be found in prominent locations and when erected were probably brightly painted; in the now blank panels that are found on many of these, the name of the individual or family might have been painted. These secular Pictish symbol stones were common before and after the kingdoms of the Scots and the Picts became amalgamated into the Kingdom of Alba around AD 843. The art style used is reflective of Continental, particularly Carolingian art influences. However, their importance here lies in the fact that they were commissioned by patrons who were in effect local kings and chiefs of clans (for want of a better description), and were designed to show them indulging in important elite pursuits, providing a rare illustration of the importance of hunting. Horsemanship is also a theme that is shown, as at the stone at Edderton.

Scenes on the symbol stones show horseback hunting of boar, hawking and hounds hunting deer. The Hilton of Cadboll stone, dating to the eighth century, shows a rare scene of a woman hunting side-saddle and dogs bringing down a deer. The stone of Aberlemno, of the ninth century, is decorated on one side with a cross and on the other a hunting scene showing stags and hounds and huntsmen on horseback. To the

36 Meigle 2 Pictish symbol stone showing hunting scenes. (Lloyd Laing)

upper right of the hunt scene is a pair of trumpeters, interpreted as 'David figures' and therefore religious iconography; however, in this instance they could easily be horn-blowing (holloaing) for the hunt. In later medieval hunting art, horn-blowing is a common theme that is depicted.

These Pictish symbol stones tell us that boars and deer were favoured quarry animals and that hawking was a well-developed sport of the elite in Britain at this time. There are references on the Continent which refer to the Kings of Lombard, Italy, using raptors to hunt from horseback in the mid-seventh century. Hunting from horseback in a manner suggestive of the medieval hunts was also shown on many stones. This strongly indicates that formal elite hunting was already fully developed here by the time the Normans had arrived in Britain. On the Continent, in Germany, the Merovingian kings were very fond of the chase, and the Lombard king's chief huntsman was his chief advisor. Hunting, especially of large game such as boar, was deemed a suitable preparation for war, not just by the Merovingians but by the Anglo-Saxon and Frankish aristocracy.

In the Anglo-Saxon period, pre-Conquest words from the Old English, such as 'haga', were associated with deer enclosures and boundary features connected with deer herding. Haga eventually gave way to the Latin 'haia', linked with 'derhage' or

37 Edderton Pictish symbol stone near Tain, Highland, Scotland. (Lloyd Laing)

38 Close-up of the riders at the base of the Edderton stone. (Lloyd Laing)

'deerhay', and at Ongar Great Park in Essex, in a will of 1045, the word 'derhage' was a term that was used. The root of the word haga is of course 'hedge' and eventually became a term for 'enclosure'. Language brings us neatly round to literature and, as mentioned earlier, *Beowulf* was one of the classic epic pieces of Anglo-Saxon literature that is familiar to most of us today. The language used to describe the forests of the period is interesting and contrasts with that used in the later Middle Ages. For example, the forests described in *Beowulf* are dark and forbidding places inspired by Germanic folklore; the following is taken from *A View to a Death in the Morning* by Matt Cartmill (1993) and highlights this eloquently:

> In the earliest English Literature, the forest is still suffused with the ghostly gloom of Germanic folklore:
> … a mysterious land,
> wolf haunted cliffs, windy headlands,
> fearful fen paths; there the mountain torrent
> falls forever under the rocks' darkness,

a flood under the earth. Not a mile hence
lies the lake rimmed with rime-covered woods;
the firm-rooted forest overshadows the water.
There each night may be seen a terrible wonder,
A fire on the flood. No man living
is so wise that he knows that ground.
Though the heath-stalker, the strong-horned stag
Hard pressed by hounds, should seek the forest
after a long chase, he would sooner yield up
his life on the shore than plunge in there
to hide his head.
Excerpt from Beowulf.

This is in contrast to this next excerpt, again from Cartmill, but taken this time from
the Robin Hood Ballads, which dates to around 1400:

In summer, when the shawes be shyne [copses are bright],
And leaved be large and long,
It is full merry in fair forest
To hear the fowlès song:

To see the deer draw to the dale,
And leave the hillès hee,
And shadow them in the leaves green,
Under the green-wood tree.

Here the forest is a much more welcoming, sweet place, in stark contrast to the forbidding forests of the Anglo-Saxon literary descriptions. Interestingly, the entomology of
the Old English word 'savage' derives from the same as for the Middle English word
'sylvan' – they come from *silva*, which is Latin for 'woods', and the differences are made
apparent by the use of language in the periods that they derive from. The ramifica-
tions of this are our evolving and changing views of wildness, and what it means in any
particular era as characterised by the prevailing socio-economic conditions of the time.
In this instance, these changing views came about because the forests were shrinking
and agriculture was expanding as time went by. As the forests became smaller and were
tamed, much of the fear of these dark impenetrable places, suffused with superstition
and full of wild creatures and magical forces, was lost. As I highlighted in the previous
chapter, in an earlier era people became increasingly divorced from the wild, and as wild
spaces shrank away from them so did their concept of wildness, and their fear of it grew
because they were not as connected to it. The wild became a hostile place filled with
wild and dangerous animals, and even mythical creatures for some. In the later Middle
Ages, it seems people had altered wild spaces so radically and made them sufficiently
small that by and large we lost our fear of them – the wild grew smaller in our psyche.

After the Conquest: poaching and hunting

In the medieval period hunting was important to all layers of society from the peasant classes to the aristocracy and the king. Moreover, the perception of lower-class hunting as poaching, done for the benefit of survival because of the wretchedness of their social station, is wholly misleading. Work by Naomi Sykes has shown, through studies of the zooarchaeological remains of fallow and red deer at a number of British sites dating from the fifth to the fourteenth centuries, that there was an obvious stratification of society visible in the osteological record. Each class did hunting and the consumption of deer differently. The divisiveness of hunting as an elite activity, brought about by restrictions, laws and ritualising the hunt, can be deceptive. The perceived elitism of hunting is very much a smoke screen of recent centuries coloured by society's own understanding of it – hunting was in fact very much a popular culture activity.

Hunting was practised, albeit differently for different layers of society, to a greater or lesser extent by nearly everyone. To the Anglo-Saxon thanes, and especially the Norman lords and kings that followed them, hunting was an activity apart; highly ritualised, it marked them out as nobles. The species they hunted, and the restrictions placed upon them and the places they were hunted, helped to further mark the hunting of these beasts of venery as symbolic of their power and status. The general conclusion is that in pastoral societies hunting is an expression of power and authority, a form of aggrandisement. In the Saxon period it was certainly so, as we saw from the Pictish symbol stones, and was more especially so in the Norman period. And not only did all men enjoy hunting universally; women were also clearly engaging in it and deriving pleasure from it. Poaching, where it occurred, was not just an activity of the lower classes; it was something people of virtually every class were engaged in and was very much a part of rural life. Country people were deeply passionate about hunting (poaching) and they were imbued with a sense of love for hunting and fishing.

Until the enforcement of the Game Laws, Roger Manning (in his paper 'Unlawful Hunting in England, 1500–1640') points out that '… hunting, [was] a common form of social intercourse and a persistent expression of culture in all societies, with its rites of passage and highly emotive bonds of fraternity …'. The changes were wrought firstly by the Normans, especially under William I, who brought Forest Law to Britain; then later came the Game Code followed by the Game Laws, which all sought (and succeeded) to turn all this on its head. The Game Laws themselves were quite absurd and attempted to restrict hunting to the privileged few. The ubiquitous hare and deer, under English common law, were regarded as *Ferae naturae*, or game that could not be profited from and had no value – and yet under the restrictions imposed by the laws could, in effect, be considered stolen. Apparently this was realised as an absurdity by the lawyers of the time who, in order to secure convictions under these laws, made the crime the circumstance under which the game was taken, and not simply the act of taking the animal. And so the following list became crimes: hunting without a sufficient estate; breaking into an enclosed park; being in possession of hunting weapons, nets or hounds; hunting at night or in disguise. As Manning noted, between the fourteenth and eighteenth centuries Parliament worked hard to make every conceivable form or circumstance in which a common man or woman might hunt a crime.

The Game Code came to define the taking of wild beasts and game as an aristo-cratic privilege, and that all deer parks, warrens and fishponds were private property. The Game Law of 1389–90 was a piece of legislation created on the back of the earlier Peasants Revolt of 1381, highlighting that the peasants and labourers could use the excuse of mounting hunting parties as a cover for uprisings against their lords. During the thirteenth and fourteenth centuries the severity of the punish-ments under Forest Law was ameliorated somewhat, especially if the offender was caught poaching outside the Royal Forests, where the offence came to be treated as trespass in common-law courts.

As hunting was considered a noble pastime it seems that the rituals, methods and places of hunting were the defining standard for each class. Sometimes the differ-ences were subtle yet telling, and very indicative of one's status in the medieval world. Recent work by Richard Almond has been at least partly responsible for changing views and perceptions of medieval hunting – a topic previously by-passed with only the briefest of mentions by other historians. This is an object lesson in how politics and public perception can affect academic objectivity – something that we more often associate with religious resistance to the debate and conclusions of scientific studies, such as evolution.

The noble art of love and sex

Venery, that is all forms of hunting that do not employ the use of a hawk, is also a word used for indulging in sexual activity. In the medieval world hunting and sex were in many ways symbolically intertwined. Looking at the depictions of hunts and hunting activities in the art of the period points to this connection, as does the litera-ture of the time. Love, hunting and sex were closely linked in the medieval mindset especially as hunting was an activity that both sexes enjoyed. Love and sex added to the popularity of hunting as a sport and in itself became part of the game of courtship. The connection between the two words may have their roots in the Indo–European word meaning 'striving' and 'desire'. Hunting, death, blood and desire make uneasy bedfellows in the modern world, yet only a few centuries ago these were common, obvious and linked aspects of daily life for many people. Certainly not concepts they felt uncomfortable with. These were very much the elemental forces in life and sur-rounded everyone in a way we can barely perceive of in a modern Western society. Death and blood were the facts of life served up at most mealtimes. The symbolism of hunting and love held a particular fascination in the later medieval world. Medieval literature and art created a vivid view of the landscape of desire and love conjoined with the skills of hunting, the prowess of the hunter and how the quarry had died. The epic late-fourteenth-century poem *Sir Gawain and the Green Knight* illustrates what I mean – here the themes of seduction and hunting are deeply intertwined. This theme follows through into a wider corpus of European literature written at this time. The reader is once again referred to the reading list and Richard Almond's book if this subject area interests them.

The etymology of the word 'venery' aside, hunting took many forms in the Middle Ages, from fishing to netting birds to hunting beasts of the chase; therefore the meaning of hunting perhaps would differ from how we might define it today. For example, in Britain we generally do not define fishing as hunting, nor would we consider shooting pheasants as hunting. One is simply fishing, the other is shooting, yet in reality, shooting a pheasant is no different from shooting a deer – both are considered forms of hunting and depending where in history you stand this would be more apparent. The rules of hunting in the Middle Ages meant that certain types of hunting, fishing and bird-netting or rabbit-netting were not hunting. Deer hunted by being chased and killed by the bow and stable method was hunting. Yet if the deer was netted and dispatched by a forester, as most were, then this was not hunting. Yet perhaps to an Ice Age hunter, every method used and all prey types were perceived as hunting; all required a measure of skill, knowledge of one's environment and seasonality. The medieval class divide perhaps also brought this into focus somewhat, as I dare say lower-class poachers may have perceived their activities and methods (of any kind) as hunting. As mentioned above, hunting in the Middle Ages was an activity done by both sexes and all classes – only the rules, methods and sometimes the quarry differed.

Hunting in the medieval period, we have seen, was deeply rooted in contemporary laws designed primarily for the protection of game, particularly deer and boar. The importance of law was paramount to hunting and all aspects of it were strictly regulated. Of particular interest here are the laws that pertain to the creation and maintenance of forests, parks and chases, for these traces still persist in the British countryside today. The forest, largely an economic and legal entity, rather than just an area of defined boundaries encompassing tree cover, was in the context of Royal Forests the king's land, and was subject to Forest Laws, codified by the king. These laws were applied after 1066 although, as has already been discussed, Cnut in the early eleventh century decreed that the New Forest was under Forest Law. Forests were in essence managed by appointed officials in the employ of the king. They were also answerable to the king and hunting was preserved there for him and to whomever he granted licence. Forests would have settlements within them, often the legacy of pre-Conquest settlement patterns, and the people who lived within them retained long-held use-rights (*usufruct*). Sometimes these rights were extinguished by the encroachment of the forest onto manorial wastes or commons and people retaliated against this by poaching. The anti-enclosure riots of the time were another response by tenants and commoners to the loss of their rights.

Forests were different to parks, which were smaller emparked areas mainly within forests that were entirely protected, and only certain rights might be granted to people who lived in surrounding settlements to collect deadwood for fires within them. I shall return to the subjects of forests and parks later. The taking of animals was restricted and the punishments were severe and included maiming (removing a hand) or imprisonment. Red deer, favoured by William I, was especially controlled, so much so that there is a sharp decline of this species appearing in urban and rural faunal assemblages after the Conquest. The people of Britain, naturally enough, viewed these harsh laws with great dismay and a good degree of contempt. Indeed, there is some archaeological evidence that red deer, which was virtually unrestricted by law and hunted by a great many people in the preceding period, was being poached after the Conquest. Eventually we see in post-Conquest rural areas a small increase in the number of red deer found in bone assemblages, indicating rural people were in fact flouting the new laws. There is a particularly telling piece of evidence that supports this which comes from the Deserted Medieval Village (DMV) of Lyveden, where the hastily butchered remains of a red deer were unceremoniously dumped down a well shaft. Before the Normans arrived the right to hunt was based more upon Roman notions, that until an animal was caught it belonged to no one or was *res nullius*.

In around AD 945 stags were commonly hunted, and in Wales texts indicated that if anyone were to appear before the skin was stripped from the animal then they were entitled to a share of the beast. King Cnut's laws (article 80), proclaimed: 'It is my will that every man shall be entitled to hunt in the woods and fields of his own property.' And later continues: 'everyone, under pain of incurring the full penalty, shall avoid hunting on my preserves.' This is a strong indication that forests existed, in a fashion, before the Conquest, and that 'laws' were always part and parcel of controlling and managing such places. The new post-Conquest laws that appeared in Britain were even more heavily enforced than they were in Normandy, perhaps an indication of the pleasure that the Normans took in subjugating the English and placing them under the yoke of the law. Showing their superior 'nobility' through these restrictions and the highly ritualised hunts that they participated in was another way of cocking a snook at the English.

The scale and significance of poaching in the Middle Ages is only just beginning to become apparent, and Naomi Sykes is one of few researchers who is focusing upon the extent of poaching in medieval England. Naomi looked at the gifting of the shoulder portions of red and fallow deer and noted that the left sides were gifted to the foresters or parkers as his fee during the highly ritualised unmaking process (explained in more detail later), whilst the right side was gifted to the yeomen. Yeomen who participated in hunts were not accommodated huntsmen, unlike the parkers and foresters, but were pressed into participating in order to facilitate a good hunt for the noblemen or the king. Naomi also observed that much of the right side portions made their way into other sites, suggesting that these portions had been filtered through the black market. These right shoulders legitimately gifted then became illicit revenue for the yeomen. We know that from the parliamentary statutes

39 Red deer

and the Royal proclamations issued that commercial poaching by gangs, particularly in venison, was a very lucrative market, especially in the south-east of England in the later Middle Ages. The gifting of venison via legitimate hunting in the earlier Norman period, and how these portions made their way into the open market, is a different mechanism. As Naomi states, the faunal evidence for this black-market produce of illicitly sold deer portions is at this time fairly tentative and requires further faunal assemblages to correlate the initial data. This is an area of research that could reveal much about wider society; its responses to elite hunting and the nature of local economies. It would also be interesting to see if the faunal assemblages corroborate what the historical texts of the time indicate, namely that poaching, especially in the later Middle Ages, was a near widespread open market activity participated in by all layers of society.

Roger Manning looked in some detail at the literature and records of poaching in medieval England and his work is nothing if not illuminating on this subject. A key feature was poaching fraternities: groups of poachers who swore oaths of loyalty to each other. The groups stayed together for up to 10 years working as trusted bands to relieve the estates of their venison, either for commercial gain or even because they were feuding with the lord. Whichever side of the law a hunter was on, hunting – or poaching – was a dangerous business and these trusted fraternities were good ways to ensure that some of the risk was ameliorated. An important part of this was swearing oaths of secrecy and exchanging bonds. However, this was not an oath of secrecy as in 'tell no one', but more a case of do not testify against your fellow poacher; and the bonds exchanged did not preclude them from talking about their exploits either. Indeed, an important part of being a gang poacher was to boast of one's exploits in the alehouses, even feasting on the proceeds of their activities there.

In a way, the Normans were a victim of their own success where hunting and poaching were concerned. In the Anglo-Saxon period, hunting was not as widely practised, it seems, as it was in subsequent periods, despite the fact that many of the game species were, ostensibly, more abundant than they were in the post-Conquest period. The Normans, in their manner, had confiscated the lands of the Saxon thanes, and effectively banned the hunting of deer, and a number of the other beasts of venery, where it had previously, in certain circumstances, been the privilege of all to hunt. Their highly ritualised and Gallicised language of the hunt; their development of hunting as an exclusive pastime of the nobility; their passing of restrictive laws; and their ostentatious self-aggrandisement through the pursuit of deer, boar and other high beasts of the chase, all conspired to make poaching a much more worthy pursuit in the Norman and subsequent periods. The Normans also made hunting fashionable, a pursuit that lower-class gentlemen, the yeomanry, and aspiring individuals wanted to be part of. Poaching then became an activity indulged in by all, from peasants, lesser gentry and the clergy to even lower-ranking nobles. Indeed, gentry households often purchased illicit venison, and a phrase or proverb in common usage during the Tudor period stated that etiquette required that guests 'Never inquire whence venison comes'. Household accounts never usually indicated where venison was acquired and was more often than not supplied by poaching gangs. Undoubtedly, though, there was a class layer for whom poaching would always remain more of a necessity than a sport, and the spoils of their activities were sold on the streets of towns and cities, notably London where James I (1394–1437), angered at the amount of venison and game openly for sale there at butchers and poulterers, lambasted the magistrates for not doing enough to halt the trade in illicit game.

Forests and parks: the driving force of the Medieval rural economy

Firstly, and most importantly, it is crucial to dispel a couple of generally held myths about medieval forests and parks:

1) Forests were not places merely covered densely with trees; they were places containing villages, hamlets, meadows, clearings, open forest and resources, such as the trees and below ground wealth such as iron and coal. For example, the De Ferrers family, who were granted lands in the Duffield Frith after the Conquest, were the *barons fossiers* or iron workers and used the local resources to start an important forging industry in Belper, Derbyshire; this continued unbroken into the Industrial Revolution as a nail-making industry before declining in the nineteenth century. By the end of the thirteenth century in the Forest of Dean there were up to 60 blast furnaces working, and the king in 1229 ordered that in Chippenham Forest, Cambridgeshire, there should be itinerant (moveable) forges to exploit the ore there. These industrial processes were carried out in the forest, sometimes posing a significant fire risk. Other industries such as charcoal burning, to provide the towns with cooking fuel for hearths and ovens, were also important. Every aspect of the forest was carefully managed for the benefit of the lord or king. Permissions were required for *pannage*, to release pigs to forage; to cut hay, *haybote*, and gather firewood, *firebote*. Even moss was gathered for the markets in the towns to use as toilet paper, and bracken, as well as being managed for deer cover, was cut for temporary carpets in peoples' homes.

2) Parks were not always grassy open places but were often covered in dense woodland, sometimes with thick understory vegetation for deer to raise their fawns in. The Royal Cheylesmore Park in Coventry used the wood resources of the park

40 Medieval blacksmiths at work

to make 300 faggots of firewood to sell, and the proceeds were used to repair the park pales and manor house in 1385 at the behest of Richard II. Later, in 1421, 12 oaks from the park were used to make repairs to the manor house. Hunts took place within parks and, as we shall see, different types of hunts took place in certain kinds of parks.

Launds on the other hand were places, enclosed like parks, where deer were put to grass from time to time, and from which hay was cut for winter fodder. In Belper, we have Far Laund just to the north of Belper Parks.

Forests were often divided into areas known as wards: the term originated from the Old English meaning to 'keep safe' or 'guard', with reference to an area or a place. This guardianship of Forests meant that each ward had keepers or officials who were responsible for them, and who kept accounts and monitored works that were required to maintain them. This ancient term still lives on in the landscape as place names, for example Hulland Ward, still exists within what was the Duffield Frith. Interestingly, it survives in politics too, as a ward is an area or administrative division in which a district councillor sits. Forests were often profitable entities that generated income for the king from the rotational harvest, such as a 10-year hag rotation of alders, chestnut and oaks for such things as scaffolding and charcoal burning. Timbers for buildings were also a prime source of income. Rentals were taken for the leases of the 'leys', which were areas of meadow within the Forest used for hay crops, and for woodland pastures for the same and for agistment (the rental received for grazing another person's animals on one's land).

Forests and parks were also expensive places to maintain and required fencing, water management systems and hunting lodges. Other buildings that might have been found in the Forest were larders. The Duffield Frith in Derbyshire, which was in the earlier thirteenth century a private chase belonging to the De Ferrers, was then commandeered from them for acts of disloyalty to the Crown by the Earl of Lancaster Edmund 'Crouchback', son of King Henry III. It became a Royal Forest in 1399 when Henry IV (b.1366; r.1399–1413) became king. The Duffield Frith, under the De Ferrers by the later thirteenth century, possessed a Great Larder, at the Manor of Beaurepaire (Beautiful Retreat), now Belper in Belper Ward. This was a place where hunted deer was salted, stored and transported to Tutbury Castle, once also held by the De Ferrers. And this Great Larder served the whole of the Duffield

41 Map of places mentioned in chapter text

Frith. Precisely where the larder itself was remains a mystery. It could be that the manor house and larder were attached and thus were one and the same; or it could be, as I suspect, that the larder referred to Belper Park itself (as it is known today), but was, in the medieval period, 'Little' or 'Lady Park'. In other instances of larders in England it is implied that the enclosed parks are themselves the larders. It has been suggested that Belper Park acted as a holding pen; a living storage place or larder for deer to be transported for great feasts at Tutbury, Kenilworth and Castle Donington and Melbourne. In some instances in excess of 30 deer, that included stags, bucks

42 Belper Parks taken during the Second World War. Note the fossilised boundary of the park preserved in the landscape

and does, were salted and transported. The wage bill for the Great Larder at Belper of £9 2s 6d was paid out in 1313. It seems likely that the park and the manor became referred to as The Great Larder of the Duffield Frith, by virtue of the role they predominantly performed in the hands of the De Ferrers, and later the House of Lancaster.

Rockingham Forest covered much of Rutland, the Soke of Peterborough and much of the north-east of Northamptonshire, but was itself part of a belt of Royal Forests that ran from Stamford, Lincolnshire, in the north, down to Oxford in the south. The administrative unit favoured here were the bailiwicks, controlled by bailiffs, appointed by the lord, and which might contain several parishes, hamlets and villages. Rockingham was made up of three such bailiwicks. These forests were administered by the king's Keeper of the Forests south of the River Trent. There was another for the north of the Trent.

Staffing of the forests and parks was a vital aspect of their management and men were carefully chosen for their roles. Iain Soden, in a recent publication, listed the staffing of the bailiwicks as follows:

> The Chief Forester
> The Bailiff (answerable to the Chief Forester)
> Under-foresters or bailiffs
> Verderer (a type of Justice of the Peace or equivalent of a coroner), two served the Bailiwick of Clyve in Rockingham Forest
> Regarder (surveyor, carried out thrice-yearly inspections)
> Lodge-keeper (maintained the hunting lodges)
> Parker (a steward of the hunting parks or launds)
> Warrener (keeper of rabbits)
> Ferreter (rabbit and vermin catcher)
> Woodward (protector of trees)
> (From Soden, I. (2008), *Archaeological Desk Based Survey of Southwick Woods, Northamptonshire* Unpublished report)

There were some variations from forest to forest; for example, the structure of the Duffield Frith was slightly different because in 1399, when the Frith and Needwood forests became proper Royal Forests, their administration was still continued by the Duchy of Lancaster. The Chancellor of the Duchy was the head official, who was the king's lieutenant, and as such held the responsibilities of administering the Honour of Tutbury for the Crown. The stewards came next in the pecking order and they were also responsible for the Woodmote Courts, which is where cases of trespass were heard. The surveyor took responsibility for the buildings and boundaries within the Frith and would probably need to be a well-educated man as his duties also required him to keep accurate records for audit. Park keepers were responsible for looking after the parks and were paid a daily rate that was commensurate with the size of the park in their care, and out of which they could pay a deputy. All these roles within the Forest staffing structure also entitled them to defined portions of venison and deer skins, as well as discounted faggots of wood, pannage rights, plus a number of other perks. Indeed, the position of park keeper was prestigious enough to attract members of the leading local families in Derbyshire, such as Roger Vernon (of Haddon). It may be that the benefits of the job meant they could take the posts and the perks whilst paying deputies to do the work, and if this was the case it seems to have been an acceptable arrangement to the Duchy.

Origins of the 'park'

The park was not purely functional as a place to hunt or as an elaborate stock pen. It was inspired by such ideas as the Garden of Eden and the teaching of the Persian scholar Achaemenid, and it was a conceptual ideal as much as a practical thing. As we have seen, the creation of parks did not start when the Normans arrived; the Romans may have had parks (*Vivarium*) in Britain as early as the first century AD at Fishbourne Palace, and there is documentary evidence to suggest that the Anglo-Saxons already had parks and established 'forests' perhaps as early as the eighth century. In the tenth century King Edmund, a keen huntsman, was hunting in what were notionally 'Royal hunting grounds'.

Columella, writing in the first century BC, describes emparked areas or *Vivarium* of woodland stocked with native and exotic beast such as roe deer or wild swine in Italy and Gaul. They may have been functional as well as attractive places, allowing the owner to keep tabs on his stock, which he would eventually sell. On the Continent, in the Frankish kingdoms, there were areas of woodland set aside for the hunting of deer as early as the seventh century. Anglo-Saxons were always aware of Continental fashions and would have adopted such practices in Britain, in areas that were suitable. Certainly, as has been seen in this book, Iron Age people probably hunted in this formal way and the Romans certainly did. However, at this point it is worth reiterating that the landscape evidence for formal hunting parks or forests, which may have existed before the Romans, would at best be very difficult or even impossible to discern. But we do now know that the Normans had introduced nothing really new into Britain in 1066. They had just brought with them a Norman way of hunting, with all of the associated laws and formalised (Gallicised) terms for places such as 'forest' and 'parks'.

The one new thing they did bring with them was a whole ritualised package of behaviours that was attached to the hunting of deer and other 'beasts of the chase', such as the unmaking of the deer. The Gallicised terminology and the strict codes of social etiquette and the unmaking were all part of the education of a Norman noble; because to know all this was to be noble. There was also a strong element of pagan, ancient Roman and Greek tradition intertwined with some Christianised language and ritual into these elaborate rites.

The unmaking

Part of this package of rituals, the unmaking was a specific way of portioning the killed deer to a certain prescribed method at the climax of the hunt. The beast was skinned, disembowelled, ritually butchered and apportioned according to ranking amongst the hunting party. Not everyone in the hunting party would be nobility; indeed the majority were of a lower status but nonetheless active participants in the hunt. Most were hunt-servants and included parkers or foresters and yeomen hired as hunters. Out of a hunting party of 10 only three might be nobility, for example. Even the dogs got a share of the entrails (on the Continent they were allowed to eat their share directly from the cavity of the disembowelled animal). The unmaking ritual was usually carried out, or at least started, by the most senior nobleman there, sometimes the king.

Descriptions of fifteenth-century unmaking tell us that the deer was turned on its back, its antlers into the ground and the throat firstly slit; the dogs which were held back would by now be braying. The flaps of the throat were opened and the dogs would rush forth for their share. They would then be called off and tethered away from the deer. From a practical dog-training point of view this provided instruction in two ways: firstly, the dog would learn to wait for its food, only moving forward on command; secondly they learned that deer was their main prey in the hunt and that it was a much more worthwhile thing to hunt the deer and participate as trained than to be distracted by other animals. A stick would then be cut, called the *fourchée*, upon which various titbits would be hung, such as the testicles, tongue and intestines, and various other entrails that collectively were considered the finest pieces of the hart and reserved for consumption by the lord. The bone of the pelvis, or *os courbin* as it was known in France, or the corbin bone here, was retrieved and thrown up for the ravens and crows – possibly by ladies if they were in attendance. In Belper Park there was once a Raven Oak possibly where the corbin was tied. The fees for the parkers, keepers and foresters were divided on the spot and the haunches and best parts of the deer returned to the kitchens of the lord.

The unmaking was widely known from the literature of the time, as we have just seen; in particular it was described in the later medieval period and most especially in Continental sources, but it was thought to be a romantic ideal, something that was rarely practised. Work by Naomi Sykes looking at zooarchaeological assemblages from high-status sites showed that the unmaking process did happen, and what's more, it happened as it was described in the literature. The unmaking was designed to be a ritualised display of status and power and was a Norman behaviour brought to Britain after the Conquest – no doubt to set themselves apart from the English.

After the Conquest the English and the Normans did not live in peace, and this led to the Anglo-Saxon lords having their lands confiscated and redistributed between the favoured Norman aristocracies and the 'Harrying of the North'. The deep feuds between the English and their Norman lords lived on well into the twelfth century. But in the fullness of time, it became difficult to distinguish between the conquerors and the conquered, as the feuds eventually dissipated. Even just after the Conquest, and apart from the more fragmented nature of the Anglo-Saxon aristocracy and land holdings, which roughly mirrored the feudal Norman state that replaced it, daily life for most was broadly the same. King Cnut, as we saw, had hunting preserves, which like the later Royal Forests had restrictions on who could hunt there. At this time, poaching must have been a rare occurrence, as there are no surviving testimonies of the punishments that might have been meted out as a result. In many instances of newly named or created Norman forests, and especially parks, there is likely to have been an Anglo-Saxon preserve that was at least broadly reflective of what it became after the Conquest. Forests were probably less formally structured but nonetheless the woodland was managed to keep in the deer and to provide hunting; they also had within them enclosed areas or 'parcum'.

The animals of the chase were subject to changing fortunes in the medieval period too. When the Normans arrived, created forests, imposed Forest Laws and brought their ritualised hunting and Continental fashions, they also brought their own preferences of the various beasts of venery. They inevitably changed the status of certain hunted animals already established in Britain. Hunting was primarily about status and control. Forest Law saw to it that exclusions could be enforced against the lower levels of society, making it illegal to hunt protected species that were reserved for hunting by the aristocracy and the king. Deer were at the top of that list. William I, who viewed himself as the protector of red deer, even the father of the deer, passed the draconian laws that included taking out the offender's eyes for killing a deer illegally. The imposition of these laws throughout Britain applied to all men, whether of high or lowly birth, and was met with disdain by all. Forest Law protected 'vert' and 'venison', the vegetation that the deer lived on as well as the deer, and it applied to boar too. This made all hunting poaching and therefore illegal; it also hindered agricultural expansion and affected many people, especially where the forests encroached onto wastes and common land. Perhaps most controversially at that time was that it applied not only to actual forest, but to wherever Royal authority decreed it should apply to. The reason for this was that eventually English kings could set the fine levels as high as they liked. And as the medieval period went on, this led to the expansion of land designated as Royal Forest. For example, the whole of Essex was eventually decreed Royal Forest. English kings could then set up forest administration to enforce the law. All of this was a very lucrative sideline for the Crown.

William I, when he started this process, did not take any heed of the resentments or complaints, nor cared whether they came from the rich or the poor – his primary concern was the protection of his deer. This period was, in terms of the severity of punishments metered out, especially upon the poor, the worst. Later, in the reigns of William Rufus (William II *c.*1058; r.1087–1100) and Henry I (b.1133; r.1154–89), blinding and emasculation was allowed as an alternative to capital punishment, but this mainly only applied to the poor. William II applied the same punishments to the rich and poor alike. In terms of the evidence for all of this maiming and death, we have only the word of the commentators of the day, such as William of Malmesbury, and William of Newburgh, who talked of Henry II's application of the capital punishments for taking a deer. None of the Court Rolls of the Forest Courts or forest pleas from the end of the twelfth to the early thirteenth centuries describe the application of capital punishments or maiming sentences. This is due to the main thrust of these documents covering boundary disputes, although some list a few trespasses.

Up to the reign of Henry III (b. 1207; r. 1216–72) things remained much the same where punishments for hunting in the king's forests were concerned. Even though the laws for quite some time remained the same, later kings preferred the application of large fines and exile rather than the more serious options open to them. However, the forest assizes of Richard I re-started the blindings and castrations. The Magna Carta attacked the unpopular Forest Law in 1215 and so a series of forest clauses were included in it, and in 1217 the Forest Charter was passed during the reign of Henry III, clarifying the earlier position stated in the Magna Carta. Forest officials, largely with the sanction of the king, imposed huge fines upon all transgressors, literally earning a king's ransom. The rules were often bent and sometimes fines were applied even outside the forest boundaries. Forest Law already deeply unpopular was no less so now. The Forest Charter was designed to impede the extortion of forest officials and made arrangements to check the boundaries of forests and ensure that they were adhered to. The Forest Charter also played a role in loosening the tight grip of the king, allowing the expansion of agriculture during the thirteenth century, but there were still issues over which the barons and the king clashed well into the fourteenth century.

In 1327 taxation income had increased sufficiently to allow the juries to recognise the forest boundaries as those accepted during the reign of Edward I (b. 1239; r. 1272–1307). The revenue raised and the offices of the forest administration were then part of a patronage system rather than being a major revenue earner. During this time a new middle class was on the ascendancy and hunting, as popular as ever, was seen less as the preserve of the nobility and something to which they could aspire. Poaching we have seen was also an indulgence of this class tier, allowing them to participate in hunting almost as their betters did when they could not hunt legitimately. Richard the II (b. 1367; r. 1377–99) imposed a statute in 1390 that effectively meant the poor were forbidden from hunting anywhere. The more symbolic issues surrounding why this statute was made will be raised again shortly. Basically, up until the reign of Henry III, people charged with poaching and without the means to pay the fines, or with no one to vouch for them, could expire in jail for years before the circuit courts could get to their cases.

The beasts of the venery

We have seen that the Romans introduced fallow deer in the first century AD and that this was a potent symbol of the Empire. They enclosed the deer in small landscape parks, such as the one at Fishbourne, Sussex, as far as is known. When the Romano-

British way of life died out, and subsequent invaders and migrations occurred, the fallow deer seems to disappear or at least become very scarce. The Normans, it seems, reintroduced the fallow deer; an animal that they considered to provide the best sport. Once fallow deer became commonplace they marginalised the native roe deer as an emparked animal, eventually replacing it. Another interesting point about roe deer is that in excavations of monastic houses that date from the seventh to the mid-twelfth century, there is a bias towards the hunting and consumption of the native roe deer (*Capreolus capreolus*), which might be for symbolic reasons as well as due to restrictions upon what monks could hunt. In Britain and France monks were granted the right to hunt the roe deer and hares because they were lesser animals than the prized fallow deer or red deer. The symbolism of the roe deer is made obvious in later medieval art and writing, where it is considered as having the virtues of faithfulness and chasteness. Then, like now, the monks probably believed in the adage that you are what you eat; in other words, they would take on those virtues by consuming the flesh of the deer. Hares, on the other hand, were not favoured by the religious orders and clergy because of their uncertain sexual orientation (they were thought to be hermaphroditic).

Roe deer was favoured on grand secular sites between the fifth and the eleventh centuries too, and was the premier beast of venery at this time. By the mid-eleventh and the twelfth centuries red deer was the more important animal. This reflected a shift in the habitat and hunting strategies that were favoured in the Saxon period compared to those of Norman period parks. In the Saxon period enclosed woodland parks with understory shrubbery were favoured and the roe deer preferred this habitat, whilst in the Norman forests and parks the cover was more open in aspect. Through open forest, over cultivated ground, horses could be used at speed and manoeuvred without hindrance. Indeed, in the forests there were unbound moors, cultivated ground and wood pasture to hunt over. By the fourteenth century the roe deer was off the list and hence had no status as a beast of the chase; it was no longer protected by Forest Law. It is unknown if this then made them a preferential 'legal' choice for poachers.

Britain's parks and forests were the preferred habitat of the fallow deer and, like that of the red deer, it was the open wood pastures, agricultural land fringed with woods, moorlands and heaths that it favoured. The fallow is smaller than the red deer and very fleet of foot. In the literature of the time it was always noted that an adult specimen of 10 points (an antler point per year) should be hunted, but the archaeological evidence from sites like Dudley Castle show that this was a literary ideal and was not always achieved and younger bucks were often taken.

Wild boar was also a highly sought-after beast of the chase and after the deer was the second most popular game animal in Britain. The Romans favoured it because of the danger aspect of hunting them – they were quite capable of injuring or killing a hunter. Like deer it was protected by Forest Law and its hunting was strictly controlled, befitting a high-status animal. What is perhaps surprising then is that after the fourteenth century there appears to be little evidence of the hunting and

43 Excavations of the north-east undercrofts at St Mary's Cathedral Priory, a house of the Benedictine order

consumption of wild swine. This is in part due to a sharp decline in their numbers in the wild, which was well under way in the thirteenth century, coinciding with the arable revolution and the now widespread domestication of the pig. Of course, until recently, spotting wild boar remains amongst domestic pig assemblages was difficult, especially as there was probably some cross-breeding going on, particularly if the pigs were allowed to graze in woodland parks. Wild boar was undoubtedly still hunted after the end of the thirteenth century and was reared and protected within the confines of parks. Wild boar eventually became extinct in England in the seventeenth century.

I have touched upon the perceptions of medieval monks as far as the sexuality of hares was concerned. In the wider world of medieval nobility the hare was another highly regarded sporting animal. The fifteenth-century *Boke of St Albans* says the hare is 'the most merveylous beste that is in this lond', and was certainly the favourite small game animal. It was often used (and recommended) for keeping one's dogs fit to hunt deer. Hare coursing was a popular sport at this time, as it was in the Roman period. In many ways hares can be perceived as a beast of venery but they were also considered a beast of the warren, which is a difference I will discuss shortly. The meat was, according to the literature of the time, highly recommended. The unmaking rituals should have been equally applied to the hare as it was to the deer, but the zooarchaeological evidence suggests that this was again an ideal that was rarely practised. At Dudley Castle the remains of hare in the medieval phases reflected the fact that smaller, younger hares were being brought back to the castle, and that this was reflective of hunting (perhaps of leverets) by hawks or hounds. Consuming younger animals was also a way of bypassing the ill effects feared by the monks of the time. So it seems that the superstitions of the age ran deep enough into the nobility to ensure that older hares were not eaten lest they turn the lord or king into a homosexual.

The fox was also a 'beast of the chase' and considered a great sporting animal, and hunting it performed the added benefit of reducing a pest in the countryside. There is a reference to foxhunting dating to 1221, within the reign of Henry III, when he gives permission to the Abbess of Barking to chase fox in Havering Park in Essex.

Parks were spaces that were stocked not just with deer but rabbits (*Oryctolagus cunniculus*) – another Norman introduction – peafowl (*Pavo cristatus*), partridges (*Perdix perdix*) and pheasants (*Phasianus colchis*). Perhaps surprising to many will be that herons (*Ardea cinerea*) and swans (*Cygnus* species) were also stock animals for parks. Freshwater fish were also stocked in fishponds, such as that at Beaurepaire, or Belper Park in 1231, when the king gifted to the De Ferrers *xx minutes luscious*, or 20 small pike, to restock the fishpond there – probably the one that is still visible from the Coppice car park in Belper. Fish were also caught in large numbers by using fish weirs; traps that were a V-shaped arrangement of posts supporting woven wicker panels that directed fish into a narrow area where they were trapped in a basket.

44 The fox; *a beast of the chase* and a pest. (Amanda Lockhart)

45 Belper Parks fishpond

46 A Malaysian fishing basket of a type used in a fish trap similar to the one that could have been used at Captains Pingle. (See fig 47)

A reasonably well-preserved example of a fish weir was excavated by the author in 2006 at Captains Pingle, Barrow-upon-Trent, Derbyshire, dating to the Anglo-Saxon period. This fish weir was found on the edge of a palaeochannel. The timbers produced radiocarbon dates which indicated that the structure was in use between the seventh and ninth centuries AD.

Rabbits were introduced by the Normans and kept in enclosed areas or warrens; the mounds especially created for their burrows were called pillow mounds. Rabbits provided a valuable resource and were kept and bred for their meat and furs. Sometimes the warren might be located within a park where the parkers would be responsible for their management, whilst outside the parks, warreners were responsible for them. In English place names, localised references to rabbits or their warrens abound,

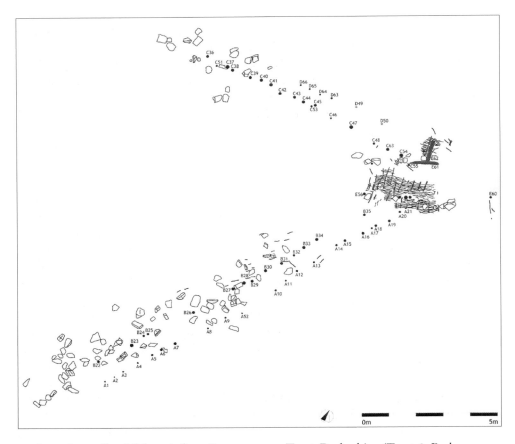

47 An early medieval fish weir from Barrow-upon-Trent, Derbyshire. (Trent & Peak Archaeology: David Walker)

such as Coneygrey Farm in Pentrich, Derbyshire. Another form exists in place names proper at Warenford, Northumberland. As an animal for hunting they were considered lowly creatures by the aristocracy, and were in effect farmed for the meat and fur they provided. Ferreting and netting, however, was considered an appropriate ladies sport. A term often encountered in relation to forests and Forest Law is the 'right of free warren', and this was the right granted by the king to local lords of the manor to be able to freely hunt animals such as badger (smoked badger ham being a particular favourite of the time), fox, hare, partridge, pheasant, rabbit, squirrel, wildcat, otter and marten. The hare was considered the principal beast of the warren and in the royal manor of Somerton they were covered by Forest Law. The right of free warren was a valuable privilege to the lord, which prevented others hunting beasts of the warren in his demesne, especially where they lay in Royal Forest lands. However, this right is not to be confused with the rights of the bigger magnates to hunt deer and boar in their own private forests – which was something entirely separate.

At Chatsworth House there is a warren within the grounds of the current house which is marked upon William Seniors' map of 1617, where an open area was known as 'cunigre'; today eight pillow mounds can still be traced. This warren may well have had a medieval origin, and contemporary strip lynchets and ridge and furrow, part of the village of Edensor's open field system, were taken into the warren; a warrener's lodge survived in the area until shortly after 1773.

The noble art of hunting

Hunting, as we have seen, was viewed as good preparation for war, a kingly and noble pursuit, and a display of knowledge and courage redolent of chivalric heroism. Though it was popular to be a pious Christian as a nobleman, the ideals of chivalry, emulation of the Burgundian courts of France, and the ritual and language of hunt-ing, were all evocative of Greek and Roman paganism. In particular, the animalism aspects of these ancient religions and the celebration of wild bull hunting were what the nobility found most appealing.

The origins of the noble aspects of the hunt emerged on the Continent after the fall of the Roman Empire, and influenced the many European kingdoms that appeared after. The courts of the Carolingian kings were particularly influential in spreading the idea that nobility and hunting went hand in hand – they themselves were influenced by ancient Persian traditions, such as hunting on horseback using raptors. Figure 48 shows two depictions of hawking from horseback; one is from a Pictish symbol stone and the other is from an Assyrian depiction. The Lombardy kings of Italy in the sev-enth century placed great stock in the noble sport of hunting on horseback using raptors and were emulated throughout many kingdoms across Europe.

The chase was viewed as being the most similar activity to war, where one might endure such privations as intense cold, heat, lack of sleep, hunger and fear. Knowledge of horsemanship was required for war, as was a knowledge of arms and their use. Hunting gave the noblemen all this training and developed and honed their skills.

48 Assyrian and Pictish versions of hunting with raptors. (Lloyd Laing)

49 An eighteenth-century etching of raptors. (After Edward Gibbon *The History of the Decline and Fall of the Roman Empire, 1776–88*)

In essence there was the noble hunting of the sporting variety, where a whole day could be spent in the pursuit of a single stag; but the king required far more venison than could be provided in a day's sport. Most deer were captured using traps, pitfalls, nets and other methods by foresters and parkers. For the king and other nobles to use these methods to catch deer was not sporting, and therefore simply not done. Parkers and foresters would capture deer in greater numbers using these methods and the resulting carcasses were salted and transported in larders as we saw at Belper,

Derbyshire. None of this meat would find its way to the peasants' table, as it was destined for the king's houses and estates, or as gifts to other nobles – it was protein for the ruling classes, not the commoners – widespread poaching notwithstanding.

Not all hunts would have taken place within the parks; the *par force de chiens* is a hunt that requires a great deal of open ground following a healthy, strong red deer. Reasonable and unencumbered ground such as open forest and cultivated land was the requirement. This is not entirely unlike a modern foxhunt. A deer hunt, to qualify as *par force de chiens*, had to be a highly ritualised event, very specific in the way it was organised to provide the exact sporting hunt required. A strong deer would be selected and parted from its group, pursued by hounds and hunt servants with the noble hunters chasing on their mounts. This hunt was designed to last all day; the deer, once exhausted, would be killed by a sword to the heart if the hunt was a success. Again, this was preparation for warfare and gave the hunter a chance to form a bond with his quarry.

As part of the basic training for war, young noblemen were required to learn to ride horses from the age of seven or eight. Horsemanship was a difficult and intense learning process and meant that all aspects of horse handling were taught alongside the handling of weapons on horseback and cross-country riding in a company. Learning to handle the dogs was also a key skill that was taught from a young age. As in all important things in a young noble's life, starting early and building skills from a young age was critical in a nobleman's education.

One of the methods of hunting in the forest, one that was preferable to more open ground, was using dogs. Humans and dogs would work in partnership, with the dog picking up the scent and the mounted hunters driving the game into concealed archers. The bow and stable hunt, in contrast to the *par force* hunt, was best used in parks rather than forest. The principal quarry of the bow and stable hunt was the fallow deer which, unlike the red deer, tends to maintain a pack or herd structure during flight and has far less stamina. Nets were also employed to catch fallow deer. The ritual unmaking applied to both forms of hunting and quarry.

There is some debate as to the role of parks in hunting, or indeed if the killing that went on in parks can actually be deemed hunting at all, because of the nature of the game (fallow were in essence a farmed animal within the park) and the proximity of the enclosing park pales effectively rendering the deer as captured animals and not wild animals. Bow and stable hunting in these circumstances may not fulfil the requirements to be classified as noble hunting *per se*. Animals must be wild for the action of killing it to be considered noble hunting; and if the perception of the game within an enclosed park was almost that of a farmed animal, and that killing it within the confines of the park did little to stir warrior tendencies or emotions, then was it truly hunting? There is evidence that suggests that the hunting of deer within parks was carried out by servants such as professional hunters and parkers, who effectively harvested the deer for the lords' table. Parks were also perhaps a place where courtly women could hunt away from the prying eyes of society in an age that valued the seclusion of young noblewomen. This near invisibility was seen as an asset to their virtue and important to future matrimony. Falconry too was an important form of hunting and one that noblewomen could participate in.

Falconry

Another method of hunting in the park and forest, one used by both men and women, was hawking or falconry, which has a history that is nearly 4000 years old. As we have seen above, the use of raptors in the ancient world, by the Persians for example, was seen as something to be emulated by the ascending European kingdoms after the fall of the Roman Empire.

The use of raptors was another area, particularly in the medieval period that was subject to peculiar customs and rituals that, once again, were all about power and status. The bird used in the hunt would indicate one's status, for example. Hawks were favoured in England, particularly peregrines, merlins and hobby. There were classifications of 'hawks of the tower' that included the peregrines, hobby, sakers and lanner whilst the 'hawks of the fist' were pre-eminently the gyrfalcon and goshawk, sparrow hawk and the merlin (see Fig. 38). The literature of the time makes many references to the tercel, which is the male peregrine, which being smaller (by about a third) than the female was suitable as a hawk of the fist. The link between species of raptor and status was made obvious in the fourteenth century texts, and the gyrfalcon and tercel were at the top of the list and considered kingly birds, whilst for women the merlin was considered suitable and for a young nobleman a hobby was appropriate. There has been some debate as to whether these social distinctions, as elucidated in the chosen raptor species, were actually real, but given the obsessive preoccupation with the appropriate types and forms of hunting to go with status, the status of the quarry animal and the method of its dispatch, it would be entirely reasonable to suppose that it is correct. If it is not entirely accurate it would still be broadly reflective of the underlying social insecurities of the age.

To flush and locate game, dogs were used in falconry (as they still are). They were also used to assist bringing down larger prey that would be a struggle for the bird. Dogs that were shown in medieval illustrations to be similar to pointers were the preferred option but all kinds of dogs were used including terriers, greyhounds and spaniels. Today, pointers are often used to flush grouse, and the sport of hunting with falcon, man and dog is known as air coursing. Spaniels had a particular aptitude for flushing birds, particularly quails and partridges. Setters were chosen for their quiet stalking abilities and they could be trained to keep an eye on their masters and respond to hand signals. If a hawk was to bring down larger birds such as cranes, herons and even bustards, then a fast dog was needed to give aid quickly to the hawk; some contemporary authorities recommended a medium-sized greyhound for this.

Training dog and hawk was a tricky business as the puppy had to be habituated to the bird from puppy-hood, and this included being fed at the same time as the bird.

They were also trained to follow the bird and be used to its scent, and a captured domestic goose would be used to train both bird and dog to capture without each injuring the other. In training both hawk food and dog food were important motivators. When prey was captured the falcon would be rewarded with a portion of it, but if the bird was expected to fly at other animals that day then the titbit offered would be accordingly smaller. Parts given to the bird was often something like the heart. John Cummins describes from fourteenth-century sources great hunts with the king which took place in France that used up to 30 birds and brought down all manner of prey from herons to ducks. These descriptions were written by Gace de la Vigne, and one of his accounts describes what was needed for a good day's hunting; the following is from John Cummins (p. 215):

> Gace's third account (ll. 10257–344) is of hunting with sparrow hawks, and this is where the ladies come to share the foreground. After a description of the ideal sparrow hawk, we learn that to make the most of the bird a man should be between twenty and forty years of age, mature but agile; one should also, because of the social nature of the sport, be courteous and debonair, since it is a great revealer of personality. One needs a stout steady-going horse, another in reserve, four spaniels to quest and retrieve, two in the morning and two in the afternoon. The other requirements are good company; lone hawking is poor sport. The company should be blithe and beautiful: knights and squires not overburdened with wealth, ladies and maidens, each bearing a sparrow hawk.

Ladies and hunting

Falconry, as hunting, particularly within deer parks, seems to go hand in hand with ladies of the court in the medieval period. As was touched upon earlier, young women of the court were educated in the art of hunting but their chastity was to be protected as being vital for their future marriage prospects and this meant they could not be seen in public too often. Unlike the men, women could not therefore be allowed to practise falconry in open forest and so their activities were likely to have been confined to the parks where they could not be observed. Also, killing their quarry using hawks allowed the ladies participating not to be directly responsible for the kill; in other words, the action of killing was kept apart from them by use of the bird as a vector in the quarry's death. Bow and stable hunting in parks might be another method where the driving of the deer into the hands of waiting bowmen also allowed the woman not to be directly involved in the killing of the deer yet be an active participant in the hunt to the full. Naomi Sykes suggests that ladies' hunting was one of the functions of medieval parks. She also suggests that distance and vectors, such as the birds or the bowmen, acted to sanitise the sport of killing for lady hunters.

The species that tended to be used to stock parks were those favoured for hunting using falcons, such as heron, pheasant and partridge. At high-status sites in the mid-twelfth century the zooarchaeological assemblages point to these species being hunted in increasing numbers. Parks were stocked and managed with the intention of ladies' hunting taking place within them, the prey species being specially selected for this purpose. In some medieval illuminations ladies were depicted ferreting and netting pillow mounds for rabbits, again using a vector, the ferret, to initiate the kill; thus, this was considered an appropriate activity for ladies of the court, but perhaps in only those instances where warrens were within parks. Seals depicting ladies hunting are also a common feature of this period. It seems that during the Middle Ages women could be educated in the rules and techniques of hunting and indeed that women actually participated in hunting and not just falconry, but the study of the role and extent of female participation is still a relatively new study. There is little doubt that in time much more will be learned about the role of women in *par force* hunting, for example.

Interestingly, ladies never really played a role in foxhunting until the later nineteenth century because it was viewed as being too dangerous and unbecoming. Somewhere between the medieval period and the later post-medieval period the participation and role of women in sport hunting slipped. It would be an interesting area of study to see what had changed in this time.

Symbolism in Medieval hunting

Hunting provided a service too, especially in rural areas where parks, woodlands and chases were close to towns and villages, and where predators such as foxes and pests, like some types of birds, could pose a problem. A fox taking a goose, or killing a number of hens or a lamb would be a big economic blow to a family. The noblemen were in a way duty-bound to provide this service to the Church and to society. This thread follows through into later foxhunting as a method of controlling rural pests. Ironically, this foxhunting, which started more as predator control, survived into more modern times better than most other forms of elite hunting.

One of the primary functions of hunting was providing pleasure – perhaps this was the conscious mainstay of hunting – across all levels of medieval society. Hunting, as we have seen, was something that was enjoyed by nearly everyone in all tiers of medieval society – whether legitimately or illegitimately. Hunting by the nobility was about social reproduction, reaffirming the class system and the place of the nobility within it, and strengthening their hold on society through the perceptions that ritualised noble hunting was exclusively the domain of the ruling class. In this way it worked very well. Hunting, landownership, ostentatious displays of wealth, power and status, reinforced by ritual and exclusivity, helped maintain the status quo for a long time. Central to this was the core belief that hunting certain game in a particular way showed that you were nobility, that you were a gentleman. There are of course nuances of meaning or classification within the range of 'gentlemen' that are beyond the scope of this book, but in later medieval Britain, this included men from royalty down to honoured clerics and freemen.

During the medieval period the best writers of hunting and hawking manuals were those of the higher aristocracy and even royalty. The language used in these manuals was often designed to reaffirm the role of nobility in hunting; designed to exclude the lower classes by its use of terminology and description of methodology – in other words, snobbery. None of these manuals were concerned with hunting as a way of sustaining life and capturing animals for nutrition, rather they described the courtly and noble chase of exclusive beasts of venery. In later medieval England, this kind of hunting was almost certainly done in an effort to keep hunting and hawking perceived among the general population in this way; to ensure that these sporting endeavours remained the preserve of the privileged few, especially to keep at bay the new socially mobile groups that were catching them up in terms of wealth. In the Statute of 1390, Richard II decreed 'that people could not hunt with hounds, ferrets and snares' if they did not have 'lands and tenements to the value of 40s a year, or any priest or clerk if he has not preferment worth £10'. To use the words of Richard Almond:

> The statute tells us in the clearest terms that other classes were hunting, possibly in aristocratic ways, and that by so doing, the commons were challenging the ancient privilege of those whose status was based upon that most incontestable of measures, land ownership and occupation.
>
> R. Almond (2003), *Medieval Hunting*, Stroud: Sutton Publishing

This statute effectively started the concept of hunting as a gentleman's pursuit and reflected the situation of the landed gentry going into the eighteenth century. The basis of the laws that followed the 1390 statute was to provide a sense of law and order for the landed classes of that era, and this had been achieved over time by discarding the antiquated laws that had existed during the Middle Ages (excepting for the Tudor and Stuart revival of the capital sentences that were favoured in Norman times).

Disafforestation had started, albeit in a piecemeal fashion, after the signing of the Magna Carta in 1215 and, despite baronial arguments over certain unfair aspects of Forest Law, the nobility saw their status and power, as defined by the act of venery, threatened by the common people who, after 1327 when Forest Law was considerably watered down, were now able to hunt. The statute of 1390 sought to make the position of the nobility unassailable but eventually even this failed. With a relaxation of the laws and a changing society, disafforestation became increasingly inevitable, and by the late seventeenth century places like the Duffield Frith were disafforested.

Disafforestation was a long, slow and tortuous legal process and was driven by the needs of agriculture and the requirement for more land leading to encroachments on the wastes and of course forests. Local wealthy landowners saw it as an opportunity to increase their land holdings, and the smaller copyholders saw an opportunity to safeguard their rights to the remaining common ground that they and their forebears had enjoyed for so long. In all, the process had taken well over 100 years. In the Duffield

Frith, Belper Manor was in serious decline by about the time of the Reformation, and the deer in Belper Park, by 1581, 'were utterlie destroyed an gone' according to George Sellers, the then collector of Belper, who was informing a visiting commission of enquiry that was looking into the state of the Duffield Frith. It seems that even by the earlier part of the seventeenth century the park pales were down and the manor house was a ruin. Manor farm was constructed at about this time using stone from the manor house. Southwick Woods, once part of Rockingham Forest, Northamptonshire, shrank over time as its plantations were cut down and utilised after disafforestation. The lodges within the forest declined and became lost, as they did in most places. Remarkably, the survival of the plots within the wood after the nineteenth-century felling meant that they were replanted with trees more recently.

Forest Law was finally abolished in 1660 along with a package of other royal rights (in the Restoration), but not before, under Charles I (b.1600; r.1625–49), a full revival of the law in the 1630s. This was one of a number of public relations disasters that saw Charles trying to recover land for the Crown and the Church, fining encroachers upon Royal Forests, even though their boundaries had not been officially acknowledged for many years. This was all apparently part of a cunning ploy to regain popularity by repealing the fines at a later date, which apparently worked.

The surviving landscapes of forests and parks

In this section I want to look at the landscape evidence for hunting and what this can tell us about the evolution of hunting and its decline in the landscape. Some of this evidence is from archaeological sites but much of it lies in the visible traces of medieval parks, such as their boundaries and even surviving trees. Much of the evidence is also encapsulated within the landscape of place names.

So what is the nature and extent of the surviving evidence of the medieval forests and parks in Britain? Well, there is plenty of evidence if one knows where to look. Some examples are more famous than others, such as the New Forest in Hampshire, Sherwood Forest on the Nottinghamshire/Derbyshire border, and Bradgate Park with its rare survivals of ancient medieval park trees near Leicester; and these are all places visited by thousands of people every year. Of the forests, only the New Forest survives in anything like its original medieval administrative form, including its forest courts and its officials; although Dean Forest and Epping Forest do have surviving traces of their old administrative structures too and common rights are still exercised.

There are many less well-known specimens of remnant landscapes from this period dotted about the landscape; for example, in Derbyshire there is Belper Parks, discussed in the text above, and great houses such as Chatsworth also have remnants of the medieval deer parks that were once administered as parts of those estates now incorporated in Capability Brown's seventeenth-century parkland landscape as a few dotard oaks.

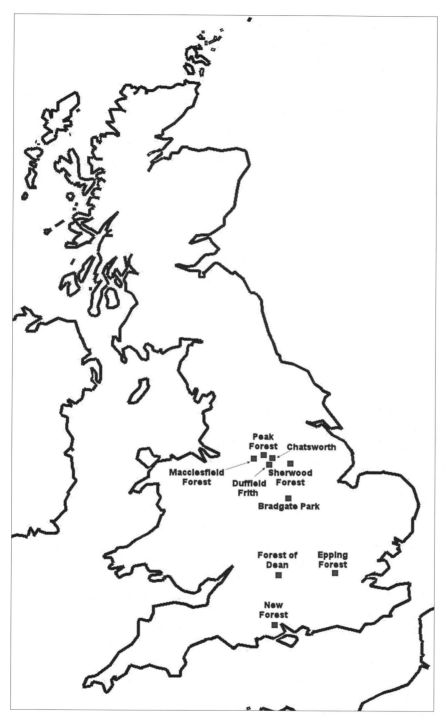

50 Map showing places mentioned in the text

Place names of the forests survive best of all down to the present. For example, there are a number of places like Morley Park, Ravensdale Park and, of course, Belper Parks that were all once deer parks within the Duffield Frith. There are many more place names in the landscape associated with forests, such as names that incorporate 'ley' from the Old English for 'Leah', perhaps originating from 'light' meaning glade or clearing within the forest; places such as Ripley therefore mean something like 'long clearing in the forest'. These names cannot occur in isolation and be presented as evidence that there once existed a forest there – other place-name evidence can complement this such as the 'ton' or 'tun' elements, meaning a settlement on land from which trees had been long cleared; so, for example, Alfreton or 'Alfic's tun' is fairly close to Ripley, Ilkeston and Shipley, all of which were known to be subject to Forest Law in the twelfth century. Other names make reference to parks that once existed such as 'Park Lane', 'Park Farm' and 'Lodge Farm' for example; these are common enough but some caution should be exercised because not in all instances do they point to the existence of a medieval park. Near to Belper is a little hamlet called Shottle Gate, indicating the presence of an entrance to the former park there. Also in the Belper area are other place names that indicate their former use within the Duffield Frith, such as Far Laund.

Place names and topographical names containing 'hart' are also common in the landscape, such as Harford, Gloucestershire; Hartford, Cheshire; and Hartforth in Yorkshire's North Riding. In Derbyshire, close to the delightfully and obviously hunting-related place name of Buckland Hollow, are the hamlets of Lower and Upper Hartshay, close to the Hartshay Brook. In Herefordshire there is a boar-related place name Boresford, and hunting dog related Rochford's in Essex and in Worcestershire, from *roecc* meaning 'hunting dog' and derived from Old English.

In the Peak District there was another Royal Forest, Peak Forest, which has its own place names that have continued down to the present, most notably Chapel-en-le-Frith and the village of Peak Forest, where there was a foresters' hall. This Royal Forest, established in the Norman period, was in Saxon times part of the royal manor of Hope, probably similarly used as a forest. In the Norman period Peveril Castle in Castleton, Derbyshire, was the administrative centre of the forest, whilst the forest courts were held in Chapel-en-le-Frith, Tideswell, Hope and Castleton, where there was also a gaol. On the moors of the Macclesfield Forest near to the hamlet of Macclesfield Forest was a foresters' chamber and gaol.

Little physical evidence of the former extents of the Peak, Duffield Frith or Macclesfield Forests survives, with the exception of the fossilised outline of Belper Parks and the abundant place-name evidence. Careful work studying old maps, documents and aerial photographs has in some instances retraced the outlines of former parks and the boundaries of forests. Mary Wiltshire, Sue Woore, Barry Crisp and Brian Rich did this in their book *Duffield Frith* to great effect. One of the most tangible forms of surviving evidence in the Duffield Frith are the foresters' chapels, at Belper (St Johns), Heage (St Luke) and Turnditch (All Saints). All built

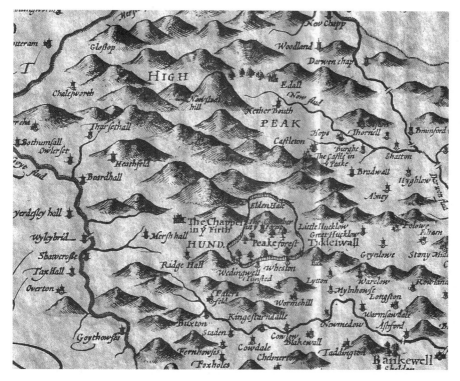

51 Speede's map of *c.*1610 of Chapel-en-le-Frith and the Peak Forest

at roughly the same time in the thirteenth century they became parish churches later in life and have been fairly extensively modified throughout their histories. St Johns Chapel is perhaps the best preserved of the three. Another very visual form of evidence in the Peak Forest comes from the grave slabs of the foresters, such as those at St Helens, Darley Dale, with swords on them seen in Colour plate 17; at Chelmorton, one example shows axes and horns.

Belper Park, or Little or Lady Park as it was also known, can be found close to the market place of Belper town, Derbyshire; it survives as a neat outline of its park boundary, as can be seen in Fig. 42. Leaving Belper market place on the town's south side, the Parks, as it is known today, is a Local Nature Reserve managed by the Friends of Belper Parks. It is immediately visible when one enters the Coppice car park there. The partially wooded hill that is visible here would have had the manor house roughly where the Coppice car park is. From here much of the progress of the hunt could be watched and has led to the speculation that one of its earlier names, 'Little' or 'Lady Park', originated from this small park and was well suited to ladies' hunting. Being sited here, next to the Great Larder of the Duffield Frith, this park's primary function was probably as a live stock park, where deer were netted, killed, salted and transported in numbers.

52 Thirteenth-century St John's Chapel, Belper, Derbyshire. One of three foresters' chapels built in the Duffield Frith

Occasional hunting in this small park could easily be supported alongside its other functions, especially with the manor providing such a good vantage point. In their book *Duffield Frith*, the authors note that there was not the high numbers of deer killed here as there were at other Frith parks in the records of the fifteenth century. The capital messuage of the Frith was sited at Ravensdale Park in Hulland Ward, Muggington Parish, where coursing took place at its deer course – the only known one in the Frith. A deer course is known from Windsor Little Park, Bedfordshire, for example. Deer coursing was a grand and complicated spectator sport and hunters used hounds and horses to chase the deer along a strip of land, which at Ravensdale Park is still marked out by field boundaries that conform to its ancient shape. The strip of land was carefully chosen as a highly visible stretch where spectators could see the whole event from multiple vantage points. Often a long stretch of valley alongside a stream edge would be chosen and spectators could be ranged on the opposite side. So the Ravensdale Manor, it can be assumed, took on a special importance because of this; to be seen hunting as part of a grand spectacle did much to aggrandise the lord or king, hence its designation of Capital Messuage of the Frith.

This is further supported by the location of Mansell Park, and its own lodge, Shuckton Manor, less than a mile to the west of Ravensdale; both Mansell and Ravensdale parks were roughly 3 miles in circumference (*c.*200 acres each), and capable of providing plenty of hunting for the nearby capital messuage. The manor at Belper, whilst still a high-status building, was not as grand as Ravensdale, but might accord with its role as a noble ladies' deer park, providing special sport that was more spectator orientated from below the park, or allowed ladies of the court just to watch the deer. In its own right, this idea of watching deer to appreciate the aesthetically pleasing was suitably noble. Ladies did certainly participate in hunts and indeed played an important part in the unmaking process. It has been recorded that

53 Speede's map (*c.*1610) of part of the Duffield Frith, showing the deer parks within it. Note Belper Parks is not recorded at this time

ladies would tie the corbin bone, the ravens fee, and raise it into the canopy of a tall tree. In Belper Parks there was a Raven Oak recorded in 1560, and today there is a Raven Oak Road.

It is interesting to note that in Speede's map of 1610 (see Fig. 53) Belper Parks has already gone. We know that by the seventeenth century the Belper Park was in decline and the pales were down. In contrast, the larger Morley Park and Ravensdale Parks were still emparked.

At Belper Parks the location of the lodge or manor is beneath earthwork terrace features, visible in the field below the Coppice car park; these were the gardens of eighteenth- to nineteenth-century cottages, long since demolished. In 2000 I undertook a small evaluation on these terraces using students from Liverpool University. Below the terraces was rubble overlying a wall foundation from which was recovered a piece of thirteenth-century pottery. There are a number of other features within the parks that could be traced to medieval documents at the Public Record Office and the County Records Office at Matlock, Derbyshire. These include a fishpond adjacent to the Coppice Brook and a highly visible mill leat or race, running parallel to the brook.

Another Derbyshire landscape that shows much evidence of its former use as a deer park is the Chatsworth estate. Here remnant parts of the medieval (Tudor age) deer parks are still visible in the form of ancient oaks that dot the current parklands just to the north and south of the house (see Colour plate 15). These are some of the most important collections of ancient oaks in Britain, with some being in excess of six centuries old. At Chatsworth, parks of varying ages surrounded the

54 Deer in Chatsworth Park

old house. The tree-covered slopes to the east of the house, Stand Wood, lead to a gritstone shelf which incorporates the Tudor-age park. William Cavendish and his wife Elizabeth of Hardwick, better known as Bess of Hardwick, established the deer park in the latter half of the sixteenth century when the house was built. Much of the land adjacent to the river only became parkland in the eighteenth and nineteenth centuries. This parkland incorporated trees of the older deer park into the new landscaping, which is believed to be the work of Lancelot Capability Brown started in the mid-eighteenth century. One of the more remarkable features of the sixteenth-century hunting landscape is The Stand (which now gives its name to the landscaped 'Stand Woods'), a hunting tower, where the movements of deer could be observed from the high prominent position it occupies on the escarpment of the ridge behind Chatsworth house. Its use was not confined to just a vantage point for observing deer because in Elizabethan times there was a fashion for having buildings like this that operated as a kind of resort away from the main house; an informal gathering place for certain types of function that escaped the rigid norms and formality of the main house. It also made the most of the strongly contrasting views of the wild and domestic landscapes that could be had from here across the Derwent Valley and away to the west, something that appealed to the aesthetic sensibilities of the time.

Remembering that in the Norman period Belper was called by the De Ferrers 'Beaurepaire', meaning beautiful retreat, parks were as much about creating Godly beauty on earth, making a personal Garden of Eden, as it was for the practical keeping of stock. The influence of those early ideas emerging from Persia and the East were foremost behind the creation of these landscapes by emparking. Managing these places and stocking them with native and exotic animals such as fallow deer were partly about creating an ideal. This resembled, both conceptually and in practice, the idea of creating landscape parks and gardens, the taming of nature by man, the creation of the Golden Age landscape gardens and houses. Parks were clearly a precursor to these ideas of nature and perfection giving inspiration to celebrity landscape gardeners such as Capability Brown. We have seen already that The Stand at Chatsworth, erected perhaps in the 1570s, was designed to capture views of the wild and domesticated landscapes of the Peak, to frame and make references to their differences as much as to view the deer. Hunting parks and forests clearly had some influence on the later manufactured 'natural' landscapes and parks of the seventeenth, eighteenth and nineteenth centuries. Indeed, they were very much the precursor of those Age of Enlightenment landscapes.

The age of great hunts

Hunting and stately homes are synonymous with horses, packs of foxhounds, deerhounds, staghounds or beagles, hedged fields and portly riders in their pinks. The British landscape we see today, for example, such as that in the counties of Rutland, Leicestershire and Northamptonshire, particularly are hunting landscapes – created and managed with the aim of providing a good day's hunting. Country crafts and practices played their part in the management of that landscape. Some of these survive to the present day such as hedge-laying and dry-stone walling, albeit in a much reduced fashion. By the beginning of the twentieth century many of these jobs

55 An example of the ancient rural tradition of hedge-laying, once common in Britain

became mechanised, replaced by the flail, or stone walls were no longer maintained and were replaced by barbed wire and wooden fence posts.

Before the first half of the twentieth century these tasks were the mainstays of country employment after the harvest and throughout the winter months. Inheritance tax laws meant that many estates became much smaller or even ceased to exist, landownership became fragmented and management methods were tailored more towards modern farming; rearing livestock or arable production, with hedge-laying and similar crafts seen as no longer cost effective. Now only a few of the larger surviving country estates are able to continue some of these activities where it is affordable. Some of these estates rely upon the incomes provided by sport shooting and a few have some income provided by hunting with hounds.

Chatsworth: a great country house estate

Great houses like Chatsworth retain something of their earlier hunting associations, with features like parkland trees becoming incorporated into the later landscaping schemes. Windsor Great Park with its ancient pollarded oaks is another example, and these oaks are considered to be amongst the oldest living trees in the country.

Derbyshire is blessed with a number of fine country houses and one of the best, Chatsworth House, is still a functioning estate owned and maintained by the current Duke and Duchess of Devonshire. However, they are, like most similar stately homes in the UK, reliant upon the business of tourism than many other aspects of estate business. The Chatsworth Show and the Chatsworth Horse Trials are also important revenue streams, which complement the nature of the estate and the overall business. The country show and the horse trials especially have strong hunting connections. Both are fairly modern spin-offs of hunting: one showcases the crafts and skills associated with rural life and hunting; and the other showcases the skills required for successful mounted hunting. A medieval house, attributed to the Leche family of at least fourteenth-century date, which in turn may have had a Saxon foundation and lies somewhere to the north of the current house, was demolished and the new one built by Bess of Hardwick. The original plans were dated 1551 and the house was completed some 25 years later in 1576, with construction taking 15 years. As Bess's fortunes increased during these years the plans may well have been revised, and the completed building was much grander than originally intended.

Chatsworth passed to William Cavendish on Bess's death, and eventually William, his great-great-grandson, the 4th Earl of Devonshire, commissioned William Talman to redesign and rebuild the south front. A rise in Cavendish's political fortunes subsequently elevated him to the status of duke in 1667. The rebuild, which began in early 1687 and took on elaborations befitting a ducal seat, saw a new Great Hall, east front and east wing, which was all completed by 1669 in the Baroque style. What may have been the finest gardens in England at this time, with their stunning terraces, parterres and complex waterworks, survived until the 1730s. Then the gardens and parks underwent one of a series of redesigns. Eventually the duke and Talman fell out and he was sacked, leaving the Elizabethan west front to dominate the Derwent Valley until the very early eighteenth century, when it too was fabulously rebuilt by an unknown designer that was, perhaps, in some way directly influenced by Talman himself. The north front and probably the Cascade House were built a little later by Thomas Archer. Archer was then responsible for some of the redesigns and alterations to the east and west ranges, part of which was later rebuilt, to the detriment of the overall look, by Wyatville according to Maxwell Craven and Michael Stanley in *The Derbyshire Country House.*

At Chatsworth the current stables attest to the importance of horses to the aristocracy after the medieval period, and like all other parts of the house and estate their location and design has changed over time, probably being rebuilt to match the current flavour of the building at the time (see Plate 19). Currently they reflect the overall look, feel and grandeur of the house. The 'new' stables were designed and built by James Paine, a noted second-generation Palladian architect. The duke met Paine in his capacity as the Master of the King's Horse, when Paine was the Clerk of Works at Newmarket. Clearly some sort of professional friendship was struck between the two men. Following the building of the new stables Paine went on to make a number of changes to the house and a number of buildings in the Chatsworth landscape and parks. The stables have been described as 'one of the grandest' to be built in that century in England. The design is influenced by a number of other buildings, such as the Royal Mews in London, and draws upon Italian designs to create the most lavishly decorated and ornamented stable block of the time.

Overall, the hunting landscape of Chatsworth consists of a deer park, the Old Park now incorporated into the later landscaped parks as a number of ancient pollarded trees (see Colour plate 15). The oldest surviving parts of its boundary consists of a part orthostatic and part boulder wall, 1.5 to 2m high to deter leaping deer, and runs close to the edge of the southern boundary. Smaller deer enclosures, known as 'Newe Park' and 'Roe Park', were in the vicinity of the gardens, easily visible from the house and were probably designed to provide a pleasing ornamental view. A medieval warren was incorporated into the Chatsworth landscape sometime in the medieval period, and a warrener's lodge was built, the accounts of which can be found from 1601.

As we have already seen, the construction of The Stand to watch the deer roaming over the Derwent Valley was probably constructed in the 1570s. The pleasures of hunting were also the pleasures of landscape and the appreciation of the aesthetic beauty of nature. Chatsworth's earliest landscapes defined these ideas quite well but they also showed how the evolution of that thinking in turn encapsulated ideas and influenced the appreciation or thinking of later ages of aesthetic beauty, especially those about the taming of nature. In this new era ideas about changing social conditions and knowledge went hand in hand with the appreciation

56 Inside the stables at Chatsworth; Grade I listed and still retaining the stalls within

of the aesthetic beauty and appreciation of nature, which became known as the Enlightenment period. Arguably those same thoughts, ideas and subsequent social changes, became ever more interlinked through time and they can be traced down to today.

The changes and evolution of this thought down through time can be linked to the anti-hunt movements of recent decades. Ironically, the beginnings of this movement happened because the nobility regarded hunting highly, indeed as the highest form of cultural aestheticism, and that they had a heightened appreciation of the form and nature of certain prey, namely deer, and their landscapes. Of course, some of these were idealised landscapes and as such only they, through this great appreciation, were worthy to hunt these creatures. As we now know, the emergence of these ideas perhaps started as far back as the Roman period in Britain. Therefore, the reasoning behind the modern anti-hunt movement could be viewed as the appreciation of nature brought into the modern era, discussed, intellectualised and enacted upon with reference to modern evolved sensibilities that had their roots in the Enlightenment. However, in the Enlightenment and in the lead up to it, hunting was a form of aggrandisement and to build 'Great Houses' was also a form of aggrandisement, so the two are inextricably linked. Without hunting it is highly probable the impetus to build great houses would have been somewhat reduced and our heritage considerably impoverished as a consequence.

Enclosing commons in the nineteenth century

During the nineteenth century there came a radical change, a shift in the politics of landownership that was met with almost universal condemnation throughout the nation by the masses of poor country people who used the commons – the Enclosure of the Commons was gathering pace. Acts were passed, such as the General Enclosure Acts of 1801, 1836 and 1845, which were designed to speed up the process and allow farmers to enclose land without reference to Parliament. This continued until a radical piece of legislation effectively halted the process, the Enclosures of the Commons Act of 1876, which was a triumph for the Commons Preservation Society who had campaigned to ensure that open areas like Hampstead Heath and Epping Forest remained places that could be enjoyed by the public. Again, arguably this was part and parcel of the evolution of thought that had begun in the Enlightenment. This final phase of enclosing the commons was started around 1750 by the major landowners to take land out of common use, allowing them in effect to do away with the rights of common, and privatise and charge rents for the land and thus quash traditional common usage rights such as quarrying, peat cutting and pasture. In areas like the uplands of the Pennines this was to have a dramatic effect.

Kinder Scout, for example, was enclosed by a number of stone walls where previously there had been none. The effect of this is quite dramatic if one looks down into the Hope Valley: here the irregular shapes and sizes of older established walls, which emerged over long spans of time, can be seen in contrast to the long straight walls creating large regular enclosures established around the mid-nineteenth century. One of the key aims of this was to keep the sheep off the high Kinder Moors, to allow the gamekeepers to provide good grouse-rearing country and better shooting sport. On Kinder Scout it was not until the 1930s that this position radically changed again with the Mass Trespass of 1932, providing the impetus for a wider movement that was to allow public access to some of Britain's most cherished places. Even more recently Open Access, a recent and long-fought-for piece of legislation, has been rolled out onto some of Britain's upland areas, including Kinder Scout, which has been in the hands of the National Trust for over 20 years.

Piecemeal enclosure also took its toll upon former forests, a process which began in Saxon times and gathered pace in the medieval period, when it was known as assarting. In some instances this activity shows up in field-name evidence with fields' names like 'sarts' or 'serts'. Eventually this even spread to old parks too, some of which had fallen out of use in the sixteenth or seventeenth centuries, such as Belper Parks and Morley Park in Derbyshire, and Ongar Great Park in Essex, to name just three examples, where enclosures would have begun to erode their old recognisable shapes from the landscape. By 1800 there were still unenclosed lands consisting of pasture, wood pasture and woodland that were once part of Royal Forests and wild upland areas, such as Wychewood in Oxfordshire and Peak Forest

57 A view over land that was once part of the Peak Forest

in Derbyshire. It was these lands that were part of the Peak Forest, which during the first half of the nineteenth century were enclosed and divided up, and included Kinder Scout.

Shooting: country estates and game shooting

In the post-medieval period, and more particularly in recent centuries, the great estates have tended to be less involved in hunting on horseback, preferring instead to hunt using guns; pheasant, grouse, partridge, quail and various other birds being favoured for sport shooting. The Scottish Highland estates in particular came into their own in this sport in the late nineteenth and early twentieth centuries for not only grouse shooting but stag hunting. Some of these estates still run very lucrative enterprises based upon tracking and shooting stags. Some are today hotels, such as Ballathie in East Perthshire, which continues to offer shooting and fishing in its grounds. This estate passed from the hands of the Drummond family, who held it in the seventeenth century, to the Richardsons in the nineteenth century, who held it until it was sold in the mid-twentieth century. It became a hotel in the 1970s.

58 Fetternear House, near Kemnay in Aberdeenshire, during excavations in the late 1990s

Game shooting and the development of the breech-loading gun go hand in hand because the sportsman no longer had to muzzle-load his gun after each shot. This laborious task having been done away with meant that the sport hunter could now quickly load his gun and discharge a steady stream of shot at flying birds. Driven shoots became particularly popular with teams of assistants required to flush and drive the game birds over the heads of the guns. The system of landownership that Britain had meant that this was still very much a sport for the wealthy, with land used as preserves for the rearing of game for the shoot. Large sums of money were invested in the redesign of estates to accommodate the sport and to manage and stock a good estate for the shoot. The apogee of the great driven game shoots was the Edwardian period, shortly before the Great War changed the fortunes of the Empire.

Another place with a long history and where game shooting still continues today is Fetternear House near Kemnay in Aberdeenshire. During the medieval period this was the summer residence of the Bishop of Aberdeen; it was then rebuilt in the sixteenth to nineteenth centuries but possibly incorporating parts of the earlier palace. It was the Leslies of Balquhain, who intermarried with several other Scottish families including the Irvines of Drum, who took on the palace after the Reformation and built the house. In the later post-medieval period the Leslies ran a noted shoot from Fetternear, which declined in the earlier twentieth century after a fire in 1919, causing the house to be abandoned. Descendants of the Leslies continue to own the estate and shooting still remains part of a more diverse business.

Welbeck Abbey in Nottinghamshire, which straddles the Derbyshire/Nottinghamshire border, continues a long tradition of private sport shooting, which

59 Crags Lodge, Welbeck Estate, Nottinghamshire and Derbyshire

is usually by invitation only. As described in an earlier chapter the estate also shoots within Creswell Crags gorge from time to time. The management of game, land and woodland requires considerable staffing to ensure that the hunt is successful. The Welbeck estate employs a number of gamekeepers who live on the estate, often strategically placed to manage the certain areas where they live. Poaching is one of many problems that the keepers have to contend with; another is the growing numbers of tourists to the crags, but this is an issue that has yet to manifest itself into a real concern that requires active management; time will tell what measures may be required in future to mitigate against its impact upon the game and the shoot.

7

The Evolution of Hunting: Weapons and Techniques

The evolution of weapons for hunting paralleled those of warfare at various points in prehistory and history, so that the history of hunting weapons is also the history of weapons for warfare. This evolution of weapons has been dealt with in detail by various authors for various specific periods, both for hunting and for warfare, so only an overview is offered here for the purpose of stitching together the disparate periods and providing a sort of narrative that makes sense within the context of this book. I will try to avoid the constant comparisons of hunting weapons to weapons of warfare, which is not the topic of this book; however, there will be the odd comparison, for the two subjects are necessarily and inextricably linked. I will start with the oldest weapons, the ancient flake tools and then the sharpened wooden staves passing through into the Upper Palaeolithic period and the leaping advances in hunting weapons, such as the atlatl (spear thrower), the bow and arrow and the changes in lithic technology and the appearance of hafted composite weapons, which might well have had their origins in the Middle Palaeolithic. These are subjects that have been touched upon to a greater or lesser extent elsewhere in the book but are worth discussing again here in the context of their evolution and uses in hunting.

Developing hunting skills was an important aspect of daily life, particularly but not solely confined to prehistoric people. Passing those skills onto succeeding generations was also of vital importance to the survival of a group, and elaborate methods of ensuring those skills were passed on were developed over time. Mechanisms such as rites of passage for boys, particularly male initiation ceremonies, were played out with strong references to hunting. This is a particular feature noted in recent or still extant indigenous hunter-gatherer societies. This ensured the desirability of accepting that in order to be a good hunter it was critical to be a full member of one's society. Strategies were critical to ensure that enough food was hunted whilst expending the minimum amount of energy and time. At Solutré we saw that carefully built corrals were a useful strategy employed there, ensuring that maximum game were killed with minimal effort – but these sorts of strategies required planning and teamwork. Danger to the hunter was to be avoided too and strategies had to take this into account. To lose a hunter was not just to lose a friend and a member of one's society; it was also the loss of a hunter who could help to ensure the group's survival.

The uses of hunting weapons are largely self-explanatory, but ethnography, for example, tells us that weapons such as spear throwers were used by Australian Aborigines as digging sticks. In the Mesolithic, and more particularly in the Palaeolithic, weapons probably had more than one function. Hunters could spend multiple days away from their transitory homes so dual or multi-functionality is perhaps an overlooked aspect of ancient hunting weapons.

Tools and weapons in the Palaeolithic

From the Palaeolithic the tools that have survived the best are the lithics. Usually when we think of prehistoric stone tools we think of flints, but in the earliest prehistory, more often than not, they were of basalt, mudstones, andesite, chert, quartz and obsidian, as well as flint; in other words, whatever was available and usable. All of the geologies I have just listed could vary in quality so selection was part of the tool-making process. I will try to avoid descriptions of the manufacture and categories of tools by typology and so on, as these issues have been dealt with elsewhere by others in a far better way than I could; instead I will just concentrate on the broader descriptions of more general typologies, and anyone who is interested in chasing up the details can refer to the Select Reading List. One thing to note is that the sequences within Britain do not necessarily have parity with the sequences within Africa, and thus Mode I and Mode II traditions will date quite differently to those same typological sequences for Africa.

The oldest tools, 2.5 million years old, come from sites in East Africa, the so-called Oldowan technology: simple pebble and flake tools used to cut flesh and break bones belonging to the Pliocene epoch (between five million and two million years ago) and our earliest hominid ancestors, broadly classified as Mode I tools. These tools were made from locally procured fine-grained basalt and could also be used for making and sharpening digging sticks for getting roots and tubers, which were undoubtedly the mainstay of the diet. During this time it seems that scavenging was perhaps the main mode of meat-getting subsistence, with hunting perhaps being a more opportunistic affair, i.e. if game could be caught and trapped because it was very young, very old or injured, or was even just stumbled across, then it was killed and consumed. Roughly pointed or ready sharp sticks or club-like branches were probably used and stones were probably thrown to stun prey. Using sticks to jab, branches as clubs and stones to stun, even kill if delivered correctly, puts distance between the human and animal, an important consideration when hunting, especially as some animals, even relatively small ones, could inflict injuries on the hunter. Hunting techniques and skills were no doubt refined somewhat over time.

Although not contemporary with the Oldowan, the nearest British manifestation of this tradition is the Clactonian (named after Clacton-on-Sea, Essex, where these tools were first found), which contain simple cobble and flake tools. These tools were also found in Swanscombe, Kent (*c.*500,000 BP) and Pakefield, Suffolk (*c.*700,000 BP) – see Fig. 3. Generally Clactonian tools and sites are found within river valleys and their ancient channel deposits and gravel terraces. They are classified as Mode I tools within the UK, but more recent research suggests that the Clactonian may only be a response to the limited quantity of usable, workable stone available locally, as they also turn up occasionally in later tool industries. In other words, the hominids were responding to situational needs and availability of raw materials, and there was some overlap with the Acheulian, Mode II technologies typified by bi-faces, such as those in Fig. 60.

Following on from the Pliocene and into the early Pleistocene came the Acheulian (starting about 1.6 million years ago in Africa) tool-kits of the Lower Palaeolithic period; hand axes typified this tool-kit and here argument has raged over the effectiveness of these as tools, let alone as hunting weapons. The teardrop-shaped or ovate hand axe (known as a bi-face: a tool with two faces that meet to form a single edge) was often a large unwieldy instrument that was flaked all around the edges and was probably unusable as a tool without slicing open the hands of the user. It has been speculated that the axes were probably show items that were created and curated as prestige objects by hominids as part of a formal mating display to attract females. These hand axes can be found across much of the Old World from Africa, through Europe (including Britain), Asia, South-east Asia, including Indonesia, and are the tools of *Homo erectus* and *Homo heidelbergensis* and *Homo neanderthalsis*.

The numbers that these tools have been found in suggests that there might be something in this display theory, but there are plenty of smaller, less-worked bi-face hand axes which could be used as tools for butchery or the manufacture of sharpened spears. However, it was the flakes that were the important by-products of this process because they provided the all-purpose cutting edges for skinning, butchery and working wood into spears. Acheulian tradition hand axes existed for many millennia and, with changes in the methods of flaking, the Levallois technique (Mode III) was also used by Neanderthals until the Châtelperronian/Aurignacian periods. There is evidence that the use of hafted spears dates to the Middle Palaeolithic and to Neanderthals (and possibly even earlier than this to *H. heidelbergensis*, although the evidence is at the present time slight). The flakes, which were the by-product of hand axe-making, as well as from prepared cores, could also provide the edges for use in simple hafted spears. The start of the Mode III Middle Palaeolithic industry in Africa was around 300,000 to 250,000 BP and appears shortly after in Europe. It seems that the industry grew out of the earlier Mode II tradition and there are a few European sites where a precursor of the Levallois technique appears around 420,000 BP, and in Britain at Purfleet, Essex, just

60 Replica Mode
II-type hand axe.
(Photographed
courtesy of Creswell
Crags Heritage Trust)

under 300,000 BP. The Mousterian is part of the Mode III package of traditions and is based upon Levallois flakes; a variant of the tradition was dated to 64–67,000 BP at Lynford, Norfolk, and examples also occurred in Creswell Crags.

The weapons of the Lower to Middle Palaeolithic, despite a richness of stone tool artefacts, are a little-known aspect of the cultural and subsistence behavioural package. As we saw in an earlier chapter, the occurrence of sharpened thrusting javelins probably happened at least 410,000 years ago, with tentative evidence of a similar weapon being used at Boxgrove and dating to around 500,000 BP; a shift to hafted composite weapons occurred around 45,000 BP, coinciding with the appearance of modern humans in Europe. Up to this time the lithic technologies were focused upon the production of tools for cutting, skinning and scraping, and were therefore dominated by a simple tool-kit of hand axes, flakes and scrappers. With the arrival of the modern humans in Europe, and perhaps having its origins in Eastern Europe, the Aurignacian assemblages were a huge leap forward in terms of the range and uses of lithic tools. The primary advantage of the Aurignacian assemblage was that it was a blade-based technology, whereas the preceding Mousterian culture was a flake-based tool-kit; although blades did sometimes occur, they were not the dominant tool form that became the basis of the whole assemblage. This meant that the development of hafted composite weapons was possible, although again, evidence for hafted thrusting spears in the Middle Palaeolithic manufactured by Neanderthals notwithstanding.

In the early Upper to late Upper Palaeolithic (see Time Chart in Plate 2) the changes in lithic technologies were nuanced and subtle, but each one reflected developments over time that themselves were reflecting changes in environment and climate, game species, mobility, strategies of hunting and the developments in weapons that were ultimately influenced by all these factors. This is why the study of lithics is so important as reflectors not only of changes of environment, climate and species hunted, but as a mirror to changing society and its development over time due to these factors – because, as we all know, necessity is the mother of invention.

At the end of the Middle Palaeolithic and into the early Upper Palaeolithic, the change from flake-based to Mode IV blade-based technologies, we have seen, was not an overnight switch from one to the other. Rather the transition was made over a fairly long period of time, reflective of a unique set of circumstances that prevailed at the time – the coexistence of two hominid species within Europe – the Neanderthals and the Cro-Magnons (modern humans). There is intense debate about the nature and driving mechanisms of these changes, some of which I mentioned in an earlier chapter, which is worth going into detail about here. The Aurignacian technology and behavioural package lasted about 18,000 years, between 45,000 and 18,000 BP, and included the development of burins to bore holes into materials like hide, wood, bone and ivory, which in turn led to the development of composite bone and ivory points for hafting and the atlatl or spear thrower, as well as the use of well-developed flint knives.

The debate comes into this because the Neanderthals and moderns coexisted side by side in some parts of the world, particularly in regions of Israel and in Europe just either side of the Pyrenees. It is believed that the modern humans developed the Aurignacian tool-kit in the Balkans region and it spread into Western Europe soon after, and that in places such as Israel and the Pyrenean region, Neanderthals copied the technologies before becoming extinct, or were being absorbed into the modern human population, part of the 'multi-regional theory' of modern human origins, and had the technology more by default. This facie of the Aurignacian technology was called the Châtelperronian and is characterised by a hybrid of Mousterian and

Aurignacian stone tool elements, in other words part blade-based and part flake-based with a developed bone industry. This makes it possible that the Neanderthals created an Aurignacian-like technology before modern humans were properly established in Europe and were on the road to 'modernity' before modern humans were. Others have suggested that the technology was created by the Neanderthals and that modern humans developed it into a fully fledged tool assemblage. Mentioned earlier, Levallois points, dating to the Middle Palaeolithic in the Near East (Syria) and discovered embedded in the neck bones of wild ass, suggests very strongly that Neanderthals were creating hafted spears and using them as projectile weapons in excess of 50,000 years ago. The osteological evidence suggests that the force and trajectory of the spear required to kill the ass came from a spear throw (see Fig. 22 for an example of an end piece of an ornate late Upper Palaeolithic version). Also, an analysis of the use-wear patterns of stone points from Kebara Cave, Mount Carmel, Israel, suggests that hafted weapons were used here by archaic *Homo sapiens* between 50,000 and 60,000 years ago. Taken together with the possible evidence for hafting from Schöningen, Germany, dating to 400,000 BP and by *Homo heidelbergensis*, this adds more weight to the argument that Neanderthals could have achieved high levels of sophistication before the arrival of modern humans in Europe. The importance of these points will be returned to shortly.

This debate becomes important; especially in Western Europe, as it is shortly after this time that the earlier examples of the spectacular Palaeolithic cave art appears. For example, Chauvet Cave in the Ardèche region, with its spectacular drawings of felines, horses and rhinos, dates to around 32,000 BP, well into the Aurignacian and shortly after the assumed disappearance of Neanderthals from Europe. Portable art of a similar age has been found in Germany and Austria, such as the Vogelherd animals (see earlier chapter) and the 'Dancing Venus' of Galgenberg (Austria). These first flourishes of artistic behaviour overlap with, or roughly correspond with, areas where Neanderthals and modern humans coexisted together for the longest times. Whilst I am not suggesting that the Neanderthals were the artists of some of these great works, it does raise an important question about the catalysts for the emergence of these bodies of art, their links with the changing environment, unusual social conditions, changing tool technologies and perhaps hunting strategies, even combining with questions about the nature of symbolic behaviour and ontologies in this period. Clearly there are many unresolved issues surrounding these matters, which are only now drawing attention.

In terms of the evidence in Britain at this time, things are perhaps slightly simplified by the fact that there is no Châtelperronian culture so far visible in the archaeological record. Even Aurignacian sites are rare with just seven find spots, including Paviland Cave. More significant was a nineteenth-century discovery of a lozenge-shaped bone point dating to around 28,000 or 29,000 BP; work by Paul Pettitt and Roger Jacobi on this implement, and a reassessment of British and German dates for the Aurignacian, showed that in northern Europe there was unlikely any settlement by these groups of people, and that they made their way to these latitudes only in the later Aurignacian.

In Britain this was likely to have been for a short period between 32,000 and 28,000 BP, and it has even been suggested that this makes it possible there was a late survival of Neanderthal populations in northern latitudes during this time. Pettitt and Jacobi then go on to suggest that due to the late arrival of the modern humans, and the existence of already long-established Neanderthal populations in northern Europe, there was probably a complex social geography at work during the 29th millennium BC. The site of Bamford Road in Ipswich provides a potential date of 35,000 BP for the appearance of modern humans, and their early Upper Palaeolithic tools of leaf points and blades that overlapped with a small ovate Levallois hand axe in the same stratigraphic unit. However, as Pettitt and Jacobi have pointed out, there are perhaps problems with dates at some sites (particularly those given for the German and Austrian sites), and on balance it seems that the Bamford Road date range could fall into a later date banding more consistent with the dates given above. The nature of these problems is likely due to having insufficient numbers of dates by the various dating techniques available; an area that has been a crucial development in ensuring secure dating of late Upper Palaeolithic artefacts and contexts in recent years.

What the nature of the relationship between modern humans and Neanderthals at the end of the Middle Palaeolithic and early Upper Palaeolithic in Britain must have been like we can only guess. This is an important area of study and one that will test archaeologists and paleoanthropologists for some time to come.

In the Upper Palaeolithic the number of blades struck from a core was far higher than was previously achieved, making much better and more efficient use of the raw material. Even the curvature of the blade could be controlled by precision striking using soft and hard hammer tools. Raw material quality was of course an important consideration, as the range of tools to be made from the flint was much higher than seen before and required higher-quality nodules, and once obtained the material should be used carefully and sparingly. Transportation of raw material over greater distances occurred and was no doubt bolstered by trade and exchange networks at this time.

Other composite weapons made of bone that we saw in an earlier chapter, such as the split-base bone spear heads and barbed tips, were also critical developments and they required the use of well-made fit-for-purpose stone tools to manufacture them (see Fig. 13). Barbed bone points have been found at a number of British sites such as Gough's Cave and Avelines Hole, Somerset. From Kent's Cavern, Devon, and also dating to the LUP, a three-barbed harpoon was found, no doubt used in hunting or even fishing. In Cosquer Cave, France, the rock-art there may show a depiction of a seal being harpooned. Items such as bone needles to make hide garments were also important, as were the hides themselves. So the whole of human society in the Upper Palaeolithic required the necessary skills and quality raw materials to ensure their survival and their continuing development during the Ice Age. This is a facet often not comprehended when considering the range and diversity of the lithic, bone and ivory tool and artistic assemblages of the Upper Palaeolithic. Humans inevitably develop, sometimes slowly, sometimes quickly, but whatever the pace of development it always requires as a minimum the maintenance of the current level of technology using the best of the materials you can to achieve that. Even harder is the slow edging forward that continuing human technological, symbolic and subsistence development requires. To do this involves more energy, more population growth, more raw material and increased sophistication and learning, which must be transmitted to the next generation to ensure success. It is this slow inching forward that we can trace in the artefactual evidence alongside that of the symbolic and faunal remains, and the remains of the people themselves, when we are lucky enough to find them. During the climatically stressful times of the Ice Age, the pace and speed of that development was perhaps at times at its slowest for humans than it was at any time subsequently, and this conservatism is visible in the artefacts which do not change for long periods of time. Developments when they came were slow to spread. The pace did quicken towards the end of the Upper Palaeolithic and the closing stages of the Ice Age and into the Holocene.

The range of weapons, particularly composite spears and then arrows, relied upon flint to make them effective. Other enhancements to weapons emerged at this time, the most critical being the atlatl or spear thrower. A number of these have been found in Europe and they were often highly decorated and made of bone or antler (see Fig. 22). Wooden ones may have existed but they are unlikely to survive down to the present. A description of atlatls and their uses have already been discussed in Chapter 2, and we have also seen that Neanderthals may have used these. But these were perhaps the great leap forward in the Upper Palaeolithic hunting weapons arsenal and were critical in delivering greater range and power to projectile weapons. Their use in hunting would have necessitated new skills and techniques. Whenever new weapons or enhancements appear in hunting, so do prey animals that can be hunted, and this consequently shows in the archaeological record. Changes may occur in the type and sizes of game that are hunted with new favoured game animals replacing those that were hunted before. For example, in the Upper Palaeolithic modern humans favoured the faster, medium-sized game such as deer and horses, and using their better communication skills and teamwork they could potentially corral and kill large numbers of these. This in turn may have led to increased ritual aggregation and feasting activities at certain key places in the landscape, and no doubt had an important cumulative effect upon the development of ritual and social evolution of modern humans.

There is no doubt also that the changing weapons technology also enabled humans to capture, perhaps by trapping or using bow and arrow, smaller game such as hares that were valued for their furs during the colder stages of the Upper Palaeolithic, as can be attested by their numbers in the caves at Creswell Crags gorge. These smaller game species were perhaps also hunted for trading pelts for lithic raw material. Aggregation locales may have been key places for trade, playing a role alongside intergroup relations as well as forging new alliances, perhaps through marriage.

Sometime in the Upper Palaeolithic, and although there is little direct evidence in Britain, many researchers believe that bows and arrows were likely to have been used. The indirect evidence comes from a number of reputed flint arrowheads that are of

Upper Palaeolithic origin, whilst the direct evidence comes from a Continental site called Stellmoor in Germany excavated just prior to the start of the Second World War. The Stellmoor site was a waterlogged site on the edge of a former lake that produced over 100 well-preserved pine arrow shafts, which were designed to come apart so that a new tanged flint-tipped foreshaft could be added, thus making the main shaft and its fletchings reusable. Also, the ends of wooden bows were recorded at Stellmoor. Luckily, a series of high-quality photographs were taken of the shafts because they were subsequently destroyed during the war. The site of Stellmoor was on the edge of the North German Plain at the mouth of a steep-sided valley, ideally suited to the interception of reindeer (*Rangifer tarandus*) herds that passed through the valleys. Thousands of reindeer bones were recovered from the lake muds, many with the tanged flint points still embedded in them.

The Mesolithic: the bow and arrow comes of age

There is good evidence for the use of the bow and arrow in the Mesolithic, especially from sites like Starr Carr and the various open lithic scatters around Britain. During the Mesolithic there was a new development, which showed its earliest manifestations at the end of the late Upper Palaeolithic, and that was the production of microliths. Microlith technology was used to create a new generation of easily maintained hafted composite weapons and was based upon the creation of tiny triangular bladelets; these were removed from a core and retouched to their final form, resembling small blade-edged points that could be set into slots and resin along the shaft of a wood or bone arrow point or spear. This greatly increased the cutting edge length of the projectile and made them more maintainable, as only small pieces of flint needed to be replaced if they were lost, it also made them usable for longer when they were broken. Previously, the loss or snapping off of a part of the projectile meant that it was no longer usable, but with a microlith hafted bone point, for example, there would usually be enough of the cutting edge left to do a sufficient job to bring down prey. All in all, therefore, the microlith was another significant advancement in lithic and hunting technology.

Evidence for the use of the bow and arrow in the Mesolithic is much more equivocal for Britain, with the eighth millennium site of Starr Carr in North Yorkshire producing almost 200 barbed antler points and more than 240 microliths. Debris from the production of barbed antler points was also found here. It is clear that in the early Flandrian the use of the bow and arrow had become much more widespread. From the Trent Valley we have a number of Mesolithic flint scatters, and the remains of at least one aurochs with microliths embedded in its soft tissue from the quarry at Bleasby, Nottinghamshire. Leicestershire has also produced a number of Mesolithic flint scatters, including a few microliths from a site at Wymondham, which also contained a few early Neolithic flints recovered during a watching brief for a new ménage.

61 Microliths from Bleasby Quarry in the Trent Valley, Nottinghamshire. These were discovered in close association with the vertebrae of at least two aurochs found in a palaeochannel in 2002 (see Colour Plate 4). (Barry Lewis)

The exploitation of sites on the higher ground was much more a feature of this period than any preceding it and the wildwood habitat required the changes in technology that happened at this time. Aurochsen, wild boar, ox, roe deer and red deer were all ideally suited to this environment. Things like uniserial bone points continued to be used into this period but it was the dominance of composite tools based upon microlith technology that typified the lithic assemblages of the time. The only new addition was the flaked adze or axe, which emerged as a useful woodsman's tool, enabling the construction of shelters and general carpentry – but was no doubt put to other uses such as the manufacture of traps or to aid the clearance of small areas in conjunction with fire to attract game to the lush new growth.

It is hard to imagine the tree cover during this time – vast forest would have covered much of the British landscape, from coast to coast and north to south. Only into the later part of the Mesolithic and into the Neolithic did man's impact upon the landscape begin to show by changing and creating new habitats. Humans had to adapt and change. Game procurement patterns, for example, had to adapt to not only rapidly changing vegetational cover due to clearance, but to changing climate, and in some places rising sea-levels. Worth mentioning at this point is the possible use of fire to encourage acorn growth in the Mesolithic at two British sites, both in Yorkshire: Malham Tarn and Starr Carr. Acorns are a resource which, if treated correctly, might well have been an important source of carbohydrate in the hunter-gatherer diet. The use of fire in some instances might have been to encourage acorns and not just as a method to exploit game.

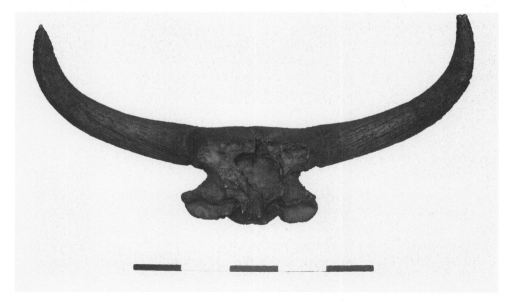

62 Aurochs skull – cast. Scale is 50cm. (Photographed courtesy of Creswell Crags Heritage Trust)

In terms of raw material for the production of stone tools chert was much more widely used in some areas, despite its slightly inferior quality when compared to flint, but the general vegetational, glacial drift sediments and soil coverage meant that flint had become a rarer commodity in certain locations. At Creswell Crags there have been a few discoveries of Mesolithic deposits, and stray finds within the gorge and the caves that indicate that people travelled to and from the higher ground of the Peak. Their movements may have coincided with the spring and summer movement of wild herds in the late Pleistocene and early Holocene and later to procure chert too, bringing it with them to use in Creswell. Chert has been found in places further away than Creswell, occasionally in the Trent Valley, but these tend to be stray finds of discarded tools rather than evidence of any kind of trade. Flint procured from the Trent Valley could also end up at Creswell and in the Peak. Transhumance patterns were an important part of the inland hunter-gatherer lifestyle, perhaps more critical than the movements of the more sedentary coastal hunter-fisher-gatherers who were exploiting a more specialised coastal marine environment.

The uplands were, however, intensively exploited and the high numbers of sites in the Pennines and the North York Moors display rich lithic scatters containing large numbers of microliths, particularly at locations that command good views of the landscape, indicating that these sites were above the contemporary tree-line. Such scatters are found from time to time eroding out of the peat on the higher moors of the Peak District. The better sources of chert in the Peak District are in the Wye Valley near Bakewell, which was exploited well into the Neolithic. The quality of the chert here could be almost as good as flint.

There are, of course, whole classes of simple weapons that are worth at least a mention at this point, as not only are they likely to have been used in the Palaeolithic, but they survived in some form or another into recent centuries or even decades – not necessarily in Britain but certainly somewhere in the world. These are weapons such as the slingshot, a simple strap or thong of leather twirled to launch a stone, and the boomerang, for which there is tentative evidence in the Solutrean period on the Continent. Even simple sticks and stones could be used to hunt to great effect.

The Neolithic

The Neolithic was a time of emerging agricultural practices in Britain, and the older hunter-gatherer mode of subsistence was slowly, in some places rapidly, being pushed aside and replaced by settlements, fields and enclosed herds of cattle, sheep and goats. Hunting was still highly important but becoming less of a focus in many peoples' lives. The process of sedentism had begun in the Mesolithic, especially around the coastal areas of Britain and along estuaries, which though specialised were resource rich and people could settle for longer, and their transhumance patterns, though still seasonal, were perhaps occupying areas or territories that were smaller than in previous times – a few kilometres from hill to beach rather than from distant plains across hills and valleys to rocky gorges. The resource-rich, forested landscape of the later Mesolithic was very different to that of the tundra and permafrost of the late Pleistocene, and was more favourable to transhumance within defined areas. By the Neolithic things were changing again, as people became increasingly settled and as human populations grew and sea-levels rose. By now Britain had long been cut off from the Continent. Trees were felled or cleared by fire and the landscape began to open up, and the methods and techniques of farming came as part of a flood of all kinds of ideas from the east. Britain was becoming more and more a modified landscape; for the first time the hand of man was visible everywhere and the balance between nature and humans started to become distorted. There were, of course, still wild places, but in the millennia to come these would become ever more squeezed as humans spread into new areas, clearing forest, planting crops and raising animals. Hunting would be quite a different affair but still the weapons evolved.

Recent fieldwork at Creswell Crags indicates that at this time the high ground above the Crags was still important to hunters. A small flint scatter was discovered here on the edge of the escarpment overlooking the current village of Creswell to its west, which contained a couple of arrowheads. This is a good vantage point overlooking the western vale and ideal for watching the movements of larger game in later prehistory. Arrowheads are relatively widespread in their distribution in Britain, indicating that hunting, in one form or another, remained important in later prehistory, despite the theories that say hunting was of relatively low importance at this time. Interestingly, there is a size correlation in arrowheads between areas of Britain where flints are more plentiful and those where they are less so. Leaf-shaped arrowheads are much smaller in western and northern Britain than in the south and the east. There is also less wastage of flint in the material impoverished areas. Often arrowheads, which are the most commonly found artefacts belonging to this period, have been taken to mean that there was warfare and conflict between groups. This is probably the case in some instances, but their presence could be equally attributable to hunting.

The majority of surviving Neolithic bows found in Europe have been made most commonly of yew and elm and are between 4 and 7ft (1.2–2.1m) in length. A yew bow of fairly crude but obviously effective construction, measuring approximately 1.5m long, was found in a peat bog near Cambridge and was dated to c.1730 BC. This example still had knots standing proud from the wood. Welsh archers favoured elm; their bows were fairly rough-hewn but were considered stout and efficient. The design of the bow remained much the same from prehistory until the Middle Ages, when it was at its peak as the common man's weapon of choice.

The use of spears and tucks and the emergence of the sword

As we move through time, stone implements are replaced by metals, first by copper then bronze and eventually iron. Flint arrowheads persisted into the Bronze Age, particularly the barbed and tanged arrowheads, which allowed them to be set and tied to the arrow shaft. Eventually bronze then iron arrowheads replaced them. Spear tips too were manufactured in bronze then iron, replacing stone and bone-tipped spears. However, one of the more radical new weapons at this time, both from a personal combat and prestige point of view, was the sword. Initially, swords in Britain were simple thrusting weapons made of bronze that were too fragile for sustained battle use. The iron replacements were much better. Many swords have been found in burial contexts dating to this time, indicating their importance as personal items and as weapons. Swords discovered in the 1970s and 1980 in the north-east of England at Hull and Acklam Wold are shown in Fig. 64. They were discovered in burial contexts belonging to the Arras tradition and were amongst a number of swords found in the East Yorkshire area. Some of the swords found were likely to have been the ones that had dispatched the grave occupants, in those instances where they were found to have been mortally wounded by swords. It is unclear whether swords were used in hunting at this time, but given that they became important to hunting in the medieval period for close-quarters dispatching of deer and boar, adding to the thrill of the chase, we can suppose that they were. Certainly the Iron Age inhabitants were famed for the use of hunting dogs, which meant that prey like deer, boar and possibly wolves and bears could be held at bay before being dispatched by the sword. This is largely supposition of course, but one that could be tested by research. We shall see the role of the sword to elite hunting in the medieval period very shortly.

In antiquity the weapons of choice were spears and the bow and arrow, but also carried for personal protection as well as final dispatching was the sword. The primary aim of using the spear and bow was, of course, to keep the quarry at a distance, sometimes a dangerous and unpredictable animal such as a boar or even a lion. Tutankhamen's tomb shows a wall painting of him killing a lion with a sickle-bladed type of sword called a *kopesh*. It is worth looking at the use of swords in hunting from the medieval period and down even into the twentieth century because, of all the weapons used, there is perhaps more symbolism in the design and use of the hunting sword than with any other weapon.

The mark of the hunter was the carrying and use of the sword in a hunt, most especially during the medieval period. Swords were often named by their owners or makers and were often viewed as an entity in their own right. The use of swords in hunting is an area shrouded in much mystery and superstition. It is perhaps no surprise that there is much mythology attributed to swords and kingliness, hunting and chivalry – look at the legends of King Arthur, Camelot and Excalibur. The swords of antiquity were made of bronze and then iron and were not terribly strong, especially as the length required, in order to allow sufficient distance between the hunter and his quarry, would further weaken the blade. Armour design in the thirteenth century improved and this required the knight and hunter to carry a straight, double-edged thrusting sword that had a stronger cross-sectional design allowing for a greater length. There are manuscript illustrations dating to the thirteenth and fourteenth

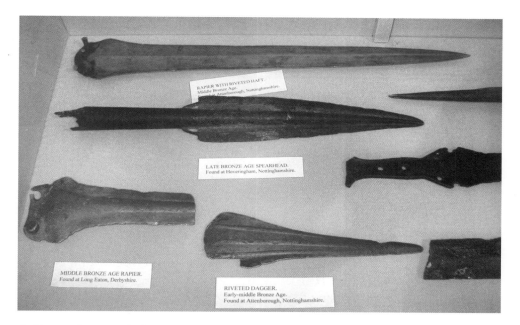

63 Bronze Age swords discovered in Attenborough and Hoveringham, Nottinghamshire, and Long Eaton, Derbyshire. (Photographed courtesy of Nottingham University Museum)

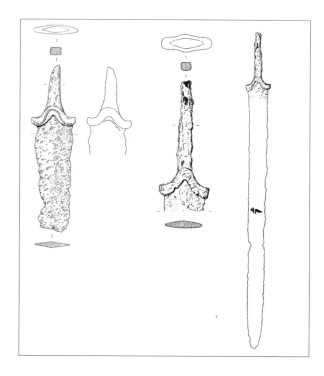

64 Iron Age swords. (After Dent, 1983, Fig. 1)

centuries that show these swords in use. For much of the medieval period, however, the sword was not really a weapon of the chase.

The fourteenth and fifteenth centuries saw the period of the Great Hunting Sword, designed to be about 4ft long, with a blunted top half to prevent damage to the hunter's legs in close action, according to Gaston Phoebus, a writer on hunting in the fourteenth century (the Count Gaston de Foix). However, there is little evidence that this protocol of having a blunted blade was ever followed when this design became the weapon of choice. In Count Gaston's work he described killing a boar without the use of mastiffs to hold it at bay and using a sword, a great and noble feat, fairer than using a spear. In illustrated works dating to the fourteenth and fifteenth centuries there are a number of scenes that show hunters attacking bears and lions, both on foot and on horseback, with swords. In one example a horseman leans from his saddle and thrusts his sword into a boar – a highly dangerous procedure.

By the fifteenth century a highly specialised hunting sword for use on horseback was developed: a riding sword. The majority of these were single-bladed and many were also decorated with hunting and religious scenes; they were strong and triangular in section and had treble grooves running the full length of the blade, designed to be cutting and thrusting blades. Boar swords, known as 'tucks', were fighting swords that appeared during the fifteenth century and had a strong square or octagonal section. From the mid-sixteenth century there is an account from the King's Armoury (after Henry VIII's death), listing the presence of tucks and boar spear swords. In the Tower Inventories, dated 1611 and 1629, 'tuckes for the wild boar' are listed. The passing of time and changing fashions dictated many of the trends for types of sword and their lengths or weights during this period.

Another type of fighting sword, called the 'hand and half sword', was also used as a hunting sword, and contained a set of eating knives in the scabbard. This sword dates to the early sixteenth century and was used against large animals from horseback, and was the preferred weapon of the wealthy hunter. The hunt, as already explained in an earlier chapter, could vary slightly, and in this instance consisted of a chase through countryside or park using dogs to flush, with the nobleman using his heavy sword to administer the 'kill' against the boar, stag or bear. Against a boar or bear, very formidable animals to take on with only a sword, which could bring the hunter easily within striking distance of the animal, a strong spear was favoured as the means of dispatch.

By the seventeenth and eighteenth centuries hunting swords were becoming more ornate and less used in the hunting field as an actual weapon. They were much more an item of dress and called 'hangars'. Because hangars were often made of brass or silver and were poor quality weapons, they could only be used if really required, and often unreliably, especially at close quarters. Something like mass production went on in Europe for the production of hangars, especially in Solingen, Germany, where all lengths and shapes of blades were made and shipped to other centres on the Continent and in Britain for hilt makers to finish the swords. In this period, the nature of hunting was rapidly changing and elites were inclined to ride with a pack of hounds in a foxhunt rather than indulge in the dangerous pastime of killing bears and boars at only arm's length.

Ornately made swords were at their height at this time and the symbol of the running wolf on the blade of a sword was supposed to represent the quality of the blade. Often this could be forged and the quality could well be suspect. Also, blade-makers invariably put on the blade what the owner wanted. Often, the hunter wanted magical symbols placed on the blade to aid his hunting or to bring luck. Indeed, such swords were thought to bestow ability on the owner to do great deeds. Most of these types of symbols, some of which were Cabbalistic in nature and were known only to the owner or the designer of the spell sold to the sword owner, were made and used by huntsmen in Germany, which is where much of this industry was centred.

Guns began to supersede the use of swords in hunting and, inevitably, there were craftsmen keen to incorporate the best of these two worlds. For example, some sword and gun makers manufactured combinations of flintlocks and hunting swords with matching hunting designs upon them. The Napoleonic Wars brought a halt to the manufacture of fine hunting swords, after a time when Napoleon had established workshops to produce highly decorated presentation swords. During the earlier twentieth century there was a brief revival of this mainly Germanic tradition: Heinrich Himmler, Hitler's deputy, had commissioned the creation of fine decorated hunting swords and knives for his SS.

Guns

Gunpowder, probably first invented, likely by accident, by the Chinese as part of an alchemical search for everlasting life, may have first been created in the ninth century AD. The mixture of saltpetre and sulphur, two constituent ingredients of gunpowder, is known from many medicinal combinations of the period. Its first military use dates to around the mid-eleventh century when it was used for incendiary devices, smoke bombs, and with the inclusion of nitrates gunpowder was quite sophisticated by the twelfth century. By the fourteenth century they had developed the cannon, the cannon ball and grenades that were capable of breaking their metal cases. Between 1240 and 1280 the Arabs had gunpowder; perhaps the technology was imported from China or introduced by invading Mongols, or even, as some researchers have suggested, they invented it before the Chinese did. There is even a report that the cannon was used in anger in Seville in 1248.

Roger Bacon, an English philosopher, Franciscan friar and early man of science, who had proved influential to Arabic medieval science, described in his *Opus Majus* how to make gunpowder. The first handgun to emerge in the fourteenth century was a tube of metal, mounted upon a wooden haft with one end closed off and fired by means of a smouldering piece of glowing cord, which was a complicated and unreliable method of firing. The weapon was of little use to either warfare or hunting.

Traditional hunting methods continued unabated until the sixteenth century, when a radical redesign and modification of the gun came along which was much more accurate and consistent – the matchlock. This weapon had a stock that could be held against the shoulder or cheek, and a priming pan and touch-hole that could have a slow burning match lowered into it via a lever or trigger; this would then ignite the charge and send a flame through the touch-hole into the main powder charge inside the gun thus firing it. The matchlock soon took a hold in the hunting world and became more technically sophisticated, and a hunter could, if he was able to stalk within range, bring down birds and animals. The matchlock guns were expensive though and they remained a weapon only for the wealthy. As in earlier periods, the idea of stalking and shooting game became a popular aspiration amongst the lower classes, so much so that Henry VIII in 1533 passed an act that said unless you had an annual income worth £100 per year, you were forbidden to fire a handgun. Henry was a shooting enthusiast and, like his *par force* devotee forebears, was keen that the new sport of shooting and hunting with a gun remained the preserve of the elite classes.

These early guns were far from perfect and had their fair share of problems, including the match alerting game to the hunter's presence, and the wind and damp conditions putting out the match. The ingenuity of the early gun makers came to the fore, however, and mechanical methods were eventually developed. The wheel-lock, a clockwork-like mechanism that worked, in a way, rather like a modern disposable lighter, was spun by pulling the trigger, spinning the wheel against a piece of iron pyrite clamped in the cock that sent sparks into the priming pan, firing the gun. The wheel-lock was much more popular on the Continent than it was here because the mechanism was complex, fiddly and expensive. It remained a weapon of war rather than being used for hunting. However, in Eastern Europe, and especially Germany, a robust wheel-lock was made, the *tschinke*, which, after the English Civil War in the 1650s, saw a great influx of these guns – replacing the now outdated and unpopular matchlocks.

In the mid-sixteenth century the Dutch were making a new mechanism that used flint and steel to ignite the priming pan, the 'snaphance', which had a cock containing flint that struck a moving steel, known as a 'frizzen'. Again, like the matchlock and the wheel-lock, this mechanism required the hunter to open the priming pan, which could be problematic in inclement weather – further improvement was needed. This came in the seventeenth century with the invention of the true flintlock. The flint struck the frizzen and the pan cover flipped open to receive the sparks, thus igniting the gun without loss of charge and less risk of weather ingress into the pan. It was also much easier to load and far more reliable than its predecessors. During this period when flintlocks were popular for hunting, pistol and sword combinations were manufactured.

There is little wonder that the flintlock lasted for more than two centuries, being perfected and engineered into some classic designs still found desirable by modern collectors. Several of the manufacturers of this period are still manufacturing guns today, and the shapes and styles we recognise now were being formed in the seventeenth century and evolving over time. There was a desire for the earlier flint-locks to be ornately decorated, but by the end of the eighteenth century, especially in Britain, there was a movement away from this, concentrating more upon the efficiency of the gun as a hunting weapon.

At about this time, in part due to the gun becoming eventually cheaper and more widely manufactured and therefore more accessible and reliable, its use in hunting by all classes of society widened. Despite being far better than their predecessors, these weapons were still prone to problems, especially weather-related ones. Flintlocks were prone to misfiring too. However, guns, because they were commonly used in war as well as by hunters, were proliferating in numbers, especially by the time the next great mechanical development in guns came along; this was the percussion system in 1807.

Developed and patented by Reverend Alexander Forsyth was a gun that could be fired by igniting a chemical charge, which was capable of exploding simply by being struck by a blow. Whilst this method was frowned upon by some at the time, partly due to the fact that the charge could not be used to propel the projectile because the force of the explosion was too great, it eventually caught on and there was a rush of gun makers keen to develop the best way of taking this idea forward. By the 1820s the percussion shotgun was favoured by hunters. This relied upon a hammer hitting a nipple that was primed with a small quantity of detonating material. When struck this sent a jet of flame into the powder charge. This popular weapon remained in existence until the twentieth century before finally disappearing. All of these guns were muzzle-loaders, which was their one main drawback – they could be fiddly and time consuming to load and required the hunter to carry various other items such as powder, wadding and ramrods to repeatedly load his gun whilst on the move. At best only three shots per minute could be mustered by skilled gunmen using this complicated paraphernalia and a well-rehearsed routine. Needless to say, in a war situation such delays could be very costly indeed and accidents were common, including double charges going off, killing or maiming the shooter. The breech-loading gun when it came was welcomed and has remained in use ever since with only minor refinements. Firstly pinfire shotguns came along, but were quickly replaced by the centre-fire system. In both systems a cartridge was developed that held both the powder and the shot, but in the pinfire system the cartridge had a projecting pin that stuck out from it and against the breech. The centre-fire cartridge had a primer fitted to its base and a hammer struck a firing pin, which passed through a hole into the breech.

During this time of early breech-loaded guns, cartridge pistols were also available, which gave inventors the inspiration to produce a whole assortment of peculiar hunting sword and pistol combinations. By the 1870s it was possible to get a hunting hangar with a scabbard that could be folded into a gunstock. Running parallel to these advancements in shotguns was the advancement of pro-pellants, with the old smoky, slightly unstable black powder giving ground to nitro

65 A hunter and his modern 17 HMR .22 calibre magnum rifle and scope

compounds, which were stable, smokeless and fast burning. These compounds are still in use today.

Much has happened in the last century or so where firearms are concerned, which is beyond the scope of this work to describe. There are many other texts that deal with the development of firearms for hunting and the legal and political issues that now surround hunting with firearms – many of which emerged in the last century or so (see Select Reading List).

8

Hunting Today: Where to Now?

Hunting to bring meat to the table is often considered to be an acceptable thing to do by a fair proportion of people; whilst hunting purely for the sake of killing animals, such as foxes, mink or deer, for sport and using dogs, termed 'blood sports', is viewed as unacceptable by many. There are also a significant number of people who have no view either way, who are indifferent to the issues. Some key points, however, on which there have been threads of discussion throughout this book, are worth summarising. Inherent to blood sports, like foxhunting and stag hunting, is an undeniably long tradition, going back centuries; the nature of these hunts was to some degree responsible for the shape and appearance of the British countryside as we know it today.

These sports have at some time or another (and arguably still do) served a function in controlling vermin or controlling numbers of deer so as to be sustainable. The control of vermin – the function of a foxhunt – is, its proponents say, designed to maintain a healthy fox population by weeding out the old and the infirm (often the culprits that kill chickens, geese and lambs because they are easier prey). Certainly the numbers of foxes killed by this method of hunting were not huge. The current situation, which allows the continuation of the sport in a different form, is more indiscriminate in the manner of kill and less selective of its prey and allows far fewer survivors. There has not been a proper assessment recently of numbers accounted for by these methods of hunting or their effect upon the fox population dynamics.

Hunting also serves a social function. Hunts tend to bring a whole network of people together who might not ordinarily have the opportunity or reason to come together; people who are involved in the care and supply of horses, like vets, livery yard owners or feed suppliers and farmers. Hunt followers come from a number of local towns and even cities. These hunts are in a way regular and important social occasions that allow people that are separated by distance and countryside, sometimes from remote farms or communities, to meet and discuss shared interests, hardships

66 A foxhunt. Bedale Hunt in Yorkshire's North Riding, by R. W. Sallis, 2005. (GNU Free Document license, Wikipedia)

and issues. Hunting gives them a shared passion, which means that there is a great deal of solidarity of purpose about issues they feel strongly about: issues such as rural life, the continuity of rural traditions and, of course, preserving their way of life, which they see as being under threat by people in towns who do not understand rural life and can sometimes view the countryside as a place managed for the purpose of their recreation.

There are also other types of hunting that are viewed as being distasteful, such as shooting pigeons, which in some circumstances is seen as a far less discriminate form of sport hunting. Sometimes hundreds or even thousands of birds are killed in a day, and this can seem far removed from hunting for necessity. In some circumstances, these hunters provide a vital service for farmers who can see their crops decimated by pigeons. At other times, though, there can seem little justification for the indiscriminate killing of pigeons piled up before the shooters for the group photograph. Yet there are those who perform this vital service of killing a few for the pot and this can sometimes be sufficient to control the problem.

Then, of course, there is the lucrative business of grouse, pheasant and partridge shooting, which can generate vital income for the rural economy, keeping historic houses and estates as functioning entities, for example. Some shoots allow farmers to diversify and continue farming, providing an important revenue stream for them and their families. Still other farmers raise young pheasants and various other game birds to stock estate shoots, again providing important revenue.

Whether or not this is a justifiable reason to have blood sports is not the place of this book to argue. Against the backdrop of this work, which has examined hunting in nearly all its forms across a great span of time, what can one say about man's relationship with hunting? What makes us continue to want to do it? What makes some people so vehemently opposed to it? These are challenging questions that would occupy however many volumes you would care to devote to them. All I can do is give a view as objectively as I can, based upon my researches. However, all people involved in active research of any kind will know that one's views, no matter how objectively presented, will be coloured by personal experience, lifestyle and political persuasions.

There are few issues more polarising or emotive politically than those that surround blood sports, and for those who are strongly for or strongly against, almost any argument one way or the other is not viewed as unbiased or objective. Fence sitters do not do well either. So it is against this background that I have written this.

In the United States there has been a long debate about the nature of hunting, particularly by those who seemingly indiscriminately kill deer and other game, dress it, then only take a choice cut and discard the rest of the animal. This testosterone-fuelled hunting, carried out by men who spend thousands of dollars on kitting out their Bronco 4x4 vehicles, spending vast fortunes on high-powered hunting rifles and scopes to kill a few deer a year, can in no way claim to do this for reasons of economy. The claimed reasoning behind this form of hunting is that man is born to hunt; that to not hunt is to deny our instincts and that the desire to kill animals is deeply ingrained into all men and that those who do not hunt are deficient. Yet, ironically, as of the early 1990s, the number of Americans who went hunting was only 12 per cent and this is an annually dwindling number.

Some, however, hunt only when they need to hunt and use the whole carcass, and these hunters also frown upon the significant number of wasteful 'sport hunters'. Plus there is a significant number of other hunters, who hunt wildfowl and the like, who disapprove of this sort of hunting too, as do the US Fish and Wildlife agents. Hunting has since the early twentieth century in the United States been an important tool in the development of conservation, so the near indiscriminate killing of animals in this way is not viewed as anything positive. A poll in the 1990s indicated that a third of Americans would like to see sport hunting banned. In Britain, the only thing that comes close to this kind of hunting is the activities of some organised gangs of poachers, who usually confine their more destructive activities to fishing. Sometimes a badly hit stretch of river can see stocks of salmon and trout collapse due to this type of activity – which is already prohibited by law. Otherwise, the poaching of deer and other game is somewhat more difficult. Gun laws, the system of permissions and a various other restrictions prevent making this type of activity widespread in Britain.

Oscar Wilde once penned the line about foxhunters 'the unspeakable in full pursuit of the uneatable'. He was nothing if not direct (and poetic) about the issue. This is where the attention of the anti-hunt movement has turned in Britain – primarily, but not exclusively to the foxhunt. Venetia Newall, in 1983, borrowed Oscar Wilde's famous title for a paper on class aspects in modern hunting, in which she concluded:

> It is difficult not to agree with the League's assessment of hunting as: 'A senseless and cruel sport … dressed up as a noble effort to rid the countryside of a pest' (League 5). It is also aristocratic and highly formalised, with a very specific dress, etiquette, and vocabulary – thus, one 'rides to hounds,' a dog's tail is a 'stern,' the red jackets are always referred to as 'pink,' and so on. In his *Theory of the Leisure Class* Thorstein Veblen suggests that people are basically motivated by a desire for status, and leisure pursuits often serve both a latent and manifest function (Veblen, 37ff). Let us conclude therefore, with Sasson reminiscing about his army days: 'Durley was an inspiration toward selfless

patience. He was an ideal platoon officer … I need hardly say that he has never hunted. He could swim like a fish, but no social status was attached to that' (Sassoon 303).

Against the background of the anti-hunt movement, and work such as Newall's paper quoted from above, is this question: is foxhunting, hunting in most or all of its forms in the modern age witnessing the beginning of the demise of what is the longest human tradition? This is quite a vexed question in the context of modern hunting and the 2004 law that banned the killing of animals using dogs, hailed as a victory by the anti-hunt lobby; conversely, hunts have seen their highest number of newcomers to the sport. Now these hunts have become drag hunts or hunts that despatch the fox with either a rifle or raptor. So was this a hollow victory for the anti-hunt lobby? And did the rise and rise of the hunts following the ban spell a new era of enthusiastic, albeit radically curtailed, hunting, propelled back into popularity because the media focus turned on what is viewed as a typically British tradition by many country people? Or was the victory outright, and the tide of public opinion on the side of the anti-hunt campaigners, who say they will continue to fight for a ban on all forms of hunting and fishing: collectively termed 'blood sports'?

The anti-hunt movement

In order to get a balanced picture it is worth reviewing the growth of the anti-hunt movement from its earliest beginnings to weigh against the subject of this book, which has examined the start of and the growth of hunting and its waxing and waning through time. There have always been those involved with hunting or at its periphery who have voiced their rejection or displeasure to some forms of sport hunting. However, history seldom records their viewpoints. For example, monastic orders in the Middle Ages sometimes noted their disdain for *par force* hunting, but we do not get much of a sense of how deep that resentment for the activity ran due to the politics and patronage system of the time. It is in the nineteenth century that the first real shoots of the anti-hunt movement began to sprout. Britain has a deep history of animal welfare reform, starting early in the first half of the nineteenth century with a Christian evangelical committee movement intent upon banning the barbaric acts of animal baiting – The Society for the Suppression of Vice. In 1822 Richard Martin passed an Act to Prevent the Cruel and Improper Treatment of Cattle, apparently the first parliamentary animal welfare act ever passed anywhere in the world. Richard Martin was an Irish politician who, when the Act of Union dissolved the Irish Parliament, was forced to represent his constituents at Westminster in London, where, through his endeavours to prevent cruelty, he earned the nickname 'Humanity Dick'. Martin had an interesting life, which aside from politics included participating in over a hundred duels, which earned him another nickname 'Hair-trigger Dick', and he was present at the start of the American Revolutionary War and the French Revolution. Accused of parliamentary intimidation during an election, and unseated after a petition in 1826, he had to flee the country due to bad debts and spent the rest of his life in exile in France. But just two years before, on 16 June 1824, he witnessed the formation of the Society for the Prevention of Cruelty to Animals (SPCA) in a London coffee shop – although he denied being its founder, he was clearly instrumental in its early formation.

The year 1835 turned out to be a momentous year in the movement, when the acts of bear, badger and bull-baiting became illegal (Cruelty to Animals Act 1835) and Princess Victoria became the patron of the SPCA, eventually adding the title 'Royal' to it on her crowning in 1837. The 1835 act was repealed and replaced by the 1849 act, which was expanded and amended into the 1876 Cruelty to Animals Act, which included controls on the use of animals in experiments and stood until 1986. The National Anti-Vivisection Society was formed just the year before in 1875.

Henry Salt, a writer and social reformer and committed anti-vivisectionist campaigner, formed the Humanitarian League in 1891, and one of its key objectives was the banning of hunting as a sport. The Humanitarian League published a book of essays titled *Killing for Sport*, with a preface written by George Bernard Shaw, which outlined the League's stance where hunting was concerned. And in 1911 another act was passed: the Protection of Animals Act, which outlawed 'unnecessary suffering', but this still did not pertain to wild or hunted animals.

The Humanitarian League was the forerunner of the League Against Cruel Sports (or more accurately League for the Prohibition of Cruel Sports, as it was called at the time), formed in Morden, now in London, in 1923, which issued its charter, 'What we Stand For', in 1924. This was almost in response to what was seen as the inactivity of the RSPCA on the issue of hunting – an area they showed reluctance to get publicly involved in, presumably in an effort to retain their royal patronage and support; royalty, after all, were hunters and hunt supporters. The league started after Henry Amos protested about local rabbit coursing and managed to achieve a ban; spurred on by this, he organised opposition to blood sports with Ernest Bell, forming the League for the Prohibition of Cruel Sports.

Bear, bull and badger-baiting were already illegal at this point and this was the first time there was a real push for the abolition of other forms of blood sports such as hunting. This in itself raised interesting questions about class and social position in society at the time, with the ban on cock-fighting, bear-baiting and badger-baiting seen as lower-class activities being banned whilst foxhunting was not. It was as if these activities were more barbaric because they were done by the lower classes, whilst the hunting pursuits of the upper classes were much more noble.

By 1927 the league had over 1000 members, drawn from all parts of society, including the aristocracy – some of whom became ardent and influential campaigners for them. By the 1940s the league was very well established, particularly gaining the support of many famous people of the day, including actress Yvonne Arnaud, who became the president of the league from 1948–51. Later, in 1960, Patrick Moore the astronomer became its patron. The league was always able to draw upon the intellectual and artistic elite of the age, right from its inception: the league received letters of support at its formation meeting from Bertrand Russell and the soon-to-be Prime Minister Ramsey McDonald. Today, its president is the Scottish actress Annette Crosbie.

The league came into its own after the Second World War and a sustained campaign, which was supported by a couple of sympathetic newspapers (one being the *Daily Express*), a cast of A-list stars of the day and growing public support, especially away from the countryside. A new element grew out of the post-war period of intense activity, especially into the politically more radicalised 'Swinging 60s'. These spin-offs from the league gave rise to the 'Hunt Saboteur'. John Prestige formed the Hunt Saboteur Association in 1964 in Brixham, London, and groups appeared soon after in other parts of England including Devon and Birmingham. The techniques of the hunt saboteur included using hunting horns and whistles to misdirect hunts, lying false scent trails and padlocking gates to cause obstruction. Later, using film and photography to capture images and footage that aided their cause, they began to influence the wider public through the media in a way that had never been seen before. For example, they took photographs of lairs constructed on the Duke of Beaufort's land, built by the hunt to encourage their numbers. The activities of hunt saboteurs still carry on not just in Britain but also in the USA and Europe to disrupt everything from deer and hare hunts to fishing.

In 1960 Patrick Moore, a life-long animal lover and opponent of blood sports, introduced an 'anti-hunting' motion at the AGM of the RSPCA that was defeated, no doubt as a result of worries over upsetting royal supporters of the society. However, a subsequent postal vote showed that there was support from over 80 per cent of the membership for the motion, and in the 1970s a number of anti-hunt reformers were elected to the council of the RSPCA, marking the beginnings of a sea change in the organisation. In 1976 it adopted a policy to oppose all hunting with hounds. In 1970 a bill was voted on in the House of Commons to ban coursing and was won by 203 to 70 votes, but it was killed in the subsequent general election. The Wildlife and Countryside Act of 1981 was instrumental in preventing landowners from killing badgers and gave hefty fines if they did. But a legal loophole meant that hunters could kill a badger and get away with it by claiming that the hunt was after foxes. In 1985 this loophole was plugged by presuming that an offence was committed, placing the onus upon the hunters to prove that their presence and activity at a sett was not for hunting badgers.

In 1988 a coalition effort by a number of animal welfare and wildlife organisations eventually saw, after a highly successful and high profile prosecution of a group of badger baiters in Wales, the creation of the Badger Sett (Protection) Act. This finally outlawed the destruction of badger setts. Since the 1960s the activities of a number of foxhunts have come under increasing pressure and scrutiny, particularly in the 1980s and 1990s, when hunt saboteurs and animal welfare campaigners applied a vice-like grip by successfully encouraging almost continuous media coverage that showed hunts being disrupted by their efforts. This different sort of 'noble cause' was to finally turn the tide of political opinion against the foxhunter.

The demise of a tradition?

THE HUNTING ACT 2004

The history of hunting from the late twentieth century into the early millennium has been coloured by the anti-hunt movement, with their great achievement coming on Friday, 18 February 2005, when a ban on hunting using dogs became law. This is what the BBC had to say about the moment:

> At the stroke of midnight centuries of tradition came to an end, when hunting with hounds became illegal.
>
> BBC News website, 18 February 2005

The lead-up to this ban encompassed a number of earlier attempts to ban or curtail the hunting of foxes, particularly since 1949, with the introduction of two private members' bills to the House of Commons. One was to ban hunting, the other to restrict foxhunting – both failed to make it onto the statute books. It was not until 1992 that another private member's bill was proposed in the Commons by Labour MP Kevin McNamara, titled the Wild Mammals (Protection) Bill. This too was defeated at its second reading. A year later, Labour MP Tony Banks tried and failed to table the Fox Hunting (Abolition) Bill, followed by another unsuccessful attempt by MP John McFall. However, a potential victory looked to be within sight as the Wild Mammals (Protection) Bill, heavily edited, returned to Commons and passed its second reading, only to be rejected by the Lords.

In May 1997 the Labour Party, with Tony Blair as leader, won the general election, and as part of its manifesto it stated that there would be 'a free vote in Parliament on whether hunting with hounds should be banned'. Then MP Michael Foster (Labour) produced a private member's bill to ban hunting with dogs, but the government refused to grant any parliamentary time to it. This obstacle was overcome and by March 1998 the bill had its second reading. Following this, the Countryside Alliance held a huge protest rally in London, attracting over 250,000 people protesting against the bill and the threat it posed to rural life. The bill ran out of time during the report stage and pro-hunt MPs tabled several hundred amendments, blocking its progress. Foster withdrew his bill in July 1998 but predicted that foxhunting would be banned in the current Parliament.

The following year Tony Bair made an announcement, much to the surprise of some, that he planned to make foxhunting illegal before the next general election. At the time there were accusations that this announcement and sudden intent was linked to a £1 million donation to the Labour Party by the Political Animal Lobby, a wholly owned subsidary of the International Fund for Animal Welfare, a group that is also lobbying for the establishment of an Animal Welfare Commission or Ministry. This group had also made donations to the Conservatives and the Liberal Democrat parties in the past. Some political manoeuvring went on over the course of the next few months and Tony Blair reiterated that he was confident the ban would be in force before the next election, but reforms to the House of Lords made this seem unlikely.

In February 2001 hunting was suspended due to foot and mouth disease, which was raging across Britain. Also in February, another bill was passed through Commons by a majority of 179 but failed at the Lords by 317 to 68 votes; finally it ran out of time when the general election was called. The issue came back in June 2001 in the Queen's Speech, when another free vote was promised. That autumn over 200 MPs backed a motion calling on the government to honour its promises to make time to vote on a ban on hunting.

Interestingly, there had been a parallel series of responses followed by local governments; for example, in 1993 Oxfordshire County Council voted to ban hunting on land that they owned or controlled, and a Japanese researcher at Oxford University, Kaoru Fukuda, stated that 'according to the League Against Cruel Sports by 1992 over 120 local councils have banned hunting on land that they own or control'. Some responses by local authorities on such matters could be described as knee-jerk or slightly bizarre, such as the incidence of angling being banned on a stretch of river near Bewdley in 2002 by the local council, because the use of lead in weights posed a risk to swans – even though the use of most lead weights by anglers had been banned for 15 years.

In response to criticism of inactivity on its manifesto pledge to ban foxhunting Labour commissioned an inquiry led by Lord Burns to establish the facts about the sport in 1999. The report, released in June 2000, found that there were over 200 active packs in England and Wales and that the number of foxes killed was between 21,000 and 25,000 per year (see Appendix 1 for a list of packs in the British Isles active in the mid to late twentieth century). The Burns Report also found that there were a high number of foxes dug out by landowners, farmers and gamekeepers and shot each year. In Devon and Somerset, three staghound packs accounted for 160 red deer per year. Burns also reported that there would be a likely detrimental effect upon the rural economy but that the relationship between sectors of the rural economy and foxhunting was a complex one. Around 6000 to 8000 jobs were dependent on foxhunting in some form or another, and that 3000 jobs were hunt related and included businesses such as livery yards, kennel workers, knackermen and people working in the clothing industries that made the 'pinks' of the huntsmen; he claimed a ban on hunting could have a deleterious short- to medium-term effect upon the rural economy, perhaps lasting up to a decade.

Burns also found that there was far more rural community support for foxhunting than he had expected, and that the role and function of the hunt upon the social fabric of some communities was important. There is a strong relationship between farming and foxhunting, with many farmers being Masters of Hounds and participating in hunts, or at the very least having family members who participate. The social network that foxhunting provides acts to bring together people who are isolated in the countryside and supplies other benefits such as voluntary staffing for pony clubs and point-to-point meets. However, Burns also found that some rural communities found foxhunting to be 'divisive, intrusive and disruptive'. There have always been different opinions as to the necessity of foxhunting: some landowners and farmers have claimed they have lost considerable numbers of livestock to foxes, whilst others report that they have suffered only limited losses to foxes and regard the sport as unnecessary.

In terms of fox numbers, Lord Burns ascertained that there was a pre-breeding annual population of 217,000 foxes, and that most farmers and landowners believed this population needed to be managed to prevent livestock losses. The report found that foxhunting only accounted for a small number of foxes killed each year (21,000 to 25,000 per annum) but that in the upland areas of Britain dogs were better suited to controlling the numbers. The data for deer was viewed differently because there was a need for culling, and the report concluded that of the 1000 deer culled annually, hunting with hounds only accounted for 15 per cent, and that if banned, there would need to be other forms of management implemented – an already problematic issue, with higher numbers needing to be culled in certain areas due to an unsustainably large population of deer.

Viewed in terms of animal welfare, the report concluded that if hunting with dogs was banned then farmers and landowners would implement other control measures that would kill foxes more frequently and in greater numbers; it also said that fox-hunting 'seriously compromises the welfare of the fox' and that lamping had the best outcomes for fox welfare in terms of control.

In September 2001, however, hunt supporters formed a body called the Independent Supervisory for Hunting, whose role was to ensure that hunting was carried out in a 'proper and humane manner', and was heralded as the first step to strict self-regulation of hunting, something that was favoured instead of an outright ban. But a year earlier in 2000 Jack Straw, the then Home Secretary, had looked at three possible directions that the law on hunting could take, including strict regulation. After some refinement, by 2002 the House of Commons and House of Lords had before them three options to choose from: 1) a complete ban; 2) keeping the status quo, unregulated hunting; or 3) a compromise of licensed foxhunting. Predictably, the Commons opted for an outright ban whilst the Lords chose licensing. Following on from this came the 'Liberty and Livelihood' march on 22 September 2002, which saw 400,000 marchers take to the streets of central London, their main focus being to voice their opposition to the hunting ban.

In December 2002 the leader of the Commons revealed the Hunting Bill that would allow some foxhunting to continue under a strict licensing system but would outlaw hare coursing and stag hunting. He hoped that the compromise outlined in this document would prevent it falling at the mainly pro-hunt Lords. Four days later a motion was tabled by Tony Banks proposing a complete ban on hunting, which passed by 362 votes to 154. Two days later again, after a day of intense debate in the Commons, the Hunting Bill was turned into an outright ban, with an identical number of votes in favour. It then cleared the Commons after a third reading on 10 July 2003. It reached the Lords in October and a cross-party group of peers virtually rewrote the bill, rejecting the MPs' complete ban on hunting in favour of licensing fox and stag hunting and hare coursing. Back in the Commons the anti-hunt MPs voted for it to be rewritten yet again to become a complete ban, and it was again rejected in the Lords; once again it ran out of parliamentary time.

2004 proved to be an eventful year for the government and the Hunting Bill with the announcement that there would be another free vote on the issue in September, followed by another vote in favour of an outright ban from the Commons. This saw violent demonstrations outside Parliament with a number of pro-hunt supporters gaining access to the House of Commons chamber. The bill was again rejected by the Lords, despite threats from Alun Michael that if no compromise could be reached by the peers then the use of the Parliament Act would be invoked to make an outright ban law. In November 2004 the Hunting Act was pushed into law by use of the Parliament Act, with the ban due to come into force by 18 February 2005. Two legal challenges mounted by pro-hunt supporters and then the Countryside Alliance were rejected by the High Court and finally the Court of Appeal.

Given the different opinions or views on the necessity of foxhunting versus other forms of control, and what constitutes reasonable treatment of the quarry, means there has been some exploration of how rural and urban society view hunting. It has been mentioned from the Burns Report that there was significant rural support for foxhunting, which is very likely to be at odds with the data obtained from cities and towns. MORI carried out a poll for the BBC in February 2005 on the issue of hunting, posing the question: 'To what extent do you support or oppose a ban on hunting with dogs?' This showed that pro-hunting had 26 per cent support, anti-hunting 47 per cent support, whilst 27 per cent said that they did not know or were of no opinion on the issue. Overall the results showed that less than 50 per cent of the population favoured the ban on hunting, ostensibly showing that the nation was very much divided on the issue. At the time the biggest complaint about the hunting ban was the amount of parliamentary time devoted to the issue, which had detracted from what many thought were more pressing issues.

The Hunting Act 2004 heralded a major change in the way of life of many rural communities, signalling for them the end of several centuries of rural tradition. In essence, the Hunting Act 2004 comprises the following legal points:

> It is an offence to hunt a wild mammal with a dog
> Some forms of hunting are exempt including:
> Using no more than two dogs to flush out a mammal to be shot
> Flushing a mammal from cover in connection with falconry
> It is a defence to believe that the hunting was exempt
> (BBC website. The Hunting Act 2004 is reproduced in full in Appendix 2)

Since the ban on hunting there has been an increase in the popularity of hunting with hounds, with many more subscribers to hunts throughout the country. Many hunts have now become drag hunts, or they work within the letter of the law and use dogs to flush the foxes, but then use raptors or a rifle to kill them. Both methods account for higher numbers of kills and the use of a raptor is not the least stressful way to be killed. Saboteurs, controversially, have now cast themselves in the role of 'hunt monitors' to ensure that the hunts do not illegally kill foxes. Recently, accusations have been cast against monitors for their possible role in the death of a hunt supporter in Warwickshire, after they used a camera mounted upon a motorised model helicopter, which crashed into him. Also, many hunts report that the tactics of monitors border or even transgress from reasonable behaviour by the way they can obstruct the progress of hunts and harass the participants. This has now opened a debate about the wisdom of allowing former saboteurs to cast themselves as suitable people to monitor hunts.

A realisation of our nature?

Hunting in the British Isles, particularly foxhunting, is held up by many as being symbolic of Britain and a sport that defines our Britishness. *The Spectator* magazine in April 2008 used an image of a hunter clearing a fence on its front cover, with the headline 'England Rides Again' to proclaim that the English were reclaiming their identity and redefining St George's Day as a day for the English to celebrate their Englishness (see Colour plate 22). Some argue that foxhunting is quite the opposite and that it defines the worst of Britain, being a country that is rooted in an ancient and elitist barbaric sport.

Opinions vary as to the value of the foxhunt in controlling numbers of foxes in rural areas, with geographers and biologists sometimes presenting differing views. A study in rural Wiltshire conducted prior to the ban indicated that the role of hunting was purely sporting and had limited value in controlling fox numbers. It cited the results of an earlier nationwide (England) study, that recorded foxhunting with dogs only had a 5 per cent effect upon fox mortality. The authors also added that hunting in Wiltshire was tolerated rather than encouraged by farmers. Curiously, this was at odds with another study and a widely known statistic that many Masters of Hounds in Britain are farmers.

Geographers from Newcastle University disputed the findings of the Burns Report, which claimed that hunting has an effect upon the rural economy and that by switching to non-quarry hunts there could actually be an economic benefit derived from the lack of disruption and reduced damage to property that hunting causes. Another study carried out during the one-year ban on hunting between 2000 and 2001, due to foot and mouth disease, looked at fox faecal densities in selected areas and compared them to the year before; it found that there was no perceptible difference in fox numbers. Another study examined the land management practices of 92 hunts covering 75,514 km² and found that they were active in maintaining and improving 24,053 (+/− 2441) ha (a conservative estimate) of woodland. They had at sometime in the preceding five years tree-planted, coppiced trees or had performed perimeter management, and in all instances where these works had occurred, the researchers noted an increase in plant, insect, and particularly butterfly diversity.

These differing views and studies highlight many social concerns and animal welfare issues to hunting with dogs; they also indicate key benefits too. However, it is public perception that holds sway, and perhaps more critically their perception of the class system and hunting's role in reproducing that system for the benefit of a social elite. The sport is certainly cheaper (relative to income) and more inclusive than it used to be, but the perception of it being an expensive upper-class sport is difficult to shake. Hunting with dogs, hawking, game shooting and fishing are at a defining moment in their history, and all these sports are critically examining themselves with an eye to the future and possibly their very survival. It is the positive benefits, such as conservation and countryside management, that they hope the urban population will see and benefit from by allowing and encouraging the survival of these sports.

All this comes at a time when there is a dawning realisation that humans have perhaps never really fitted in to the natural world as we thought we had. The idea that man and nature coexisted in harmony when humans were in their hunter–gatherer state is slowly being turned on its head by evidence from the southern hemisphere, which strongly indicates that humans caused the extinction of megafauna in Tasmania and Australia. This evidence suggests that the extinction of megafauna, such as the giant wombat, 3m-tall kangaroos and marsupial lions, long thought to have been made extinct by the changing climate, were actually made extinct in a 2000-year period-shortly after humans arrived during a phase of suitable and stable climatic conditions.

After a revaluation of the data there is evidence that suggests this pattern was repeated elsewhere, such as in Europe, Britain and North America. It seems that humans actually did hunt these animals to extinction, or at the very least contributed to their demise along with other factors such as changing climate. It took time for humans to realise their impact upon the wildlife and the effect this was having on them in turn. Sometimes, it seems, humans learnt too late and killed off their food sources. This paints a far from perfect view of man-the-hunter living in harmony with his fellow creatures, as hunter-conservator and custodian of a pristine wilderness habitat; all the evidence points to humans being destroyers and alterers of their environment, adapting it to suit their needs. From the cutting of the wildwood after the end of the last glacial and into the Bronze Age, and beyond to the creation of deer parks (possibly as early as the Roman period in Britain) and the forests in the medieval period, the extinction of the boar, bears and the wolf, hunting along with farming has always played a part in changing the British environment and landscape.

Recently, relatively speaking, people have noticed the effects of humans on the environment, and realised that what we see in the 'natural' world, particularly in Britain, is really the work of man's heavy hand. We have seen too that the accelerating pace of animal extinction is the result of climate change and overpopulation, yet because humans need time and space to change and make changes we are effectively powerless to stop the extinctions. In other words, for the most part we care about the world that we live in, but we are constrained by our need for economic growth and improving our standard of living and having useful items of technology. We wish to be able to drive our cars by ourselves to work and to travel cheaply and more frequently to overseas destinations. We want the better houses, better forms of entertainment, better schools and better hospitals, and all this has a cost – particularly on the natural world. A result of the collective ability to see our impact on the world is the capacity to see what needs to be done to correct our mistakes, or at least ameliorate our impacts on the environment. All this is too big a topic for this book but hunting is part and parcel of the subject of where our food comes from and how it is produced.

Organic farming, once the norm, was then replaced in the Agricultural Revolution by intensive farming, familiar to most by the term 'factory farming', but has returned to us once again in recent decades. People realise that this is one way we can engage with the natural world favourably and probably with benefit to our health and well-being. Even more recently there has been a movement towards buying beef and lamb at the farm gate, so to speak, directly sourcing from the farmer for the freezer. Also increasing in popularity is growing vegetables at home, and rearing chickens for eggs and meat. The media has become suffused with programmes such as *River Cottage* and *Jamie at Home*, and various specialist magazines as well as many newspaper articles are expounding the virtues of organic home-grown vegetables. Like the fox, the home-rearing of chickens has spread to urban areas too – and with this has come a realisation that the fox can be a menace, sometimes killing all the chickens kept by a household.

In the 1980s it was estimated that over 400,000 Bovine Spongiform Encephalitis (BSE) infected cattle entered the human food chain and was directly linked to the emergence of variant Creutzfeldt-Jacob Disease (CJD), which by April 2008 had killed 163 people in Britain. Also, the issue of battery chickens for producing eggs: Edwina Currie's inappropriate comments about salmonella in eggs in 1988, and the more recent controversy surrounding the production and rearing of factory chickens for meat by celebrity chefs, has done much to galvanise support for organic and home-grown and produced foods. An interest in wild foods has grown alongside this minor revolution and there has been a significant growth and attendance of agricultural and game fairs in recent years. For example, the CLA game fair, now in its 50th year, had a record 150,000 plus visitors – a new record. All this may account for the rise in the popularity of shooting and fishing in recent years as well.

A final word

Before I finish there are a couple of points to note. Firstly, and perhaps most critically, there has been little work of the nature of the current book which seeks to join up all of the periods of hunting, to give an overview and consider issues that might arise when doing so. Secondly, there seems to be a political element that has been difficult to avoid in the writing of this work; it pervades some areas of the academic research into this topic in the form of a general distaste for dealing with this subject, especially where any form of elite hunting is discussed. Inevitably, much of a work like this will focus upon elite hunting, and makes specific areas of research linked to this topic difficult to find decent, current and relevant research on. Other researchers, such as Richard Almond, have commented on this in their works too.

There are whole areas, even in prehistoric archaeology, which have been affected by a reluctance to research the topic of hunting, possibly because there is simply a general distaste by researchers, and more significantly within academia generally, for the topic of hunting, its attendant symbolism and the socio-political issues it gives rise to. I hope that I have shown that by taking a 'holistic' approach to the subject it need not be affected by the weight of political baggage related to current issues surrounding blood sports and elite hunting. Hunting, like most human endeavours, is simply a way of life for some people in Britain today; but in the past it was for most or all people, depending where in time you stood. As such, to enrich the disciplines of archaeology and history, and bring hunting into the research mainstream – where it deserves to stand – this nettle must finally be grasped.

We have seen that there is a connection between prehistory and the present which suggests that the origins of our land tenure may be based upon forms of ancient land tenure associated with hunting. Traditionally, archaeologists and landscape historians have examined land tenure as having its origins in agriculture, which I would suggest is looking at the issue backwards. As archaeologists and historians we follow trends through time, and the social and physical (such as landscape) effects they had on the way to the present. Yet where this issue is concerned we have tended to work from the modern agricultural point of view, apply it to the past and then work forwards again whilst looking at those societal and physical changes with skewed vision. The reason we do this is, I suspect, largely lost to us, but it probably started in the early days of these disciplines, particularly archaeology, with the assumption that as agriculture is a wonderful thing and was, in its early days, of such earth-shattering importance, it must have radically shifted our perspective on the world.

We have since learned many things about the early Neolithic: it was neither unexpected nor particularly earth-shattering for the people of Britain, nor indeed in many places in the Near East or Europe. It came slowly – not by great invasions of people carrying boats full of grain and sheep. Yet knowing this we seem reluctant to shift our own perspectives on some key elements of the past. I suspect we would gain new perspectives on the nature of land tenure and landscape archaeology if we did.

In summary, what I have shown here in this book is that hunting has been a critical and inescapable thread running throughout the full length of human occupation of the British Isles (some 700,000 plus years), it is our longest continuous tradition, it has shaped land tenure as we understand it today and it has been hugely influential in shaping the British countryside and its landscapes. It has shaped rural traditions, and links us inescapably to the very food we eat in ways that we are scarcely aware of. Most importantly, hunting is hugely undervalued in the contribution it makes to the archaeology and history of the British countryside, and I hope that this book has made a critical first step in taking a more holistic view of the role and importance of hunting in archaeology and landscape studies.

Appendix I

List of Hunts in Britain and Ireland in the Mid-Twentieth Century

List of Hunts in 1952
(Possibly revised in 1975: From Summerhays' *Encyclopedia for Horsemen*)

Foxhounds

ENGLAND AND WALES

Aber Valley	Snowdonia
Albrighton	Staffordshire and Shropshire
Albrighton Woodland	Shropshire, Staffordshire and Worcestershire
Ashford Valley	The Weald of Kent and the Ashford-Tenterden-Headcorn district
Atherstone	Greater part in Leicestershire and Warwickshire
Avon Vale	Melksham, Devizes and Trowbridge
Axe Vale	Seaton, Axminster and Honiton
Badsworth	Adjoining Grove and Bramham Moor in Yorkshire
Banwen Miners	West Glamorgan
Barlow	North-east Derbyshire and small part of Yorkshire
Beaufort's, Duke of	Gloucestershire, Somerset and Wiltshire
Bedale	North Riding of Yorkshire
Belvoir (*beevor*)	(Duke of Rutland's) Leicestershire and Lincolnshire

Berkeley	Gloucestershire. Adjoining Cotswold and Ledbury, and in the east the Beaufort
Berkshire, Old	Berkshire and Oxfordshire. Adjoining the Heythrop in the north, the V.W.H. (Crickdale) in the west, and the Craven in the south
Bewcastle	Borders of Scotland, Northumberland and Cumberland
Bicester (*bister*) and Warden Hill	Oxfordshire, Buckinghamshire and Northamptonshire
Bilsdale	Thirsk, Stokesley and Helmsley, Yorkshire
Bisley and Sandhurst	Surrey and Hampshire
Blackmore and Sparkford Vale	Dorset and Somerset
Blankney	Lincolnshire and Nottinghamshire
Blencathra	Cumberland
Border	North-west Northumberland, Roxburghshire
Braes of Derwent	South Northumberland and north-west of Durham
Bramham Moor	The West Riding of Yorkshire, adjoining the York and Ainsty in the north and east and the Badsworth in the south
Brecon	Breconshire, but does not include Tallybont and district
Brocklesby	Lincolnshire
Burton	The northern half of Lincolnshire
Cambridgeshire	Cambridgeshire, Huntingdonshire and Bedfordshire
Carmarthenshire	Best Centres, Carmarthen, St Clears, Whitland and Llanboidy
Cattistock (catstock)	Dorset and small part of Somerset
Cheshire	Most of Cheshire
Cheshire Forest	The Wirral Peninsula
Chiddingfold, Leconfield and Cowdray	Surrey and Sussex
Cleveland	North Riding of Yorkshire
Clifton-on-Teme	Worcestershire and Herefordshire
College Valley	Northumberland
Coniston	Partly in Westmoreland, partly in North Lancashire
Cornwall, East	Liskeard district

Cornwall, North	From Boscastle and Padstow Bay on the north coast, to Fowey in the south
Cotley	Devon, Somerset and Dorset
Cotswold	Gloucestershire
Cotswold, North	Gloucestershire and Worcestershire
Cotswold Vale Farmers'	Around Cheltenham and Gloucester
Cottesmore (*cotsmore*)	Rutland, Leicestershire and Lincolnshire
Crawley and Horsham	Sussex, from Rudgwick to the sea
Croome and West Warwickshire	Worcestershire, Warwickshire and Gloucestershire
Cumberland	Wholly in Cumberland
Cumberland Farmers'	Around Penrith and Carlisle
Curre	Monmouthshire, around Chepstow
Cury	The Lizard peninsula to the sea
Dartmoor	Devon
David Davies	Montgomeryshire
Derwent	The North Riding of Yorkshire
Devon, East	South-east Devon
Devon, Mid	The Dartmoor district
Devon, South	Dorset. Best centres, Dorchester and Blandford
Dulverton, East	South-east edge of Exmoor
Dulverton, West	North Devon and West Somerset
Durham, South	County Durham. Best centres, Darlington and Stockton
Eggesford	Devon. Best centres, Eggesford and Okehampton
Enfield Chace	Hertfordshire and Middlesex
Eridge	Sussex. Best centres, Tunbridge Wells and Crowborough
Eskdale and Ennerdale	Cumberland, Westmoreland and Lancashire
Essex	Best centres, High Roding, Harlow, Ongar and Dunmow
Essex, East	North-west and East Essex
Essex Farmers'	Mostly between Rivers Crouch and Blackwater
Essex and Suffolk	Partly in Essex and partly in Suffolk
Essex Union	South-east Essex around Billericay and Chelmsford
Exmoor	Devon and Somerset

Farndale	North Riding of Yorkshire. Best centres, Castleton and Kirby Moorside
Fernie	South Leicestershire
Fitzwilliam (Milton)	Northamptonshire and Huntingdonshire
Flint and Denbigh	The western parts of Flintshire and Denbighshire
Four Burrow (*forbrer*)	The Truro, Falmouth and Helston districts of Cornwall
Garth and South Berks	Principally in Berkshire, with corners of Surrey, Hampshire and Oxfordshire
Gelligaer Farmers'	North-east Glamorganshire and parts of Monmouthshire
Glaisdale	The North Riding of Yorkshire. Best centres, Glaisdale, Leadholm, Danby End and Roxby
Glamorgan	Cowbridge district of Glamorganshire
Goathland	The North Riding of Yorkshire
Gogerddan	The west of Cardiganshire
Golden Valley	Herefordshire and Radnorshire
Goschen's, Mr	West Sussex, Hampshire and Surrey
Grafton	South Northamptonshire and North Buckinghamshire
Grove and Rufford	Nottinghamshire, Yorkshire and Derbyshire
Hambledon	Hampshire
Hampshire ('H.H.')	Aldershot to Winchester, and Basingstoke to West Meon. Best centre Alton
Haydon	The south-west corner of Northumberland
Herefordshire, North	Hereford, Leominster and Bromyard
Herefordshire, South	Between Hereford, Ross-on-Wye, Perterchurch and Whitchurch
Heythrop (*heethrop*)	Oxfordshire and Gloucestershire
Holderness	The East Riding of Yorkshire
Hursley	Part of Hampshire and Wiltshire between Winchester, Salisbury and Southampton
Hurworth	Between South Durham and North Yorkshire
Irfon and Towy	North Breconshire

Isle of Wight	Newport, Ryde, Shanklin, Sandown and Freshwater
Kent, East	Canterbury, Folkstone and Ashford
Kent, West	Sevenoaks and Tonbridge
Lamerton	West Devon and north-east Cornwall
Ledbury	Herefordshire, Worcestershire and Gloucestershire
Ledbury, North	North of Ledbury and Malvern, on the borders of Herefordshire and Worcestershire
Llandeilo	Carmarthenshire and Glamorgan
Llangeinor	Glamorgan
Llangeitho	Mid-Cardiganshire
Llangibby	Monmouthshire
Lonsdale, North	The portion of Lonsdale not including Low Furness and the Duddon Valley
Ludlow	Shropshire, Herefordshire and Worcestershire
Lunesdale	North, south and east Westmoreland and parts of North Lancashire and the West Riding of Yorkshire
Melbreak	West Cumberland
Mendip Farmers'	Bristol, Bath, Wells and Shepton Mallet
Meynell (*menel*) and South Staffordshire	Derbyshire, South Staffordshire and Warwickshire
Middleton	The North and East Ridings of Yorkshire
Milvain (Percy)	Northumberland
Monmouthshire	The northern half of Monmouthshire and small coverts in Herefordshire
Morpeth	South Northumberland
New Forest	Hampshire, and a small part of Wiltshire
Norfolk, West	Best Centres, East Dereham, Swaffham, Fakenham and King's Lynn
Northumberland, North	Cornhill-on-Tweed, Berwick and Wooler
Nottinghamshire, South	Nottingham, Newark and Bingham

Oakley	Bedfordshire, Buckinghamshire, Northamptonshire and Huntingdonshire
Pembrokeshire	North of Milford Haven in Pembrokeshire
Pembrokeshire, South	The Tenby and Pembroke districts with some coverts in Carmarthenshire
Pendle Forest and Craven	*see* Harriers
Pennine	The Pennine Range, from Malhamdale and Wharfedale to Edale and Derwentdale
Pentyrch	East Glamorgan, between Cardiff and Pontypridd
Percy	Northumberland
Percy (West)	Northumberland
Portman	Dorset, Wiltshire and Hampshire
Puckeridge and Thurlow	Hertfordshire, Essex, Suffolk and Cambridgeshire
Pytchley	Northamptonshire and Leicestershire
Pytchley, Woodland	Northamptonshire
Quorn	Mainly in Leicestershire, with coverts in Derbyshire and Nottinghamshire
Radnorshire and West Herefordshire	North-west Herefordshire and parts of Radnorshire
Royal Artillery	Wiltshire. Between West Lavington, Wylye, Salisbury and Tidworth
Saltersgate Farmers'	Yorkshire. Between Whitby and Pickering
Seavington	Dorset and Somerset
Sennybridge and District Farmers'	Breconshire, around Sennybridge and Brecon
Shropshire, North	Shrewsbury, Wem and Wellington
Shropshire, South	South of Shrewsbury
Shropshire, West	Around Oswestry
Silverton	The Exeter district of Devonshire
Sinnington	The North Riding of Yorkshire
Snowdon Valley	Caernarvonshire
Somerset, West	Between the Bredon Hills and the sea

Somerset Vale, West (formerly Quantock Farmers')	From Bridgewater to the Quantock Hills
Southdown	The Sussex Seaboard
South Wold	Lincolnshire. Extending from Louth, adjoining the Brocklesby, to Boston in the south, and from the sea to the Burton country in the west
Spooner's and West Dartmoor	Chiefly on Dartmoor
Staffordshire, North	North of Stafford town, bordering Shropshire, Cheshire and Derbyshire
Staintondale	North Riding of Yorkshire, between Scarborough and Whitby
Stevenstone	North Devon
Suffolk	West Suffolk
Surrey and Burstow, Old	Surrey, Sussex and Kent
Surrey Union	The North Downs from Horsham to Guildford
Sussex, East, and Romney Marsh	Battle, Hastings, Bexhill, Eastbourne and West Kent
Tallybont	Breconshire, bordering Monmouthshire
Tanatside	East Montgomeryshire to the borders of Shropshire
Taunton Vale	The Taunton district of Somerset
Tedworth	Wiltshire and Hampshire
Teme Valley	Radnorshire, Herefordshire and Shropshire
Tetcott	Devon and Cornwall
Tetcott South	The borders of north-west Devon and Cornwall
Tickham	North Kent
Tiverton	Devonshire, with a small part extending into West Somerset
Tivyside	North Pembrokeshire and south Cardiganshire
Torrington Farmers'	Devonshire, between Dolton and Barnstaple
Towy and Cothi	North Carmarthenshire. Best centres, Cilycwm and Llandovery
Tredegar Farmers'	The south-west district of Monmouthshire
Tyne, North	The Wark and Falstone districts of Northumberland
Tyndale	Northumberland

Ulleswater	Westmorland and Cumberland
United	Shropshire and Montgomeryshire
Vale of Aylesbury	Buckinghamshire
Vale of Clettwr	North-east Carmarthenshire
V.W.H.	Gloucestershire and Wiltshire
Vine and Craven	Hampshire, with a small portion in Berkshire and Wiltshire
Warwickshire	Warwickshire, Gloucestershire, Worcestershire and Oxfordshire
Warwickshire, North	Entirely in Warwickshire, from Rugby to the Worcestershire border
Western	West Cornwall
West of Yore	Yorkshire, west of River Yore from Rippon northwards
West Street	Kent, Sandwich, Dover and Herne Bay districts
Whaddon Chase	Buckinghamshire
Wheatland	South Shropshire
Williams–Wynn's, Sir Watkin	Denbighshire, Flint, Cheshire and Shropshire
Wilton	South of Salisbury to the north Dorsetshire border
Wiltshire, South and West	Shaftesbury and Warminster
Worcestershire	Central Worcestershire from the Hereford to Warwickshire borders
Ynysfor	South Caernarvonshire and North Merionethshire
York and Ainsty, North	The West Riding and North Riding of Yorkshire. Best centres, Harrogate and Boroughbridge
York and Ainsty, South	North, west and south of York
Ystrad	Aberdare and Rhondda Valleys
Zetland	South Durham and North Riding of Yorkshire

SCOTLAND

Berwickshire	Best centres, Duns, Coldstream and Greenlaw
Buccleuch's, Duke of	Roxburghshire, Selkirk and Berwickshire
Dumfriesshire	Best centres, Lockerbie
Eglinton	Ayrshire. Best centres, Ayr, Troon and Kilmarnock
Fife	Best centres, Cupar and St Andrews
Jed Forest	Roxburghshire. Best centres, Jedburgh and Hawick
Lanarkshire and Renfrewshire	Almost wholly in Renfrewshire, adjoining the Eglinton
Lauderdale	In Roxburgh, Berwick, Selkirk and Midlothian
Liddesdale	Roxburghshire
Linlithgow and Stirlingshire	Midlothian, West Lothian and Stirlingshire
Lochaber and Sunart Farmers'	Inverness-shire and Argyllshire

IRELAND

Avondhu Hunt Club	Co. Cork, Waterford and Tipperary
Ballymacad	North Co. Meath, bordering on Caven and Westmeath
Bermingham and North Galway	North of Co. Galway and South Mayo
Carberry	Entirely in Co. Cork
Duhallow	Co. Cork. Best centre, Mallow
Dungannon	Private footpack
Galway, County ('The Blazers')	Best centres, Loughrea and Athenry
Galway, East	Co. Galway and Co. Roscommon
Island	Wexford. Best centres, Gorey, Ferns and Enniscorthy
Kildare	Kildare and Dublin, with portions in Meath and Wicklow
Kilkenny	Best centre, Kilkenny
Kilkenny, North	Best centre, Freshford
Laois (Queen's County)	Queen's County. Best centres, Abbeyleix, Athy, Maryborough and Stradbally
Limerick	Co. Limerick
Louth	Louth, Meath, Dublin, Cavan and Monaghan
Macroom	Mid Co. Cork
Muskerry	Co. Cork. From Carrigrohane Bridge to Macroom

Ormond	South Offaly and North Tipperary and Limerick
Strabane	On the borders of Counties Tyrone and Donegal
Tipperary	Co. Tipperary
Tipperary, North	From Coolbawn in the north, southwards to Killaloe
United Hunt Club	Co. Cork
Waterford	Between the sea and the Comeragh Mountains
Waterford, West	Centres are Cappoquin, Lismore and Ardmore
Westmeath	Westmeath County
Wexford	Co. Wexford
Wicklow	South Co. Wicklow and North Co. Wexford

Staghounds

ENGLAND

Devon and Somerset	West Somerset and North Devon
New Forest Buckhounds	Centres are Lyndhurst, Brockenhurst and Stoney Cross
Quantock	The Quantock Hills
Tiverton	Almost wholly in Devon, south of the Taunton-Barnstaple railway

IRELAND

County Down	Best centres, Belfast, Ballynahinch, Newcastle and Downpatrick
Ward, Union	North Co. Dublin and South Co. Meath

Harriers

ENGLAND AND WALES

Aldenham	Hertfordshire, Buckinghamshire and Bedfordshire
Axe Vale	*see* Foxhounds
Bolventor	Cornwall
Cambridgeshire	Within the territories of the Puckeridge and Thurlow and Cambridgeshire Foxhounds

Clifton Foot	North Somerset
Cotley	*see* Foxhounds
Dart Vale and Haldon	The greater part of South Devon from the Dart Valley to the Exe
Dunston	South Norfolk
Easton	East Suffolk
Edmonstone	Midlothian and East Lothian
Eryi	Caernarvonshire and Anglesey
High Peak	Bakewell and Buxton, Derbyshire
Holcombe	Central Lancashire
Minehead	West Somerset and Exmoor
Modbury	South Devon
Norfolk, North	the North of Norfolk
Pendle Forest and Craven	East Lancashire and the West Riding of Yorkshire
Rockwood	The West Riding of Yorkshire
Ross	South Herefordshire
Rufford Forest	Nottinghamshire
Sennowe Park	Norfolk
South Pool	The Kingsbridge district of Devon
Taunton Vale	Around Taunton, Devon, and in Somerset
Vale of Lune	The border of Lancashire, Westmorland and Yorkshire
Waveney	Suffolk and Norfolk
Wensleydale	Watershed of River Ure and above Aysgarth
Weston and Banwell	Somerset
Windermere	Around Kendal and Windermere, Westmorland

IRELAND

Antrim, East	Between Belfast, Antrim and Larne
Antrim, Mid	Mid-Antrim and South Derry
Bray	Counties Wicklow and Dublin
Clare, County	Around Ennis
Derrygallon	West Dunhallow and North Cork
Down, North	The north part of Co. Down
Dublin, South County	South part of Dublin County
Dungarvan	Co. Waterford
Fermanagh	Fermanagh, parts of South Donegal, South Tyrone and West Monaghan
Fingal	North Co. Dublin and South Co. Meath
Iveagh	Co. Down and North Armagh

Killeagh	Co. Cork
Killinick	South Co. Wexford
Killultagh, Old Rock and Chichester	Co. Antrim
Kilomganny	South Kilkenny and a small part of South Tipperary
Limerick	Co. Limerick
Little Grange	Co. Meath
Longford, County and Roscommon	Bordered by counties Cavan, Westmeath,
Naas	County Kildare
Newry	Counties Down and Armagh
Route	North Londonderry and North Antrim
Sligo, County	Whole of Co. Sligo and part of Roscommon
Stonehall	Co. Limerick
Tara	Centre and north of Meath and parts of Cavan
Tynan and Armagh	Co. Armagh
Tyrone, South	Co. Tyrone and parts of North Monaghan and South Derry

Draghounds

ENGLAND, WALES AND CHANNEL ISLANDS

Cambridge University	Cambridgeshire, East Essex, Newmarket and Thurlow, Fernie, Belvoir, Oakley and Woodland Pytchley country by invitation
Cheshire, North-East	North-east Cheshire and north-west Derbyshire
Jersey	Jersey C.I.
Mid-Surrey Farmers'	The old Surrey, Burstow, West Kent, Southdown, Eridge, Crawley and Horsham, and Chiddingfold, and Surrey union countries
Oxford University	Oxford and Bicester
Staff College and Royal Military Academy	From Wokingham and Arborfield to Basingstoke and Aldershot

Appendix II

Hunting Act 2004

By Kind Permission HMSO
Part 1: Offences

1. Hunting wild mammals with dogs
A person commits an offence if he hunts a wild mammal with a dog, unless his hunting is exempt.

2. Exempt hunting
   (1) Hunting is exempt if it is within a class specified in Schedule 1.
   (2) The Secretary of State may by order amend Schedule 1 so as to vary a class of exempt hunting.

3. Hunting: assistance
   (1) A person commits an offence if he knowingly permits land which belongs to him to be entered or used in the course of the commission of an offence under section 1.
   (2) A person commits an offence if he knowingly permits a dog which belongs to him to be used in the course of the commission of an offence under section 1.

4. Hunting: defence
It is a defence for a person charged with an offence under section 1 in respect of hunting to show that he reasonably believed that the hunting was exempt.

5. Hare coursing
   (1) A person commits an offence if he:
        (a) participates in a hare coursing event,
        (b) attends a hare coursing event,

(c) knowingly facilitates a hare coursing event, or

(d) permits land which belongs to him to be used for the purposes of a hare coursing event.

(2) Each of the following persons commits an offence if a dog participates in a hare coursing event:

(a) any person who enters the dog for the event,

(b) any person who permits the dog to be entered, and

(c) any person who controls or handles the dog in the course of or for the purposes of the event.

(3) A 'hare coursing event' is a competition in which dogs are, by the use of live hares, assessed as to skill in hunting hares.

Part 2: Enforcement

6. Penalty

A person guilty of an offence under this Act shall be liable on summary conviction to a fine not exceeding level 5 on the standard scale.

7. Arrest

A constable without a warrant may arrest a person whom he reasonably suspects:

(a) to have committed an offence under section 1 or 5(1)(a), (b) or (2),

(b) to be committing an offence under any of those provisions, or

(c) to be about to commit an offence under any of those provisions.

8. Search and seizure

(1) This section applies where a constable reasonably suspects that a person ('the suspect') is committing or has committed an offence under Part 1 of this Act.

(2) If the constable reasonably believes that evidence of the offence is likely to be found on the suspect, the constable may stop the suspect and search him.

(3) If the constable reasonably believes that evidence of the offence is likely to be found on or in a vehicle, animal or other thing of which the suspect appears to be in possession or control, the constable may stop and search the vehicle, animal or other thing.

(4) A constable may seize and detain a vehicle, animal or other thing if he reasonably believes that:

(a) it may be used as evidence in criminal proceedings for an offence under Part 1 of this Act, or

(b) it may be made the subject of an order under section 9.

(5) For the purposes of exercising a power under this section a constable may enter:

(a) land;

(b) premises other than a dwelling;

(c) a vehicle.

(6) The exercise of a power under this section does not require a warrant.

9. Forfeiture
   (1) A court which convicts a person of an offence under Part 1 of this Act may order the forfeiture of any dog or hunting article which:
       (a) was used in the commission of the offence, or
       (b) was in the possession of the person convicted at the time of his arrest.
   (2) A court which convicts a person of an offence under Part 1 of this Act may order the forfeiture of any vehicle which was used in the commission of the offence.
   (3) In subsection (1) 'hunting article' means anything designed or adapted for use in connection with:
       (a) hunting a wild mammal, or
       (b) hare coursing.
   (4) A forfeiture order:
       (a) may include such provision about the treatment of the dog, vehicle or article forfeited as the court thinks appropriate, and
       (b) subject to provision made under paragraph (a), shall be treated as requiring any person who is in possession of the dog, vehicle or article to surrender it to a constable as soon as is reasonably practicable.
   (5) Where a forfeited dog, vehicle or article is retained by or surrendered to a constable, the police force of which the constable is a member shall ensure that such arrangements are made for its destruction or disposal:
       (a) as are specified in the forfeiture order, or
       (b) where no arrangements are specified in the order, as seem to the police force to be appropriate.
   (6) The court which makes a forfeiture order may order the return of the forfeited dog, vehicle or article on an application made:
       (a) by a person who claims to have an interest in the dog, vehicle or article (other than the person on whose conviction the order was made), and
       (b) before the dog, vehicle or article has been destroyed or finally disposed of under subsection (5).
   (7) A person commits an offence if he fails to:
       (a) comply with a forfeiture order, or
       (b) co-operate with a step taken for the purpose of giving effect to a forfeiture order.

10. Offence by body corporate
   (1) This section applies where an offence under this Act is committed by a body corporate with the consent or connivance of an officer of the body.
   (2) The officer, as well as the body, shall be guilty of the offence.
   (3) In subsection (1) a reference to an officer of a body corporate includes a reference to:
       (a) a director, manager or secretary,

(b) a person purporting to act as a director, manager or secretary, and

(c) if the affairs of the body are managed by its members, a member.

SCHEDULES

Section 2

SCHEDULE 1: Exempt Hunting

Stalking and flushing out

1. (1) Stalking a wild mammal, or flushing it out of cover, is exempt hunting if the conditions in this paragraph are satisfied.

(2) The first condition is that the stalking or flushing out is undertaken for the purpose of:

(a) preventing or reducing serious damage which the wild mammal would otherwise cause:

(i) to livestock,

(ii) to game birds or wild birds (within the meaning of section 27 of the Wildlife and Countryside Act 1981 (c. 69)),

(iii) to food for livestock,

(iv) to crops (including vegetables and fruit),

(v) to growing timber,

(vi) to fisheries,

(vii) to other property, or

(viii) to the biological diversity of an area (within the meaning of the United Nations Environmental Programme Convention on Biological Diversity of 1992),

(b) obtaining meat to be used for human or animal consumption, or

(c) participation in a field trial.

(3) In subparagraph (2)(c) 'field trial' means a competition (other than a hare coursing event within the meaning of section 5) in which dogs:

(a) flush animals out of cover or retrieve animals that have been shot (or both), and

(b) are assessed as to their likely usefulness in connection with shooting.

(4) The second condition is that the stalking or flushing out takes place on land:

(a) which belongs to the person doing the stalking or flushing out, or

(b) which he has been given permission to use for the purpose by the occupier or, in the case of unoccupied land, by a person to whom it belongs.

(5) The third condition is that the stalking or flushing out does not involve the use of more than two dogs.

(6) The fourth condition is that the stalking or flushing out does not involve the use

of a dog below ground otherwise than in accordance with paragraph 2 below.

(7) The fifth condition is that:

    (a) reasonable steps are taken for the purpose of ensuring that as soon as possible after being found or flushed out the wild mammal is shot dead by a competent person, and

    (b) in particular, each dog used in the stalking or flushing out is kept under sufficiently close control to ensure that it does not prevent or obstruct achievement of the objective in paragraph (a).

Use of dogs below ground to protect birds for shooting

2. (1) The use of a dog below ground in the course of stalking or flushing out is in accordance with this paragraph if the conditions in this paragraph are satisfied.

  (2) The first condition is that the stalking or flushing out is undertaken for the purpose of preventing or reducing serious damage to game birds or wild birds (within the meaning of section 27 of the Wildlife and Countryside Act 1981 (c. 69)) which a person is keeping or preserving for the purpose of their being shot.

  (3) The second condition is that the person doing the stalking or flushing out:

    (a) has with him written evidence:

       (i) that the land on which the stalking or flushing out takes place belongs to him, or

       (ii) that he has been given permission to use that land for the purpose by the occupier or, in the case of unoccupied land, by a person to whom it belongs, and

    (b) makes the evidence immediately available for inspection by a constable who asks to see it.

  (4) The third condition is that the stalking or flushing out does not involve the use of more than one dog below ground at any one time.

  (5) In so far as stalking or flushing out is undertaken with the use of a dog below ground in accordance with this paragraph, paragraph 1 shall have effect as if for the condition in paragraph 1(7) there were substituted the condition that:

    (a) reasonable steps are taken for the purpose of ensuring that as soon as possible after being found the wild mammal is flushed out from below ground,

    (b) reasonable steps are taken for the purpose of ensuring that as soon as possible after being flushed out from below ground the wild mammal is shot dead by a competent person,

    (c) in particular, the dog is brought under sufficiently close control to ensure that it does not prevent or obstruct achievement of the objective in paragraph (b),

    (d) reasonable steps are taken for the purpose of preventing injury to the dog, and

    (e) the manner in which the dog is used complies with any code of practice which is issued or approved for the purpose of this paragraph by the Secretary of State.

Rats

3. The hunting of rats is exempt if it takes place on land:
    (a) which belongs to the hunter, or
    (b) which he has been given permission to use for the purpose by the occupier or, in the case of unoccupied land, by a person to whom it belongs.

Rabbits

4. The hunting of rabbits is exempt if it takes place on land:
    (a) which belongs to the hunter, or
    (b) which he has been given permission to use for the purpose by the occupier or, in the case of unoccupied land, by a person to whom it belongs.

Retrieval of hares

5. The hunting of a hare which has been shot is exempt if it takes place on land:
    (a) which belongs to the hunter, or
    (b) which he has been given permission to use for the purpose of hunting hares by the occupier or, in the case of unoccupied land, by a person to whom it belongs.

Falconry

6. Flushing a wild mammal from cover is exempt hunting if undertaken:
    (a) for the purpose of enabling a bird of prey to hunt the wild mammal, and
    (b) on land which belongs to the hunter or which he has been given permission to use for the purpose by the occupier or, in the case of unoccupied land, by a person to whom it belongs.

Recapture of wild mammal

7. (1) The hunting of a wild mammal which has escaped or been released from captivity or confinement is exempt if the conditions in this paragraph are satisfied.
    (2) The first condition is that the hunting takes place:

(a) on land which belongs to the hunter,

(b) on land which he has been given permission to use for the purpose by the occupier or, in the case of unoccupied land, by a person to whom it belongs, or

(c) with the authority of a constable.

(3) The second condition is that:

(a) reasonable steps are taken for the purpose of ensuring that as soon as possible after being found the wild mammal is recaptured or shot dead by a competent person, and

(b) in particular, each dog used in the hunt is kept under sufficiently close control to ensure that it does not prevent or obstruct achievement of the objective in paragraph (a).

(4) The third condition is that the wild mammal:

(a) was not released for the purpose of being hunted, and

(b) was not, for that purpose, permitted to escape.

Rescue of wild mammal

8. (1) The hunting of a wild mammal is exempt if the conditions in this paragraph are satisfied.

(2) The first condition is that the hunter reasonably believes that the wild mammal is or may be injured.

(3) The second condition is that the hunting is undertaken for the purpose of relieving the wild mammal's suffering.

(4) The third condition is that the hunting does not involve the use of more than two dogs.

(5) The fourth condition is that the hunting does not involve the use of a dog below ground.

(6) The fifth condition is that the hunting takes place:

(a) on land which belongs to the hunter,

(b) on land which he has been given permission to use for the purpose by the occupier or, in the case of unoccupied land, by a person to whom it belongs, or

(c) with the authority of a constable.

(7) The sixth condition is that:

(a) reasonable steps are taken for the purpose of ensuring that as soon as possible after the wild mammal is found appropriate action (if any) is taken to relieve its suffering, and

(b) in particular, each dog used in the hunt is kept under sufficiently close control to ensure that it does not prevent or obstruct achievement of the objective in paragraph (a).

(8) The seventh condition is that the wild mammal was not harmed for the purpose of enabling it to be hunted in reliance upon this paragraph.

Research and observation

9. (1) The hunting of a wild mammal is exempt if the conditions in this paragraph are satisfied.

(2) The first condition is that the hunting is undertaken for the purpose of or in connection with the observation or study of the wild mammal.

(3) The second condition is that the hunting does not involve the use of more than two dogs.

(4) The third condition is that the hunting does not involve the use of a dog below ground.

(5) The fourth condition is that the hunting takes place on land:
(a) which belongs to the hunter, or
(b) which he has been given permission to use for the purpose by the occupier or, in the case of unoccupied land, by a person to whom it belongs.

(6) The fifth condition is that each dog used in the hunt is kept under sufficiently close control to ensure that it does not injure the wild mammal.

SCHEDULE 2: Consequential Amendments

Game Act 1831 (c. 32)

1. In section 35 of the Game Act 1831 (provision about trespassers: exceptions) the following words shall cease to have effect: 'to any person hunting or coursing upon any lands with hounds or greyhounds, and being in fresh pursuit of any deer, hare or fox already started upon any other land, nor'.

Game Licenses Act 1860 (c. 90)

2. In section 5 of the Game Licenses Act 1860 (exceptions) exceptions 3 and 4 (hares and deer) shall cease to have effect.

Protection of Animals Act 1911 (c. 27)

3. In section 1(3)(b) of the Protection of Animals Act 1911 (offence of cruelty: exceptions) a reference to coursing or hunting shall not include a reference to:
(a) participation in a hare coursing event (within the meaning of section 5 of this Act), or
(b) the coursing or hunting of a wild mammal with a dog (within the meaning of this Act).

Protection of Badgers Act 1992 (c. 51)

4. Section 8(4) to (9) of the Protection of Badgers Act 1992 (exception for hunting) shall cease to have effect.

Wild Mammals (Protection) Act 1996 (c. 3)

5. For the purposes of section 2 of the Wild Mammals (Protection) Act 1996 (offences: exceptions) the hunting of a wild mammal with a dog (within the meaning of this Act) shall be treated as lawful if and only if it is exempt hunting within the meaning of this Act.

Section 13

SCHEDULE 3: Repeals

Short title and chapter	Extent of repeal
The Game Act 1831 (c. 32)	In section 35, the words 'to any person hunting or coursing upon any lands with hounds or greyhounds, and being in fresh pursuit of any deer, hare or fox already started upon any other land, nor'.
The Game Licences Act 1860 (c. 90)	In section 5, exceptions 3 and 4.
The Protection of Badgers Act 1992 (c. 51)	Section 8(4) to (9).

Hunting Act 2004 is reproduced under the terms of Crown Copyright Policy Guidance issued by HMSO.

Select Reading List

The following reading list is not an exhaustive list of all the references used in the text, rather it is designed to aid the reader to start their own enquiries should they require further information on specific topics. There are a number of edited volumes included below and these often contain more than one paper used in this book and are good general sources of information about hunting or aspects of landscape theory.

Almond, R. (2003) *Medieval Hunting*, Stroud: Sutton Publishing

Ashton, N., McNabb, J., Irving, B., Lewis, S., and Parfitt, S. (1994) 'Contemporaneity of Clactonian and Acheulian flint industries at Barnham, Suffolk', *Antiquity* 68: 585–9

Ashton, N. and Lewis, S. (2002) 'Deserted Britain: declining populations in the British Late Middle Pleistocene', *Antiquity* 76: 388–96

Aston, M. (1985) *Interpreting the Landscape: Landscape Archaeology and Local History*, London: Routledge

Attenbrow, V. (2002) *Sydney's Aboriginal Past: investigating the archaeological and historical records*, Sydney: University of New South Wales Press Ltd

Bahn, P.G. (1978) 'The "Unacceptable Face" of the West European Upper Palaeolithic', *Antiquity* 52: 183

——(1980) 'Crib-biting: tethered horses in the Palaeolithic?', *World Archaeology* 12, No. 2: 212–17

——(1990) 'Motes and Beams: A further Response to White in the Upper Palaeolithic', *Current Anthropology* 31: 171–6

Barnatt, J. and Smith, K. (1997) *Peak District. Landscapes Through Time*, London: Batsford

Barnatt, J. and Williamson, T. (2005) *Chatsworth: A Landscape History*, Macclesfield: Windgather Press

Barton, N., Roberts, A.J., and Roe, D.A. (eds) (1991) *The Late Glacial in North-West Europe: human adaptation and environmental change at the end of the Pleistocene*, CBA Research Report, No. 77

Barton, R.N.E., Currant, A.P., Fenandez-Jalvo, Y., Finlayson, J.C., Goldberg, P., Macphail, R., Pettitt, P.B. and Stringer, C.B. (1999) 'Gibraltar Neanderthals and the Results of Recent Excavations in Gorham's, Vangard and Ibex Caves', *Antiquity* 73: 13–23

Barton, R.N.E., Jacobi, R.M., Stapert, D. and Street, M.J. (2003) 'The Late-Glacial Reoccupation of the British Isles and the Creswellian', *Journal of Quaternary Science* 18:7: 631–43

Barton, N. (2005) *Ice Age Britain*, London: Batsford

Bell, M. and Walker, M.J.C. (2005) *Late Quaternary Environmental Change: Physical and Human Perspectives*, 2nd edn, Harlow: Pearson Education Limited

Bender, B. (ed.) (1995) *Landscape: Politics and Perspectives*, Oxford: Berg

Bignon, O. and Eisenmann, V. (2006) 'Western European Late Glacial Horse Diversity and its Ecological

Implications' in Mashkour, M. (ed.) *Equids in Time and Space: Papers in Honour of Vera Eisenmann*, Oxford: Oxbow

Bleed, P. (2006) 'Living in the Human Niche', *Evolutionary Anthropology* 15:8: 8–10

Boëda, E., Geneste, J.M., Griggo, C. with Mercier, N., Muhesen, J.L., Reyss, J.L., Taha, A. and Valladas, H. (1999) 'Levallois point embedded in the vertebra of a wild ass (*Equus africanus*): hafting, projectiles and Mousterian hunting weapons', *Antiquity* 73: 394–402

Bogaard, A. (2004) *Neolithic Farming in Central Europe: An Archaeobotanical Study of Crop Husbandry Practices*, London: Routledge

Bradley, R. (1984) *The social foundations of prehistoric Britain: themes and variations in the archaeology of power*, Harlow: Longman

——(1997) *Rock Art and the Prehistory of Atlantic Europe: Signing the Land*, London: Routledge

——(2000) *An Archaeology of Natural Places*, London: Routledge

——(2003) *Altering the Earth: the origins of monuments in Britain and Continental Europe*, Edinburgh: Society of Antiquaries of Scotland, Monograph Series 8

Brown, T. (1997) 'Clearances and Clearings: Deforestation in the Mesolithic/Neolithic Britain', *Oxford Journal of Archaeology* 16:2: 133–46

Carbonell, E., Bermúdez de Castro, J.M., Parés, J.M., Pérez-González, A., Cuenca-Bescós, G., Ollé, A., Mosquera, M., Huguet, R., Van der Made, J., Rosas, A., Sala, R., Vallverdú, J., Garcia, N., Granger, D.E., Martinón-Torres, M., Rodríguez, X.P., Stock, G.M., Vergès, J.M., Allué, E., Burjachs, F., Cáceres, I., Canals, A., Benito, A., Díez, C., Lozano, M., Mateos, A., Navazo, M., Rodríguez, J., Rosell, J. and Arsuaga, J.L. (2008) 'The first hominin of Europe', *Nature* 452:27: 465–70

Cartmill, M. (1993) *A View to a Death in the Morning: Hunting and nature through history*, Cambridge Massachusetts: Harvard University Press

Conard, N.J. (2003) 'Palaeolithic ivory sculptures from south-western Germany and the origins of figurative art', *Nature* 426: 830–2

Cook, J. (1991) 'Preliminary report on marked human bones from the 1986–1987 excavation at Gough's Cave, Somerset, England' in Barton, N., Roberts, A.J. and Roe, D.A. (eds) *The Late Glacial in North-West Europe*, CBA Research Report, No. 77

Cummings, V. and Whittle, A. (2003) 'Tombs with a View: Landscape, Monuments and Trees', *Antiquity* 77, No. 296: 255–66

Davies, W. (2001) 'A Very Model of a Modern Human Industry: New Perspectives on the Origins and Spread of the Aurignacian in Europe', *Proceedings of the Prehistoric Society* 67: 195–217

Downing, G. (1996) *Shooting for Beginners*, Shrewsbury: Swan Hill Press

Edmonds, M. (1999) *Ancestral Geographies of the Neolithic: Landscapes, Monuments and Memory*, London: Routledge

Edmonds, M. and Seabourne, T. (2001) *Prehistory in the Peak*, Stroud: Tempus

Flemming, A. (1999) 'Phenomenology and the Megaliths of Wales: A Dreaming Too Far?', *Oxford Journal of Archaeology* 18(2): 1999

Frayer, D.W. (1981) 'Body size, weapon use and natural selection in the European Upper Palaeolithic and Mesolithic', *American Anthropologist New Series*, Vol. 83, No. 1: 57–73

Gabunia, L. and Vekua, A. (1995) 'A Plio-Pleistocene hominid from Dmanisi, East Georgia, Caucasus', *Nature* 373:9: 509–12

Gilbertson, D.D. (1984) 'Early Neolithic Utilisation and Management of Alder Carr at Skipsea Witthow Mere, Holderness', *The Yorkshire Archaeological Journal* 56

Gräslund, B. *Early Humans and their World*, London: Routledge

Green, H.S. (1980) *The Flint Arrowheads of the British Isles (Parts 1 & 2)*, BAR British Series 75 (i & ii)

Green, H.S. with contributions by Aitken, M.J., Bevins, R.E., Bull, P.A., Clayton, C., Collcutt, S.N., Currant, A.P., Debenham, N.C., Embleton, C., Huxtable, J., Ivanovich, M., Jenkins, D.A., Molleson, T.I., Newcomer, M.H., Schwarcz, H.P. and Stringer, C.B. (1984) *Pontnewydd Cave: A Lower Palaeolithic Hominid Site in Wales. The First Report*, National Museum of Wales Quaternary Monographs, No. 1

Guthrie, D.R. (1984) 'Mosaics, Allelochemics and Nutrients: An Ecological Theory of Late Pleistocene Megafaunal Extinctions' in Martin, P.S. and Klien, R.G. (eds) *Quaternary Extinctions A Prehistoric Revolution*, Arizona: University of Arizona Press

Hardy, B.L. (2004) 'Neanderthal behaviour and stone tool function at the Middle Palaeolithic site of La Quina, France', *Antiquity* 78:301: 547–65

Holt, B.M. (2003) 'Mobility in Upper Palaeolithic and Mesolithic Europe: Evidence from the Lower Limb', *American Journal of Physical Anthropology* 122: 200–15

Hosfield, R. (1999) *The Palaeolithic of the Hampshire Basin: A Regional Model of Hominid Behaviour During the Middle Pleistocene*, Oxford: Archaeopress BAR British Series 286

Jacobi, R. (1978) 'Northern England in the Eighth Millennium BC' in P. Mellars (ed.) *The Early Postglacial Settlement of Northern Europe*, London

Jacobi, R.M. and Pettitt, P.B. (2000) 'An Aurignacian Point from Uphill Quarry (Somerset) and the Earliest Settlement of Britain by *Homo sapiens sapiens*', *Antiquity* 74: 513–18

Karavanic, I. (1995) 'Upper Palaeolithic Occupation Levels and Late-Occurring Neanderthal at Vindija Cave (Croatia) in the Context of Central Europe and the Balkans', *Journal of Anthropological Research* 51: 9–35

Keevil, G.D. (2000) *Medieval Palaces: An Archaeology*, Stroud: Tempus

Knight, D. and Howard, A.J. with contributions by Elliott, L., Jones, H., Leary, R. and Marshall, P. (2004) *Trent Valley Landscapes: The Archaeology of 500,000 Years of Change*, Heritage: Kings Lynn

Lavelle, R. (2007) *Royal Estates in Anglo-Saxon Wessex: Land, politics and family strategies*, BAR British Series 439

Liddiard, R. (ed) (2007) *The Medieval Park: new perspectives*, Macclesfield: Windgather Press

Lynch, A.H., Hamilton, J. and Hedges, R.E.M. (2008) 'Where the wild things are: aurochs and cattle in England', *Antiquity* 82: 1025–39

Mason, S.L.R. (2000) 'Fire and Mesolithic subsistence – managing oaks for acorns in northwest Europe?', *Palaeogeography, Palaeoclimatology, Palaeoecology* 164: 139–50

Musil, R. (1998) 'Evidence for the Domestication of Wolves in Central European Magdalenian Sites' in Crockford, S.J. (ed) *Dogs Through Time: An Archaeological Perspective*, Proceedings of the 1st ICAZ Symposium on the History of the Domestic Dog. Eighth Congress of the International Council for Archaeozoology (ICAZ 1998), August 23–29 1998, Victoria, B.C., Canada, Oxford: Archaeopress BAR International Series 889

Nash, G. (2008) 'Encoding a Neolithic Landscape: the Linearity of Burial Monuments along Strumble Head, South-West Wales', *Time and Mind: The Journal of Archaeology, Consciousness and Culture*, Vol. 1, No. 3: 345–62

——(2002) 'Constructing Hypothetical Systems of Exchange: Doing Kula in the Danish Mesolithic' in W.H. Waldron and J.A. Ensenyat, *World Islands in Prehistory: International Insular Investigations V Deia International Conference of Prehistory*, BAR International Series 1095: 19–30

——(2003) 'Settlement, Population Dynamics and Territoriality During the Late South Scandinavian Mesolithic' in Bevan, L. and Moore, J. (eds) *Peopling the Mesolithic in a Northern Environment*, BAR International Series 1157

Nash, G. and Chippindale, C. (2002) *European Landscapes of Rock-Art*, London: Routledge

Newall, V. (1983) 'The Unspeakable in Pursuit of the Uneatable: Some Comments on Fox-Hunting', *Folklore* 94:1: 86–90

Olsen, S.L. (ed.) (1996) *Horses Through Time*, Lanham: Roberts Rinehart

Page, R. (2000) *The Hunting Gene: Hunting – its People; its Wildlife and its Countryside*, Barton, Cambridgeshire: Birds Farm Books

Parfitt, S.A., Barandregt, R.W., Breda, M., Candy, I., Collins, M.J., Coope, R., Durbidge, P., Field, M.H., Lee, J.R., Lister, A.M., Mutch, R., Penkman, E.H., Preece, R.C., Rose, J., Stringer, C.B., Symmons, R., Whittaker, J.E., Wymer, J.J. and Stuart, A.J. (2005) 'The earliest record of human activity in northern Europe', *Nature* 438:15: 1008–1012

Pettitt, P., Bahn, P. and Ripoll, S. (2007) *Palaeolithic Cave Art at Creswell Crags in European Context*, Oxford: Oxford University Press

Rackham, O. (1986) *The History of the Countryside: the classic history of Britain's landscape, flora and fauna*, London: Weidenfeld & Nicolson

Richards, M.P. and Hedges, R.E.M. (1999) 'Stable Isotope Evidence for Similarities in the Types of Marine Foods used by Late Mesolithic Humans at Sites Along the Atlantic Coast of Europe', *Journal of Archaeological Science* 26: 717–22

Richards, P.M. and Schmitz, R.W. (2008) 'Isotope Evidence for the Diet of the Neanderthal Type Specimen', *Antiquity* 82: 553–9

Roberts, B.K. (1996) *Landscapes of Settlement: prehistory to the present*, London: Routledge

Roberts, M.B., Parfitt, S.A., Pope, M.I., Wenham-Smith, F.F. with contributions by Macphail, R.I., Locker, A. and Stewart, J. R. (1997) 'Boxgrove, West Sussex: Rescue Excavations of a Lower Palaeolithic Landsurface (Boxgrove Project B, 1989–91)', *Proceedings of the Prehistoric Society*: 303–58

Rodgers, R.A. and Rodgers, L.A. (1988) 'Notching and Anterior Bevelling on Fossil Horse Incisors: Indicators of Domestication?', *Quaternary Research* 29: 72–4

Rosen, S.A. (1988) 'Notes on the Origins of Pastoral Nomadism: A Case Study from the Negev and Sinai', *Current Anthropology* 29:3: 498–506

Rowley-Conwy, P. (1990) 'On the Osteological Evidence for Palaeolithic Domestication: Barking Up the Wrong Tree', *Current Anthropology* 31, No. 5: 543–7

Shea, J.J. (1988) 'Spear Points from the Middle Palaeolithic of the Levant', *Journal of Field Archaeology* 15, No. 4: 441–50

Sheldrick, C., Lowe, J.J. and Reynier, M.J. (1997) 'Palaeolithic Barbed Point from Gransmoor, East Yorkshire, England', *Proceeding of the Prehistoric Society*: 359–70

Shulting, R.J. and Richards, M.P. (2001) 'Dating Women and Becoming Farmers: New Palaeodietary and AMS Dating Evidence from the Breton Mesolithic Cemeteries of Téviec and Hoëdic', *Journal of Anthropological Archaeology* 20: 314–44

Smith, R. (ed.) (2002) *Kinder Scout: Portrait of a Mountain*, Leicester: De Montfort Press

Soden, I. (2005) *Coventry: the Hidden History*, Stroud: Tempus

——(ed.) (2007) *Stafford Castle: Survey, Excavation and Research 1978–1998, Volume II The Excavations*, Stafford: Stafford Borough Council

——(2008) *Archaeological Desk-Based Survey of Southwick Woods Northamptonshire*, Unpublished Report by Northamptonshire Archaeology 08/051

Steane, J. (1993) *The Archaeology of the Medieval English Monarchy*, London: Routledge

Sykes, N.J. 'The Impact of the Normans on Hunting Practices in England' in Woolgar, C.M., Serjeantson, D. and Waldron, T. (eds) *Food in Medieval England: Diet and Nutrition*, Oxford: Oxford University Press

Sykes, N.J., White, J., Hayes, T.E. and Palmer, M.R. (2006) 'Tracking Animals using Strontium Isotopes in Teeth: the role of fallow deer (*Dama dama*) in Roman Britain', *Antiquity* 80: 948–59

Thieme, H. (1997) 'Lower Palaeolithic hunting spears from Germany', *Nature* 385:27: 807–9

Thomas, J. (1988) 'The Social Significance of Cotswold-Severn Burial Practices', *Man*, New Series 23:3: 540–59

Tilley, C. (1995) 'Art, Architecture and Politics [Neolithic Sweden]' in Bender, B. (ed.) *Landscape: Politics and Perspectives*, Oxford: Berg

(1994) *A Phenomenology of Landscape: places, paths and monuments*, Oxford: Berg

Turner, E. (2006) 'Results of a Recent Analysis of Horse Remains Dating to the Magdalenian Period at Solutre, France' in Mashkour, M. (ed.) *Equids in Time and Space*, Oxford: Oxbow

Vekua, A., Lordkipanidze, D., Rightmire, G.P., Jordi, A., Ferring, R., Maisuradze, G., Mouskhelishvili, A., Medea, N., Ponce de Leon, M., Tappen, M., Tvalchelidze, M. and Zollikofer, C. (2002) 'A New Skull of Early *Homo* from Dmanisi, Georgia', *Nature* 297: 85–9

White, R., Bahn, P.G., Clottes, J., Cribb, R., Delpech, F., Kehoe, T.F., Olszewski, D.J., Straus, D.S. and Svoboda, J. (1989) 'Husbandry and Herd Control in the Upper Palaeolithic: A Critical Review of the Evidence [and Comments and Reply]', *Current Anthropology* 30, No. 5: 609–32

Whittle, A. (1997) 'Moving on and moving around: Neolithic settlement mobility' in Topping, P. (ed.) *Neolithic Landscapes: Neolithic Studies Group Seminar Papers 2*, Oxbow Monograph 86

Wiltshire, M., Woore, S., Crisp, B. and Rich, B. *Duffield Frith: History & Evolution of the Landscape of a Medieval Derbyshire Forest*, Ashbourne: Landmark Publishing

Index